THE SASH ON THE MERSEY:
THE ORANGE ORDER IN LIVERPOOL
1819–1982

THE SASH ON THE MERSEY

The Orange Order in Liverpool
1819–1982

MERVYN BUSTEED

LIVERPOOL UNIVERSITY PRESS

First published 2023 by
Liverpool University Press
4 Cambridge Street
Liverpool
L69 7ZU

British Library Cataloguing-in-Publication data
A British Library CIP record is available

ISBN 978-1-83764-508-4 cased

Typeset by Carnegie Book Production, Lancaster

Contents

Illustrations

Abbreviations

D.C.	Deputy Chaplain
D.D.M.	Deputy District Master
D.M.	Deputy Master
D. Scy	Deputy Secretary
G.M.	Grand Master
GOLE	Grand Orange Lodge of England
LOIE	Loyal Orange Institution of England
LOLE	Loyal Orange Lodge of England
LLOL	Ladies Loyal Orange Lodge
LOL	Loyal Orange Lodge
LRO	Liverpool Record Office
P.G.S.	Provincial Grand Secretary
R.A.P.	Royal Arch Purple
W.D.M.	Worshipful District Master WLOL
WLOL	Women's Loyal Orange Lodge
W.M.	Worshipful Master/Mistress
WMCA	Workingmen's Conservative Association
W.S.	Worshipful Secretary

For Helen

Acknowledgements

This book is the result of a number of influences, including personal background in Protestant working-class west Belfast where the Orange Order had strong support and frequent parades, reading literature on the Order in Ireland, Britain and abroad, extensive documentary research and many personal conversations. I am deeply indebted to all these sources, but there are some which particularly deserve mention. First I must acknowledge those many members in Liverpool who so readily discussed the Order, patiently answered my questions, passed me on to fellow members and invited me to open days and events. In particular I would like to thank Harry, Beryl and Hannah Roberts for their assistance and hospitality, Grand Master W.R. Bather for allowing me access to some documentation on Garston True Blues LOL 64 held in Heald Street Orange Hall Garston and for sharing recollections of events in the early 1980s. I must also thank Provincial Grand Master Steve Kingston, W.M. Vivien Cawley of Rose of England LLOL 95, Ken McGee of Ivy LOL 783, W.M. Jim Roberts of Toxteth True Blues LOL 548 for giving me access to his splendid collection of Grand Lodge annual reports, former Provincial Grand Master Billy Owens for directing me to the material in Liverpool Central Library, the organisers of the open days at Provincial headquarters in Everton and Mill Street Orange Hall and Owen Roberts for inviting me to share some early results of my work at an open meeting organised by the History and Research Lodge.

I am particularly indebted to archivist Helena Smart and the staff of Liverpool Record Office at the Central Library, who always responded to my requests with promptitude and patience. I would like to thank the anonymous reader who directed me towards the work of his ancestor Reverend Richard Hobson. I was also very well served by the staff of Special Collections in the Sydney Jones Library, University of Liverpool, Neil Sayer, archivist at Liverpool Metropolitan Cathedral and Dr Jonathan Mattison at the Museum of Orange Heritage, Belfast.

Everyone connected with the Institute of Irish Studies at Liverpool University provided warm encouragement, especially Professors Diane Urquhart, Pete Shirlow, Frank Shovlin and emeritus Professor Marianne Elliott, as did Neil

Smith and Barry Hazley. Niall Gilmartin of Ulster University generously gave me early access to his work on the flight of Belfast refugees to Liverpool in 1971. Emeritus Professor John Belchem was an early and enthusiastic source of encouragement. I owe a notable debt to Mrs Grace Sinclair and Canon Godfrey Butland, executors of Bishop David Sheppard, who arranged for me to have access to his papers at a time when they were under embargo during the preparation of his biography by Emeritus Professor Andrew Bradstock of Winchester University. Professor Bradstock kindly paused his work to send me copies of documentation on events in the city in the early 1980s. Canon Neville Black, Reverend Bill Letheren and Reverend Graham Amey were also very helpful in providing background information and Canon Butland shared his memories of the events of 1980–82. The late Reverend Brian Kennaway and my old friend Reverend Alistair Kennedy of the Presbyterian Church in Ireland provided some early guidance. Joe Flynn kindly gave me the opportunity to share some early results of the research at a typically lively conference of the Manchester Irish Education group. I owe a debt to my friend the late Frank Neal, who pioneered research on the role of the Orange Order in Liverpool history and to Councillor Roland Griffin who shared details on his ancestor Field Marshall Sir Henry Wilson but did not live to see the publication of this book.

Many friends at St Barnabas and All Hallows in Liverpool shared their experiences and memories of the Order, including Liz Creswell, Jeff Hall, Ivy Jones, Guy Snaith, Shirley Spencer and Paul Young. My near neighbours were notably supportive, so thank you Pat Krumbein, Greg Quiery, Mal, Carol, Eric and George Spanner and Seamus and Siobhan Alan and their considerably extended family. Thanks are also due to the anonymous reviewers for their encouraging remarks and Alison Welsby, Rebecca Graham and Catherine Pugh of Liverpool University Press for patient guidance. Every effort has been made to obtain permissions. Any errors of fact or omission are mine alone.

Most of this book was written during the lockdown regulations provoked by the COVID-19 pandemic. Throughout the researching and writing my wife Helen has once again been a magnificent source of patient support, taking the photographs and making everything possible and worthwhile.

Introduction: Structure, Literature and Data Sources

The aim of this book is to explain how the Orange Order, formed in the circumstances of late eighteenth-century Ireland, transplanted successfully to one of the great imperial port cities of nineteenth-century Britain, became deeply embedded within a large section of its working-class population and made a striking contribution to the development of a distinctive civic culture in nineteenth- and early twentieth-century Liverpool. A wide range of archival materials and some personal interviews are used to explore how these overwhelmingly working-class Orange lodges adopted an enduring life style based around ultra-Protestantism, loyalist royalism, ritualised meetings, mutual aid, intensive socialising and periodic public processing. It discusses how the local Conservative party, in parallel with the Order, cultivated a fervently Protestant, working-class, Tory vote which enabled it to dominate local and parliamentary politics in Liverpool well into the twentieth century. The study also traces the process by which this distinctive regional political tradition and the influence of the Order were eroded by a combination of national and local socio-economic and cultural changes.

Structure

The first chapter outlines the foundation of the Order in the context of the popularity of loyalist voluntary organisations and the specific circumstances of Irish unrest in the late 1790s. It notes the appeal of its loyalist Protestantism to English soldiers serving in Ireland and its diffusion as they returned to England, demobilised and formed local lodges, especially in the towns of the north-west, where its outlook resonated strongly with traditional anti-Catholic sentiment and wartime patriotism. It goes on to trace the development of the Order up to the early 1830s, when it encountered increasing official displeasure, leading to suppression in 1836. The factors enabling the Order's survival and re-emergence as a single national organisation in 1876, with particular strength in Liverpool, are discussed.

Chapter Two sets the Order in the context of the economic and religious landscape of Liverpool. Attention is drawn to how, well into the twentieth century, the city's local labour market was dominated by casual dock-based employment, the reliance of many working-class families on an unpredictable income and the development of residential clustering and a dense associational culture in the dockside areas. It is argued that a historic sectarian tradition was reignited by the influx of Irish Roman Catholic famine refugees in the years 1845–52 and the campaigning efforts of a cadre of Irish-born Anglican clergy whose outlook resonated strongly with the Orange tradition. It also discusses the process whereby the local Conservative party reinvented itself by taking on an ultra-Protestant outlook in sometimes uneasy alliance with the Order, thereby cultivating an ardent working-class Tory vote, enabling it to dominate local electoral politics well into the twentieth century.

Chapter Three examines the structure of the Orange Order. Drawing on some lodge records, it describes the conduct of meetings and stresses the attraction of carefully prescribed ritual, liturgy and regalia at male, female and juvenile lodge events. The evolving structure of the public events centred around 12 July is discussed, along with sporadic sectarian conflict. The processions are viewed as performances of numerical strength and respectability, plus simple enjoyment of a day out. It becomes clear that, whilst women were active in the Order from at least the mid-nineteenth century, their lodges have always occupied a subordinate though significant role. The efforts to transmit the beliefs of the Order through the work of juvenile lodges are discussed.

The fourth chapter discusses the social dimension of lodge life. Analysis of data available for one lodge reveals the overwhelmingly working-class and marked localism of membership. The intensely strong social interaction within and between lodges is analysed, along with a vibrant structure offering welfare support against times of distress. It is demonstrated that an Orange hall was a notable asset, generating income as a venue for other local organisations and making the lodge an integral part of community social capital. The role of lodges as a migrant support network is examined as they provide travel warrants, cash and information for members seeking better prospects within the United Kingdom and in the growing Orange imperial diaspora.

Chapter Five dissects the unvarying, unquestioned attachment to monarchy, country and empire. The ardent patriotism of members is examined, as demonstrated in heavy wartime recruitment, material support for servicemen, veterans and bereaved families, and the ready incorporation of commemorative memorials and ceremonies into lodge life. The extended roles for women and restructuring of lodge meetings in wartime are outlined.

Chapter Six examines how the Order defended and policed its Protestantism by monitoring and disciplining members' social behaviour. Recurring internal tensions over alcohol are discussed, especially when economic pressures led to application for a licence. There is also analysis of the relationship between lodge and church life: most members see them as mutually supportive but some clergy are unhappy at levels of attendance and practice. The strong sense of unity in opposition to the 'ritualism' of the Anglo-Catholic movement within the Church of England is outlined and the growing dismay at the ineffectiveness of governmental and ecclesiastical measures to check its progress, leading to the emergence of direct action and sectarian conflict. The emergence of an independent ultra-Protestant church and political party, and their relationship with the lodges, is analysed.

Chapter Seven discusses the role of the Order in the politics of Liverpool and the enduring interest in the affairs of Protestant Ireland. The conscious development of a distinctive populist, Protestant and welfarist appeal and leadership style by the local Conservative party, and the sometimes variable relationship with the Orange lodges in the face of the rise of the Protestant Party and the growing strength of Labour, are examined. The chapter also analyses the ongoing special interest in the affairs of Protestant Ireland as expressed verbally and in material form.

Chapter Eight examines the efforts by the Order to cope with the profound economic, social and cultural changes in twentieth-century Britain. It discusses how the hollowing-out of long-established working-class neighbourhoods by slum clearance and redevelopment, the commercialisation and professionalisation of much of the mutual aid and entertainment industries and the rise of mass media combined to challenge many of the traditional attractions of lodge life and the ill-conceived efforts to organise alternative attractions are examined. There is also discussion of dismay at the decline of religion in British life and local Orange Order reactions to the development of warmer relationships between the Christian traditions as they impacted on the Liverpool scene in the early 1980s.

In the Conclusion it is argued that the Orange Order took deep root in Liverpool because it expressed in organisational form deep-seated popular convictions and fears surrounding the need to preserve and defend the Protestant nature of the British constitution and the state church against what was seen as the multi-faceted threat from Catholic religious and political aspirations. It is argued that deep-seated socio-economic and cultural shifts in Britain as a whole, and specifically in Liverpool, rendered the Order's traditional principles and concerns of diminishing relevance to everyday city life.

Literature

Sustained analysis of the Orange Order in Great Britain has emerged slowly and fitfully. An enduring problem has been lack of access to records on the inner workings and life of the lodges. This was partly atttributable to the ethos of semi-secrecy surrounding some of the Order's rituals and ceremonies, but also partly a reaction to hostile commentary, provoking wariness of enquiry by outside analysts. Consequently, discussion was based on material from observers at public events, such as newspaper reporters or spectators, some hostile. One result was concentration by media and popular commentators on the more vivid public manifestations of Orange activity. Coverage of the annual 12 July procession has traditionally focused on the elaborate street theatre of banners, bands, singing, dancing and the colourful bodily decoration in the form of collarettes encrusted with badges of lodge rank and orange lilies. The occasional violent sectarian clashes with Irish nationalist crowds inevitably attracted attention.

Early work understandably focused on the Order's enduring strength in Ireland, with only passing reference to the lodges in Great Britain,[1] but there was gradual recognition of its presence, often alongside suggestions that it was responsible for the importation of the Irish traditions of secret societies and sectarian conflict into Britain and that its strength was maintained by Irish Protestant immigrants.[2] Some early analysis noted the appeal to working-class people of a loyalist outlook in Britain and the close social linkages amongst members, often expressed in lodge-based friendly societies.[3] The presence of a small skilled element amongst the membership was also remarked.[4] In the late 1990s study of the Order, relying largely on local newspapers, grew alongside efforts to trace the elusive Protestant element within the Irish migrant inflow. There was increasing recognition of the fact that the Order tapped into the long-standing anti-Catholicism inherent in English and British popular nationalism, and that this was utilised by local Tory parties in the mobilisation of working-class voters.[5]

The outbreak of the 'Troubles' in Northern Ireland in 1968 provoked something of a rethink in Irish Orange ranks, as members gradually came to realise that their poor public image resulted in part from neglect of modern public relations techniques along with an historic tendency to hold the media at a distance. In June 1992 the Irish Grand Lodge appointed archivists with a

[1] Hereward Senior, *Orangeism in Ireland and Britain 1795–1836* London: Routledge and Kegan Paul, 1966, pp. 151–76, Appendix C; Tony Gray, *The Orange Order* London: The Bodley Head, 1972, pp. 89–95, 121–32

[2] Lynn Hollen Lees, *Exiles of Erin: Irish Immigrants in Victorian London* Manchester: Manchester University Press, 1979, pp. 218–39

[3] John Archer Jackson, *The Irish in Britain* London: Routledge and Kegan Paul, 1963, p. 128

[4] Elaine McFarland, *Protestants First: Orangeism in 19th Century Scotland* Edinburgh: Edinburgh University Press, 1990

[5] Donald M. MacRaild, *Culture, Conflict and Migration: The Irish in Mid-Victorian Cumbria* Liverpool: Liverpool University Press, 1998; *Irish Migrants in Modern Britain, 1750–1922* Basingstoke: Macmillan, 1998

brief to collate and catalogue printed records, material objects and regalia and make them available for study under supervision.[6] In turn the English Grand Lodge launched an Education and Research Lodge in 1997, which has overseen publications and held occasional open meetings with invited speakers. There was a more open attitude towards researchers, and local lodges began to organise open days with banners and regalia on display and members available to guide visitors and answer questions.[7]

As with so much concerning the Order, a key breakthrough came via personal contact giving researchers access to documentation on a number of lodges in north-east England for the period 1850–1920.[8] This enabled a series of studies exploring the role of the local lodge in the life of members, the strength of social bonding and localism, the hearty social warmth in lodge meetings, the growth of mutualism in the form of benefit societies and the role of lodges as a support network for Orangemen migrating in search of employment. Further work discussed the development of an Orange diaspora within the British empire, a source of increasing pride amongst members at home.[9]

Women's lodges had long been remarked in newspaper reports and their regular presence in Scottish demonstrations from the early nineteenth century had been noted.[10] Study of Tyneside women's lodges revealed their activities were often extensions of domestic roles – housekeeping, child rearing, moral instruction—and deployment of these skills to advance their case for formal recognition within the movement. For women of a conservative disposition this was also a route into the wider public political arena at a time when the

---

[6] Brian Kennaway, *The Orange Order: A Tradition Betrayed* London: Methuen, 2007, pp. 192–214

[7] See for example P. Day, '"Pride before a fall?": Orangeism in Liverpool since 1945', in M. Busteed, F. Neal and J. Tonge (eds), *Irish Protestant Identities* Manchester: Manchester University Press, chp. 19, pp. 273–88; James W. McAuley, Jonathan Tonge and Andrew Mycock, *Loyal to the Core? Orangeism and Britishness in Northern Ireland* Dublin: Irish Academic Press, 2011; Deborah Butcher, 'The changing demographics of Scottish women's Orangeism', *Journal of Orange History*, 1, 2015, pp. 18–33; Keith Roberts, *Liverpool Sectarianism: The Rise and Decline* Liverpool: Liverpool University Press, 2017

[8] Donald M. MacRaild, *Faith, Fraternity and Fighting: The Orange Order and Irish Migrants in Northern England, c.1850–1920* Liverpool: Liverpool University Press, 2005, p. x

[9] Donald M. MacRaild, 'Networks, communication and the Irish Protestant diaspora in northern England, *circa* 1860–1914', *Immigrants and Minorities*, 23, 2005, pp. 311–37; '"Wherever Orange is worn": Orangeism and Irish migration in the nineteenth and early twentieth centuries', *Canadian Journal of Irish Studies*, 28–9, 1–2, 2002–03, pp. 98–117; David Fitzpatrick, 'Exporting brotherhood: Orangeism in South Australia', *Immigrants and Minorities*, 23, 2005, pp. 277–310

[10] McFarland, *Protestants First*, p. 7

campaign for female suffrage was gathering strength. Further research has traced the fading and re-emergence of female lodges to the point where by 1914 they were an indispensable dimension of the Orange movement, especially in the north of England, though progress towards full recognition has been fitful.[11]

The distinctive nature of Liverpool political and religious life and the interrelationship between the two have long been acknowledged by both practising politicians and academic analysts. There has been a tendency amongst observers and some academic analysts to assume that the historic significance of the Order in Liverpool is solely attributable to the Ulster Protestant element amongst Irish immigrants. When the July 1935 processions had to battle against torrential downpours a reporter noted 'apparently it takes more than drenching rain to daunt a Liverpool Ulsterman, for each event was carried out strictly to schedule'[12] One analyst attributed Conservative strength and Labour weakness in the city to xenophobia expressed in religious bigotry reinforced 'by Ulster immigrants who were naturally anxious to establish their own status at a higher level than that of other Irishmen' whilst making passing reference to the Orange Order but not specifying its role in city politics.[13] Another noted the extraordinarily high number of Irish immigrants, intense sectarian feeling and recurring conflict, and the strength of the Order in the city, but gave little attention to the relationship with the Conservative party and failed to grasp the nature of the relation between Orangeism and ultra-Protestantism.[14] One study recognised that Liverpool was the most notable centre of Orange strength in England, was equally uncertain in treatment of the relationship with the Protestant churches but recognised the pragmatic nature of the alliance with local Conservatism.[15] More recent work has argued that in every sense the Liverpool experience of sectarian conflict was greater in both scale and intensity than any other large urban centre in Britain because of a mix of severe urban problems, a tradition of militant Protestantism in local politics, the impact of the unparalleled number of

---

[11] James MacPherson and Donald M. MacRaild, 'Sisters of the Brotherhood: female Orangeism on Tyneside in the late nineteenth and early twentieth centuries', *Irish Historical Studies*, 35, 137, 2006, pp. 40–60; James MacPherson, *Women and the Orange Order: Female Activism, Diaspora and Empire in the British World, 1850–1940* Manchester: Manchester University Press, 2016, chp. 1: England, pp. 19–99

[12] *Liverpool Post*, 13 July 1936

[13] Henry Pelling, *Social Geography of British Elections 1885–1910* London: Macmillan, 1967, p. 247; the Protestant element in the Irish influx to Liverpool is generally estimated as one-quarter of the total: see John Belchem, *Irish, Catholic and Scouse: The History of the Liverpool Irish* Liverpool: Liverpool University Press, 2007, p. xii

[14] W. J. Lowe, *The Irish in Mid-Victorian Lancashire: The Making of a Working Class Community* New York: Peter Lang, 1989, p. 163

[15] McFarland, *Protestants First*, pp. 205–06

refugees from the Irish famine in the period 1845–52, the presence of the Order, its role in building up and perpetuating a remarkably long-lasting working-class Tory vote, the generally close though never easy relationship with the party and the impact this combination had in slowing Labour party progress in the city.[16]

The 1980s saw the publication of two works destined to become classic studies of the distinctive nature of Liverpool political life. One, on the period 1869 to 1939, traced the sometimes fractious relationships between ultra-Protestantism, the Orange Order, the Conservative party and the Protestant working class, the Liberal struggle to find a space on the city's political landscape, the hesitant progress of the Labour movement and the development of a 'boss' style of local political leadership unique in British city politics. The second focused on another unique feature of Liverpool's political life, namely the frequency, dynamics and actors in the sectarian conflicts in the city during the nineteenth and early twentieth centuries.[17] Both assigned a major role to the Orange Order and the personalities involved in articulating ultra-Protestant fears and organising opposition to what they considered Catholic inroads into the traditional British Protestant way of life. Neither had access to lodge records.

Data sources

The Orange Order consists of local 'private' lodges organised into Districts and Provinces, all under the authority of the Grand Orange Order of England. A significant part of the data bank underlying this study of the Liverpool Order consists of minute books and some accompanying documentation from Liverpool Province, three District lodges, twelve men's lodges, five women's lodges and three juvenile lodges, held in Liverpool Record Office (LRO) in the city's Central Library. Clearly these are not a representative random sample of records from the numerous lodge, District and Provincial meetings in nineteenth- and twentieth-century Liverpool (see Table 1 for an indication of how many lodges have operated). The survival of the material is down to 'the serendipity of preservation and retrieval'.[18] Moreover, some of the documentation is closed unless the researcher undertakes not to reveal personal names, which I have agreed not to do. Obviously there is much more material held by lodges but not available for

---

[16] Graham Davis, *The Irish in Britain 1815–1914* Dublin: Gill and Macmillan, 1990, pp. 120–56; MacRaild, *Faith, Fraternity and Fighting*, pp. 113–14

[17] Philip Waller, *Democracy and Sectarianism: A Political History of Liverpool 1868–1939* Liverpool: Liverpool University Press, 1981; Frank Neal, *Sectarian Violence: The Liverpool Experience, An Aspect of Anglo-Irish History* Manchester: Manchester University Press, 1988

[18] John Romer, *History of Ancient Egypt from the First Farmers to the Great Pyramid* London: Penguin, 2013, p. 109

study and at least one lodge (Garston Rose of England LLOL 95) has lost almost all of its records to water damage. However, in one case a cache of material in an Orange Hall has been loaned out and proved invaluable.[19]

Table 1   *Orange Lodges in Liverpool Province in selected years 1914–80*

	1914	1920	1938	1948	1950	1960	1970	1980
Men's lodges	79	72	67	68	55	59	54	47
Women's lodges	43	35	50	40	41	51	51	48
Juvenile men's lodges	32	25	29	24	25	22	23	23
Juvenile women's lodges	32	29	23	23	26	25	26	25
Juvenile mixed lodges	0	0	20	19	10	20	22	18

Source: Loyal Orange Institution of England Annual Reports

The quality of the documentation varies considerably in terms of fragility, legibility and detail. Some secretaries were quite open in what they recorded. The Secretary of Everett LOL 108 noted that the meeting of 17 May 1899 had a 'long and dreary discussion'.[20] Some can be quite frank about internal problems. Cases of expulsion from the Order are carefully noted, occasionally for unspecified 'conduct unbecoming an Orangeman'. One lodge brought a charge of misappropriation of lodge funds against a member, resulting in expulsion.[21] For more serious charges there was no reservation whatsoever. The minute book for Everett LOL 108 in early 1908 opens with the statement that a member of another lodge has been 'expelled for life… for misconduct with a girl of tender years'.[22]

Some secretaries were clearly conflicted by the clash between accuracy and discretion, one noting that at a meeting of Cromwell LOL 94 on 19 June 1892, which discussed an application for financial assistance, 'there was a little demur'.[23] The Secretary of LOL 28 Sons of the Boyne did not explain why the meeting on 12 September 1908 had to pass a vote of confidence in him.[24] Similarly, there is no

---

[19] I am indebted to Grand Master W.R. Bather of Garston LOL 64 for allowing me access to some records of Garston True Blues LOL 64 and Rose of England LLOL 95 held in Heald Street Orange Hall, Garston, Liverpool. The sole Liverpool Province document is held in the library at the Museum of Orange Heritage, Belfast

[20] Everett LOL 108 Minute Book 17 May 1899; Liverpool Record Office, henceforth LRO: 306.ORA/1/1/2

[21] Kirby Defenders LOL 300 Minute Book 10 October 1980. LRO 306.ORA/16/1/2

[22] Everett LOL 108 statement on first page of Minute Book, date unclear, probably April 1908. LRO 306.ORA/1/1/5

[23] Cromwell LOL 94 Minute Book 19 June 1892. LRO 306.ORA/2/1/1

[24] Sons of the Boyne LOL 28 Minute Book 12 September 1908. LRO 306.ORA/6/1/1

explanation why a meeting of LOL 3 Belfast Patriotic on 25 March 1954 expelled 11 members.[25] The result of such self-censorship can be quite startling. The minute books for Everett LOL 108 have a possibly significant gap for the period from June 1902 to 18 November 1903. The minutes for this latter meeting open thus:

> The Worshipful Master stated that owing to certain matters which had taken place recently he could no longer remain a member of the Orange Institution. He then vacated the chair and left the Lodge room.

The Secretary also left but returned and resigned. No further details are forthcoming.[26] Secretaries could be remarkably laconic, as in the report on the October 1956 meeting of Belfast Patriotic LOL 3, when '[v]arious discussions talked of in a friendly manner'.[27] In one case secretarial restraint provoked lodge members to request more detail in the minutes and subsequent records are more informative.[28]

Women's lodge minutes generally follow the same pattern as their men's lodge equivalents, but there are significant differences. For a long period, the posts of Secretary, Treasurer and representative to District in a significant number of Liverpool women's lodges were occupied by male members of neighbouring lodges. Much of the energy of the women's lodges is taken up with the organisation of catering for social events, care of the juvenile lodges and the 12 July processions. Discussion of wider public issues is notably rare in women's lodges and almost always initiated by the male officers.

Occasionally members have produced a history of their lodge, and two such accounts have been shown to me, for Garston LOL 64[29] and Ivy LOL 783.[30] The Garston booklet marks 125 years of lodge life from 1876 to 2001 whilst the Ivy history covers 1876 to 1934 and 1945 to 2005. The authors had access to lodge documentation and have been quite open in recording both highpoints and contentious issues in lodge life.

The presence of juvenile lodges in processions was often remarked by contemporary observers and academic analysts, but no sustained analysis of their activities has been attempted. Fortunately, minute books of three Liverpool juvenile lodges are available for short periods. Old Swan Star of the East LOL 105 is exclusively female,[31] whilst two, Pride of West Derby LOL 11 and LOL 12,

---

[25] Belfast Patriotic LOL 3 Minute Book 25 March 1954. LRO 306.ORA/11/1
[26] Everett LOL 108 Minute Book 18 November 1903. LRO 306.ORA/1/1/3
[27] Belfast Patriotic LOL 3 Minute Book October 1956. LRO 306.ORA/11/1
[28] Protestant Martyrs LLOL 91 Minute Book November 1967. LRO 306.ORA/15/1/3
[29] *A Glimpse into 125 Years History of Garston True Blues LOL 64* Privately published: 1977
[30] *100 Years of History.* 2005; available on disc
[31] Old Swan Star of the East LOL 105 Minute Book. LRO 306.ORA/17/1/1

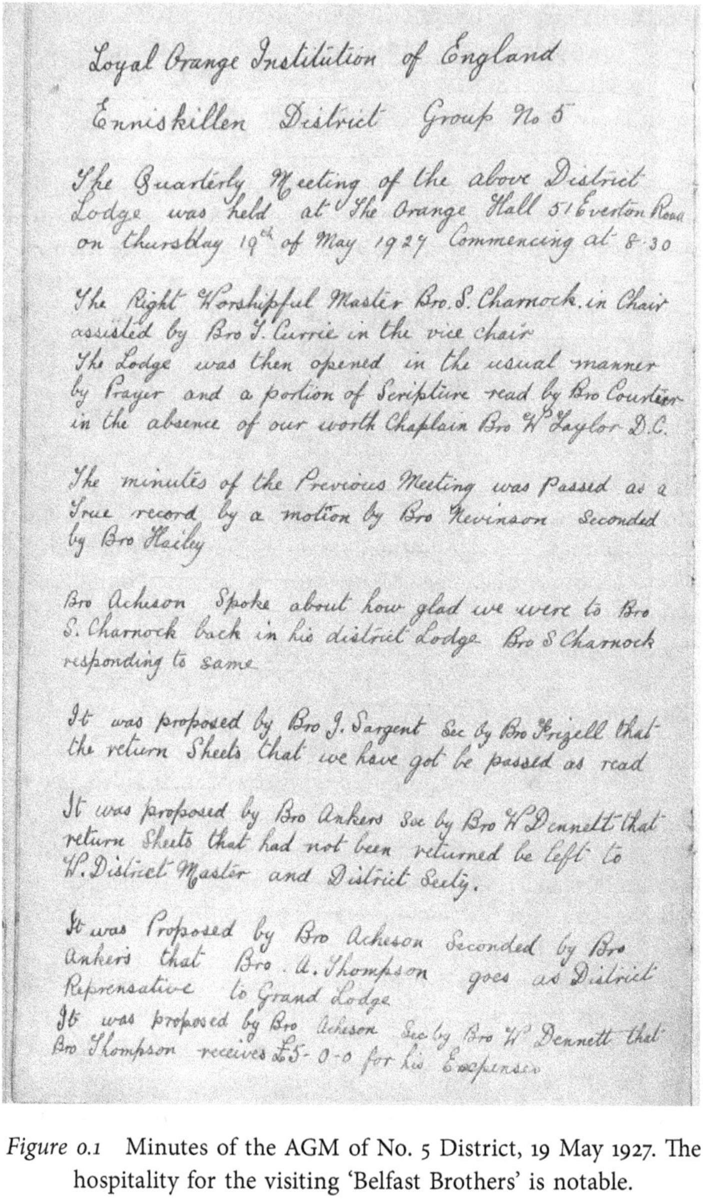

Loyal Orange Institution of England

Enniskillen District Group No 5

The Quarterly Meeting of the above District Lodge was held at The Orange Hall 51 Everton Road on thursday 19th of May 1927 Commencing at 8-30

The Right Worshipful Master Bro. S. Charnock. in Chair assisted by Bro T. Currie in the vice chair
The Lodge was then opened in the usual manner by Prayer and a portion of Scripture read by Bro Courtier in the absence of our worth Chaplain Bro W Taylor D.C.

The minutes of the Previous Meeting was Passed as a True record by a motion by Bro Nevinson Seconded by Bro Hailey

Bro Acheson Spoke about how glad we were to Bro S. Charnock back in his district Lodge Bro S Charnock responding to same

It was proposed by Bro J. Sargent Sec by Bro Frizell that the return Sheets that we have got be passed as read

It was proposed by Bro Ankers Sec by Bro W Dennett that return Sheets that had not been returned be left to W. District Master and District Secty.

It was Proposed by Bro Acheson Seconded by Bro Ankers that Bro. A. Thompson goes as District Represnsative to Grand Lodge
It was proposed by Bro Acheson Sec by Bro W Dennett that Bro Thompson receives £5-0-0 for his Expenses

Figure 0.1 Minutes of the AGM of No. 5 District, 19 May 1927. The hospitality for the visiting 'Belfast Brothers' is notable.
Source: *LRO*

It was Proposed by Bro J Sargent seconded by Bro Hailey
that Bro Thompson Receives £6·0·0 Deafeted
            Election of Officers
Bro S Charnock declaring all officers Vacant
        Bro S McCoy in the Chair Bro Ankers Vice Chair
Pro by Bro J Sargent Sec by Bro Acheson   Bro S Charnock D.M
 - - Bro Acheson - - Bro Ankers   Bro J Currie D.D.M
 - · Bro S Charnock Sec Bro Acheson   Bro Frizzell D.Y.
 - - Bro H Dennett Sec Bro Lawless   Bro H. Taylor D.C.
 - · Bro Kevinson Sec Bro Taylor   Bro A Thompson D. Secty
 - - Bro Ankers Sec Bro Thompson   Bro Rigby   Tyler
 - - Bro Thompson Sec Bro Ankers   Bro McCoy & Acheson Auditors
 - · Bro Acheson Sec Bro Taylor   Bro Ankers Foreman Com
The Master of Each Lodge form the Committee men

It was proposed by Bro Acheson seconded by Bro A Thompson
that the District Provides Breakfasts for the Belfast
Brothers that are visiting Liverpool and we also do our
best for them during their visit

There being no more Business the Lodge was Closed
in the usual manner till the Third Thursday in
September

            God Save the King

          males   Females   Jur Males
    No 1   14   No 15   15   No 3   52
    No 2   14   No 40   14   No 5
    No 3   71
    No 5   20
    No 243 14
    No 663

have both male and female members.[32] Though material is only available for 12 years in the 1950s and 1960s, it nonetheless provides invaluable insight into their work as vehicles for transmission of the outlook and values of the Order to the next generation.

[32] Pride of West Derby LOL 11 Minute Book. LRO 306.ORA/10/3/1 and LOL 12 Minute Book. LRO 306.ORA/10/3/2

I have seen one Liverpool Province Report, for 1905, in which the activities of the past year are reviewed and suggestions made for increasing membership; and records of the meetings of three Districts.[33] The great bulk of the business was to review local lodge decisions, especially on questions of discipline, and pass the more significant matters on to Province. The data bank includes documentation on the proceedings of the Province Processions Committee whose chief function was to organise the 12 July processions, review their workings and liaise with the police and transport authorities. Documentation survives for three Orange hall committees, namely Garston LOL 64 (1921–33, 1939–62), Kirby Defenders LOL 300 (1956–59) and no. 3 District (1959–65). They reveal the intense use of the hall not merely by the Order, but by individual members celebrating personal events such as wedding receptions and by the wider local community.

Some documentation has survived from other committees. In the case of Garston LOL 64 there is a Minute Book for a Distress Committee covering 2 November 1921 to 27 July 1923 detailing goods and cash provided for distressed members, and the role of women in some aspects of the work and their exclusion from others. There are occasional pieces of ephemeral literature enclosed with lodge records and, very occasionally, lists of lodge members and their home addresses. Between the dissolution of the Order in 1835 and its reconstitution in 1876, surviving lodges gradually crystallised into two groups, the Loyal Orange Institution based in Liverpool and the Grand Protestant Association of Loyal Orangemen based in Bradford under the leadership of the formidable Squire Auty. Following the merger of the two into the Loyal Orange Institution of England in 1876, annual meetings were inaugurated and an annual report issued, providing a window on the concerns of the Order at the highest level throughout the period under discussion.[34]

Local newspapers provide a vivid record of the activities of the Order when it put on public events such as the 12 July processions, church parades and public meetings, and when members were involved in sectarian clashes. Of the local press, the pro-Conservative *Liverpool Courier* was notably sympathetic in reporting the Order. From the mid-nineteenth to the early twentieth century it carried detailed descriptions of processions, the activities at the rallying point and lengthy accounts of speeches on 12 July. However, from the 1920s onwards there is a marked decline in all newspaper coverage, much less attention paid to speeches and more to the colourful nature of the event. The *Courier* can be

---

[33] Liverpool Provincial Grand Secretary's Report 1905, Museum of Orange Heritage, Belfast, Archives Department, box 14 2D; District No. 3 LRO 306.ORA/3/1/1; Enniskillen No. 5 District LRO 306.ORA/7/1/1; District No. 6 306.ORA/13/1/1 and 13/1/2

[34] I am deeply indebted to Jim Roberts, W.M. of Toxteth LOL 548 for allowing me access to his excellent collection of Grand Lodge annual reports

cross-checked against accounts in less sympathetic local publications, such as *The Porcupine*, the *Liverpool Mercury* and, later, the *Liverpool Echo* and *Daily Post*.

For much of the period there was fierce and occasionally violent public contention over matters of faith and religious affiliation. A plethora of ultra-Protestant organisations sprang up, the great majority of which faded as the issues that had provoked them passed away along with much of their printed material. However, the first annual report of the Liverpool Protestant Association of 1836,[35] the first annual report of the Liverpool Workingmen's Protestant Reformation Society for 1853–54[36] and a report of the Auxiliary of the Protestant Reformation Society for the year ending 1 March 1878 survive.[37] The short-lived League of Latimer and Ridley, founded in 1901 to oppose the advance of the Anglo-Catholic movement within the Church of England, expounded its views in the *Protestant Searchlight* and the breakaway Protestant Reformers' Church produced a monthly magazine, for which the years 1920–25 survive along with a single copy of their *Protestant Times* for October 1937.[38] In each case there was considerable overlap of membership with the Orange Order and frequent mutual citation.

As will be discussed below, many of the ardently anti-Catholic Anglican clergy who took up livings in Liverpool were Irish-born and -trained, but several graduated from St Aidan's College, Birkenhead, founded in 1847 by a Limerick-born cleric. Analysis of its archive held in the Special Collections of Sydney Jones Library, University of Liverpool, reveals the notably apocalyptic, ultra-Protestant and vehemently anti-Catholic ethos of the courses and the distinctive world view imbibed by its graduates. The archives of the Metropolitan cathedral have been consulted for discussion of Archbishop Downey's outlook on the controversy surrounding the Catholic cathedral and education in the 1930s.

Following his appointment in 1975 the Anglican Bishop David Sheppard developed a close working relationship with the Catholic Archbishop Derek Worlock and, building on local work between the churches in the preceding decades, they embarked on a joint policy to symbolise the healing of the historic sectarian cleavage in Liverpool society. In many ways the process was cemented by the visit of Pope John Paul II in May 1982 and that seemed an appropriate end point for this study. But the years immediately leading up to the widely expected Papal visit brought to a sometimes noisy climax a long-running disagreement between the Order and the Anglican cathedral authorities, reflected in Sheppard's papers lodged in the Central Library. Several people involved in the events of that

---

[35] Liverpool Protestant Association Annual Report 1836. LRO H283.05PRO
[36] Liverpool Workingmen's Protestant Reformation Society for 1853–4 LRO H284.06PRO
[37] Report of the Auxiliary of the Protestant Reformation Society 1878 LRO H284.06PRO
[38] *Protestant Times*, 16 October 1937, 8,41 LRO 331.TRA 17/3

time kindly agreed to discuss their experiences. A selection of the correspondence between the Order and the cathedral Dean has been consulted.[39]

Conclusion

Previous work on the Orange Order has long acknowledged that the Liverpool region is its greatest stronghold in England. Much early analysis focused on high-profile public events in the form of colourful processions and sectarian conflict. Shifts in the attitude of the Order to outside researchers have opened a certain amount of archival material which can be used to elaborate not only the political attitudes and activities of the lodges in the period under study but also their broader role in the life of members and the civic life of the city, and can help explain the enduring intensity of the hold which the Order once had on the everyday life of a significant section of Liverpool's Protestant working class.

---

[39] These papers had been placed under embargo whilst Emeritus Professor Andrew Bradstock of Winchester University was preparing the authorised biography of the bishop, but the executors of the papers, Mrs Jenny Sinclair and Canon Godfrey Butland, kindly agreed to allow me access for which I am extremely grateful to all concerned, especially to Professor Bradstock who sent me copies of the relevant documents. See Andrew Bradstock, *David Sheppard: Batting for the Poor* London: SPCK, 2019

1

History and Heritage

The Orange Order originated in the distinctive circumstances of late eighteenth-century Ireland, but its central beliefs and esoteric rituals found ready favour with the members of English regiments serving in Ireland. On returning to north-west England, they founded lodges in the towns where they were based or where they mustered out. These attracted not only ex-servicemen but members of the civilian population who shared the traditional anti-Catholicism of popular English and British nationalism. Despite official disapproval, an outright ban and internal schisms, Orange sentiment and lodges survived in some working-class communities, gradually re-emerging into public gaze and eventually amalgamating to form a national movement in 1876.

Foundation

The Orange Order is one long-term outworking of the British presence in Ireland. From the mid-sixteenth century successive London governments attempted to 'plant' loyal populations in various regions of Ireland. This involved the seques-tration of large tracts of land held by defeated chieftains and their replacement by Protestant entrepreneurs who, in return for grants of land under favourable terms, undertook to replace the native Catholic population with loyal Protestants who would transform local religious and economic geography. A Catholic rising in the early 1640s was followed by several years of warfare and another phase of Protestant settlement. The Restoration in 1660 ushered in a period of relative tranquillity, but this was shattered by the advent of the Catholic King James II (1685–88) who proceeded to alleviate the status of his coreligionists, much to the growing alarm of the Protestant establishment. In late 1688 William of Orange, Stadtholder of the Netherlands, responded to the pleas of powerful Whig and moderate Tory peers to accept the British throne and landed with an army in the English West Country. James fled to France in November 1688 but returned to Ireland with a largely French army in March 1689 in an attempt to regain his throne. William arrived in Ireland in June 1690 and at the battle of the Boyne in July defeated James who returned to France. These events and William's role became Orange folklore.

The resulting political settlement in Ireland imposed a succession of laws on the Catholic population which effectively removed all political rights, restricted the practice of the Catholic religion, eroded land holding rights and barred Catholics from possessing arms or holding officer posts in the army and navy. Throughout the eighteenth century Irish political, social and much of economic life was dominated by a small Church of Ireland, Anglo-Irish elite which numbered about 12 per cent of the population. However, by the 1790s there was a ferment of political ideas in Ireland, fuelled by the American and French revolutions. The Society of United Irishmen, who hoped to overcome historic divisions in the pursuit of what were seen as universal political rights, was founded in October 1791.

Some aspects of the anti-Catholic penal laws had lapsed or been modified, but every step taken to repeal such legislation reawakened traditional Protestant fears of a Catholic counter-revolution. Following a deep-seated tradition of semi-secret rural agitation common to both communities, from the early 1780s Protestant unease was expressed in clandestine groups that began to harass the local Catholic population with raids on Catholic homes where arms were thought to be held. Since these groups generally raided in the early hours, they became known as 'Peep O' Day Boys'. In response Catholics began to organise self-protection groups known as 'Defenders' who gradually evolved into a network of members bound by secret oaths and passwords. Traditional sectarian fears were reignited and small-scale armed clashes became increasingly common.

The outbreak of war with France in 1793 transformed the situation. On the political front the United Irishmen were banned and the Society went underground in May 1794, adopting an increasingly radical programme of establishing an independent Irish republic by force of arms. Their ideas increasingly permeated the ranks of local Defender groups. They in turn infected the movement with a more atavistic, *revanchist* flavour involving millenarian hopes for the overthrow of Protestant hegemony and reversion of confiscated land holdings to the original Catholic owners. The end result was an explosive mix of popular anxiety, excitement and vague expectation.[1] This reawakened the ancient Protestant nightmare of an armed Catholic population increasingly intent on violent revolution and massacre, to be achieved with the help of a hostile foreign power.[2] The interaction of these hopes and fears created an intensely

---

[1] Roy Foster, *Modern Ireland 1600–1972* London: Allen Lane, 1988, pp. 270–73; Thomas Bartlett, *Ireland: A History* Cambridge: Cambridge University Press, 2010, pp. 213–15
[2] Kevin Haddick-Flynn, *Orangeism: The Making of a Tradition* Dublin: Wolfhound Press, 1999, pp. 129–31; Senior, *Orangeism*, pp. 6–12

febrile and unstable mix of group anxieties, expectations and tensions that fed off each other.

Mid-Ulster, defined as stretching from north Armagh to west Down, had long been marked by recurring conflict between contending groups under various names and by the mid-1790s both the Peep O'Day Boys and the Defenders were active, with north Armagh in particular becoming known for its 'flaming sectarianism'.[3] The county was finely balanced in demographic terms and it has been argued that this uneasy equilibrium was gradually destabilised by economic changes leading to growing competition between Protestants and Catholics. The end result of these changes was a notable growth in the Armagh population in the 1790s, further escalating sectarian tensions.

For the Orange Order the formative conflict occurred at the Diamond crossroads, a few miles from the village of Loughgall, county Armagh, in autumn 1795. On 21 September a number of Defenders attacked the public house owned by Dan Winter, a strong loyalist who occasionally hosted Peep O'Day Boy gatherings. Winter and his associates were joined by reinforcements who fired devastating volleys into Defender ranks, causing several fatalities, with only one Protestant wounded.[4] It was the catalyst that convinced leaders of the victorious loyalists of the urgent need to replace the mosaic of locally based groups such as the Peep O' Day Boys with a more formally structured organisation. That evening they agreed to launch the Orange Society, later the Loyal Orange Institution of Ireland, named for William of Orange and dedicated to the preservation of the Protestant nature of the British throne and constitution and the reformed Protestant religion. Such loyalist groups were increasingly popular in the wartime atmosphere of the day. Following the template adopted by the many male organisations that proved so popular in the eighteenth century, and was the model adopted by both the Defenders and the burgeoning Masonic Order, local groups were to be organised as 'lodges', authorised by warrant and bound by secret oath, signs and passwords. The movement spread rapidly and on 12 July 1796, the anniversary of William's victory over James II, was strong enough to organise the first public processions of lodge members in north Armagh and west Down.[5] Large numbers of Protestants saw it as a self-defence organisation in response to the Defenders and that year it has been estimated 1,300 lodges were founded. The leadership realised the need for a wider structure. The Grand Lodge of Ireland was founded in July 1797

[3]   A. Blackstock, '"The invincible mass": loyal crowds in mid Ulster 1795–96' in P. Jupp and E. Magennis (eds), *Crowds in Ireland c.1720–1920* Basingstoke: Macmillan, 2000, p. 90

[4]   Haddick-Flynn, *Orangeism,* pp. 134–38

[5]   Blackstock, 'The invincible mass', pp. 98, 104

with William Blacker, witness of the Diamond clash, as the first Grand Master and in April 1798 headquarters were set up in Dublin.

The authorities were initially wary of a grass-roots, oath-bound organisation but, faced by growing Catholic restlessness and the threat of French invasion, the loud loyalty of the Protestant Orangemen reassured them. When, in late 1796, it was decided to raise a part-time Yeomanry, large numbers of Orangemen were recruited and, when used to enforce martial law and suppress the Defenders and the United Irishmen, the corps took on a decidedly sectarian flavour.[6] Their sanguinary role in putting down the rising of summer 1798 confirmed their reputation. In the early years of the nineteenth century they were used on a full-time basis to suppress agrarian disorder and were thoroughly disliked and feared by the Catholic population. In 1822 the Yeomanry was replaced by a new county constabulary.[7] This set a pattern whereby the authorities looked favourably on the Order when it served their purposes but would distance themselves when sectarian excesses or a changed political context rendered the relationship embarrassing or simply unnecessary.

Arrival and diffusion in England

From quite early on there was a close association between the British army and the Order.[8] Many British regiments served in Ireland during the troubled 1790s and Orange lodges were formed by soldiers attracted by their loyalism and ultra-Protestantism plus the convivial, well-lubricated atmosphere of lodge meetings. They returned to Britain with their lodge warrants and continued to meet. Thus in 1798 Colonel Stanley's regiment of the Lancashire Militia returned to Manchester with lodge warrant 220. The following year a military lodge returned to its home area of south Ayrshire, the first lodge in Scotland.[9] Ex-servicemen seeking to recapture the *camaraderie* they had enjoyed in Ireland secured a warrant from the Irish Grand Lodge and set up a lodge where they had settled down, thus founding the first civilian lodges in Britain. By 1803 there were lodges in Manchester and other textile towns of the north-west. Membership seems to have been a combination of ex-soldiers, Irish Protestant immigrants and

---

[6] Sean Farrell, *Rituals and Riots: Sectarian Violence and Political Order in Ulster 1784–1866* Lexington, KY: University of Kentucky Press, 2000, pp. 30–31

[7] Allan Blackstock, '"A dangerous ally": Orangeism and the Irish Yeomanry', *Irish Historical Studies*, xxx, 119, pp. 393–405; *An Ascendancy Army: The Irish Yeomanry, 1796–1834* Dublin: Four Courts Press, 1998

[8] David Fitzpatrick, *Descendancy: Irish Protestant Histories since 1795* Cambridge: Cambridge University Press, 2014, chp. 2: Orangeism and Irish military history, pp. 21–40

[9] McFarland, *Protestants First*, p. 49

local textile workers attracted by the combination of anti-Catholic loyalism and bucolic socialising. The first 12 July procession in Britain was in Oldham in 1803.[10]

The first clash in Britain between the Order and Irish Catholics also occurred in the north-west. On Monday 13 July 1807 a Manchester lodge in regalia proceeded to the Collegiate Church. On leaving they moved off in procession, when they were attacked. A local newspaper reported 'a very serious and alarming affray… The parading with sashes has very properly been suppressed in this town, for a few years back', implying that this was not the first such procession and not the first clash between 'a body of Orange-men, as they are termed… and a body of the Green, as they are called'.[11] The next edition condemned such processions along with 'the writing of "No Popery" upon the walls'.[12] The following month local Irish Catholics published a declaration disclaiming any responsibility and arguing that their community had suffered considerable slander by the local Orange Order.[13] Later that year a County Grand Lodge was formed, followed in 1808 by the first English Grand Lodge on the model of the Irish institution. The first Grand Master of England was Samuel Taylor, a modest landowner from the Moston district of Manchester. Analysis suggests that in 1811 the total membership of the Order in England was about 7,500 in 75 lodges of which 22 were military and 53 civilian – 35 were north of a line from Chester to Hull and of these 23 were in the textile towns of the Manchester region.[14]

The next few years were a period of considerable social unrest in Britain culminating in the famous 'Peterloo' incident in Manchester on 16 August 1819 and the Order was at pains to ensure that its structures and activities did not fall foul of the panic-stricken legislation that followed, notably the Unlawful Oaths Act (1823), Unlawful Associations Act (1825) and the Party Processions Act (1832). In fact it was widely believed that members of the Order were active in helping suppress the disorders. A local newspaper reported '[i]n a neighbouring town it is a well-known fact, to use the language of a friend of ours who knew them well, that if every Orangemen is not a spy for the magistrates, then at least every spy is an Orangeman'.[15] Recent analysis has argued that well into the mid-1830s the Order was indeed a notable element in the maintenance of law and order in disturbed urban areas.[16]

---

[10] Neal, *Sectarian Violence*, p. 18; Frank Neal, 'Manchester origins of the English Orange Order', *Manchester Region History Review*, iv,2, 1990–91, pp. 12–24; MacRaild, *Faith, Fraternity and Fighting*, pp. 37–38

[11] *Cowdroy's Manchester Gazette and Weekly Advertiser*, 18 July 1807

[12] *Cowdroy's Manchester Gazette and Weekly Advertiser*, 25 July 1807

[13] *Cowdroy's Manchester Gazette and Weekly Advertiser*, 15 August 1807

[14] Neal, 'Manchester origins'; his estimate of 100 members per lodge is generous

[15] *Liverpool Mercury*, 14 July 1820

[16] Katrina Navickas, *Protest and the Politics of Space and Place 1789–1848* Manchester: Manchester University Press, 2016, pp. 70–71

On 12 July 1819 lodges from Liverpool, Manchester and Bolton attended a service at St Peter's Church in Liverpool after which, headed by a band, they paraded through the strongly Irish Catholic Vauxhall area, sparking a riot which resulted in 11 Irish Catholics being sent to prison.[17] It was the first of a series of sectarian clashes that were to recur into the early twentieth century. The following year the Mayor requested local lodges not to parade but they refused and it was estimated 90 lodge members wearing regalia, carrying three silk banners, holding sticks and accompanied by a crowd of supporters, again paraded to St Peter's Church, reformed and paraded to a hotel, where dinner was enjoyed. Running fights developed, sticks and truncheons were used, shops closed to avoid damage, unrest continued into the evening and nine arrests were made.[18] The following year the Mayor forbade any processions and also denied the Order the right to participate in official processions marking the coronation of King George IV.[19]

For the rest of the 1820s and into the early 1830s no Orange processions were held in Liverpool on 12 July, but there were private celebrations and gatherings in public houses and the result could sometimes spill into the streets. In 1823 it was reported a constable who had just left a public house 'where an Orange Society were amusing themselves by celebrating the "glorious memory"' was knocked down and assaulted, Orangemen rushed to assist him but were attacked in turn; and five people were arrested.[20] The following year it was reported that the centre of the city was

> kept in a state of alarm, owing to the riotous conduct of a considerable number of Irish labourers who congregated... for the purpose of insulting and annoying the members of several clubs as they assembled at their usual places of annual meeting held on that day, which is also the anniversary of the Orange Societies. Such conduct is the more outrageous, as these clubs have forborne to have their usual processions on that day...[21]

In 1825 the same source declared 'we rejoice that the party processions which formerly disgraced the 12th of July have been laid aside, in despite of the real and noble examples of eternal enmity towards the Catholics'.[22] Despite the absence of large public events, it is clear that sectarian antipathy simmered at the local and personal level and could erupt given sufficient provocation.

[17] *Liverpool Mercury*, 14 July 1820
[18] *Liverpool Mercury*, 14 July 1820
[19] *Liverpool Mercury*, 20 July 1821
[20] *Liverpool Mercury*, 18 July 1823
[21] *Liverpool Mercury*, 16 July 1824
[22] *Liverpool Mercury*, 14 July 1825

This was provided when Catholic emancipation became a hotly contested issue in the late 1820s. Feelings on both sides were intense and sincere. Catholic leaders believed they had been led to expect that emancipation would follow the 1801 Act of Union between Britain and Ireland but successive bills had failed to pass.[23] The most effective advocate of the cause was Daniel O'Connell who, in May 1823, founded the Catholic Association, which developed into a remarkably effective instrument for mass mobilisation of a European peasant population. It put mounting pressure on the government by a series of massive demonstrations and a succession of by-election victories culminating in the election of O'Connell as MP for county Clare in July 1828.[24] The Tory government of the Duke of Wellington was now faced with the dilemma of either granting emancipation, thereby infuriating ultra-Protestants within their own party, or facing large-scale and possibly violent unrest in Ireland.

Parallel with the emancipation campaign there was mounting alarm in ultra-Protestant circles at the prospect of the Protestant constitution of the United Kingdom being undermined by the entry of Catholics into parliament. This led to a short-lived alliance between the Orange Order and some ultra-Protestant Tory peers. As the campaign for emancipation intensified the Duke of Cumberland, a son of King George IV, became Grand Master in 1828. Possibly flattered by royal patronage the Order saw a notable rise in membership and lodge numbers. In February 1829 Prime Minister Wellington and Home Secretary Sir Robert Peel, both long-term opponents, announced that in view of the threat to public order and good government in Ireland, they would support emancipation, which finally received grudging royal assent in April.[25]

Following this defeat the Orange Order entered a lengthy period of difficulty. The few ultra-Protestant peers who had joined drifted away. The political context altered as a series of Whig governments were elected between 1831 and 1841. Three developments converged to focus unfavourable attention on the Order. There had long been unease at the presence of Orange lodges in the military, with wild estimates concerning their numbers and possible political intentions. These suspicions were further stoked by colourful statements by some officers of the Order.[26] Research suggests there were in fact only 30 military lodges with a very modest total membership, somewhere between 500 and 1,000.[27] However, there was a complication in that the Duke of Cumberland was not merely Grand Master of the English Orange Order, but also the commander in chief of the

---

[23] Antonia Fraser, *The King and the Catholics; The Fight for Rights 1829* London: Weidenfeld and Nicolson, 2018

[24] Patrick Geoghegan, *Liberator: The Life and Death of Daniel O'Connell 1830–1847* Dublin: Gill and Macmillan, 2010

[25] Fraser, *The King and the Catholics*, p. 258

[26] Senior, *Orangeism*, pp. 259–66

[27] Neal, *Sectarian Violence*, p. 29; Fitzpatrick, *Descendancy*, pp. 21–34

British Army. Rumours circulated that, on the death of the incumbent King William IV, he planned to use the regiments in which the Order was strong to mount a coup, replacing his teenage niece Princess Victoria as heir to the throne.[28]

The reputation of the Order was further sullied by sectarian riots in Manchester and Liverpool. Following the Manchester outbreaks of 1830, 1834 and 1835, sectarian feeling lingered at local level, though there were no further conflicts there until a last minor outbreak in 1888.[29] By contrast, in Liverpool the tradition of violent sectarian conflict was to become deeply entrenched in civic life. In 1835 protracted riots were triggered by rumours that an Orange Order procession was planned and in response crowds of 'the opposite faction' began to gather around the junction of five roads at the southern end of Vauxhall Road, a strongly Irish neighbourhood.[30] The crowds forced the release of a recently arrested prisoner and the night watch intervened, but it had to take refuge in the local lockup. This was stormed by an estimated 2,000 people armed with various weapons who were eventually dispersed by police, the watch and firefighters. Throughout the following day rumours of an Orange procession persisted, 'several quarters of the town still remained in a most unquiet and unsettled state', troops were summoned, 400 special constables quickly sworn in and calm eventually restored. It was the most sustained sectarian riot the town had experienced to that date.[31]

It was the worst possible publicity for the Order when faced by a Whig party long suspicious of the military lodges, the role of the Order in the anti-emancipation campaign and its dalliance with Tory ultras. Following an alliance with O'Connell and his followers, in mid-1835 the Whig government set up a Select Committee of Parliament 'to inquire into the origin, nature and tendency of the Orange Institution in Great Britain, and to report their evidence and their opinions thereon'. Having taken evidence from witnesses, including the Grand Lodges of both Ireland and Great Britain, and examined a wide range of documentation, it produced four reports totalling 4,500 pages, the volume on England appearing in September 1835.[32] This revealed there were 381 lodges in Great Britain, of which 30 were military lodges, and 8 in overseas

---

[28] Senior, *Orangeism*, pp. 269–72

[29] M. Busteed, *The Irish in Manchester: c.1750–1921: Resistance, Adaptation and Identity* Manchester: Manchester University Press, 2016, pp. 88–92

[30] *Liverpool Mercury*, 17 July 1835

[31] *Liverpool Courier*, 13 July 1835; Neal, *Sectarian Violence*, pp. 41–43; Ann Bryson, 'Riotous Liverpool', in John Belchem (ed.), *Popular Politics, Riots and Labour: Essays in Liverpool History 1790–1940* Liverpool: Liverpool University Press, 1992, chp. 5, pp. 98–134

[32] Report of the Select Committee Appointed to Inquire into the Origin, Nature and Tendency of Orange Institutions in Great Britain and the Colonies, with the Minutes of Evidence, Appendix and Index. LRO Town Clerk's Papers 352.CLE/460

garrisons. Actual numbers in each lodge were hard to determine, but Appendix 20 of the Report lists the number of warrants in each of the 48 Districts and the total number of lodges and members in 16 of those Districts. One analysis of this patchy data suggests that total membership was about 7,800.[33] This was a movement largely concentrated in the north of the country, particularly Lancashire and Cheshire. Clearly the strength of the Order was much lower than some of the wild estimates that had circulated in the over-heated public debates. The great majority of lodges met in public houses where the political flavour was obvious, such as the Duke of York in Richmond Row, Liverpool. The third volume of the Select Committee's Report declared

> when your Committee look to the political tendency of the measures of the Orange societies in England and Ireland, and particularly to the language contained in addresses to the public, and in the correspondence with the grand officers of the Institution, and consider the possible use that made of such an organized power, its suppression becomes, in their opinion, imperatively necessary.[34]

In the parliamentary debates of September 1835 particular attention was focused on the position and rumoured intentions of the Duke of Cumberland, and in February 1836 he ordered the dissolution of the Order – the Irish Grand Lodge followed suit in April.[35]

The organisation had been dissolved but as a sentiment and a movement Orangeism survived. Quite soon after the formal dissolution other groups having the same outlook emerged and from these two in particular crystallised. One was The Grand Protestant Confederation, later Association, which came to be dominated by Squire Auty, an energetic councillor and businessman in Bradford who financed a vast range of Orange publications including a monthly newspaper. While strongest in west Yorkshire, Auty's home ground, it had branches throughout northern England and for a time was the largest single organisation within the Orange movement.[36] Its chief rival was the Loyal Orange Institution of Great Britain (LOI), whose main strength was in the Liverpool region. Despite recurring efforts to combine they went their separate ways for almost 30 years.[37]

At the grass-roots level lodges thrived and continued to meet for the traditional July dinner, toasts and songs. In 1841 a local newspaper noted that '[t]he Orangemen of Liverpool celebrated the anniversary of the battle of the

---

[33] Report of Select Committee, Appendix 20, p. 145; Neal, *Sectarian Violence*, p. 27

[34] Report of Select Committee, p. xxviii

[35] Haddick-Flynn, *Orangeism*, pp. 266–71; Senior, *Orangeism*, pp. 267–73

[36] MacRaild, *Faith, Fraternity and Fighting*, pp. 49–51

[37] Neal, *Sectarian Violence*, pp. 68–70

Boyne by dining in several parts of the town last evening. Loyal and constitutional toasts were, as usual, the order of the night.'[38] By this time a consensus had emerged in the city that there should be no public processions on either 17 March (St Patrick's Day) or 12 July, reinforced by a public plea from local magistrates in 1842. But sectarian feeling was latent. On 12 July 1842, although lodges celebrated in private, 'the town was in an exceedingly disturbed state throughout the entire day', some club houses were vandalised and four people appeared in court, but the police prevented wider outbreaks by placing a guard on club houses and patrolling districts regarded as likely to generate rioting.[39]

Though the ban on 12 July and 17 March processions was respected, Orange Order church parades did occur and lodges often joined the funeral corteges of deceased members. This may have been the reason for the decision of four local Irish Catholic organisations to celebrate St Patrick's Day 1845 with a public procession, wearing green and white scarves, bands playing party tunes and banners displaying O'Connell. In doing so they defied pleas by the parish priests of St Anthony's and St Patrick's, the two churches most closely associated with the local Irish community. Although a group of Orangemen gathered near the route, careful policing prevented serious conflict.[40] One local newspaper declared '[w]e were glad to find that none of the respectable portion of the Irish population joined in', contrasting the event with a dinner on the same day attended by 'about 100 members of the respectable Irish residents... It has seldom been our good fortune to attend a meeting where so much good feeling prevailed.'[41]

It was not to last. In June 150 Orangemen joined the funeral of a member, many wearing scarfs and 'orange favours', others black sashes trimmed with Orange ribbons. Returning by a route close to St Anthony's, rioting broke out and 'stones and brickbats were flying about as thick as hail during the greater part of the affray'. Pleas from local Catholic clergy and the arrival of police defused the situation but the following day the town was still in a disturbed state. At the trial of those arrested the magistrate deplored the breach of the ban on party demonstrations 'in a town where antagonist religious feelings were on such occasions so strongly excited' and he expressed the fear that such events were 'a practice which was calculated to renew former feuds'.[42]

Consequently, on 12 July '[i]t was not to be wondered at there should have been an Orange procession in Liverpool'.[43] The event displayed several features that would become standard for the city's July celebrations. It was estimated that

[38] *Liverpool Mercury*, 16 July 1841
[39] *Liverpool Courier*, 13 July 1842
[40] *Liverpool Courier*, 19 March 1845
[41] *Liverpool Mercury*, 21 March 1845
[42] *Liverpool Courier*, 9 June 1845
[43] *Liverpool Courier*, 16 July 1845

500 to 600 men from 30 lodges, carrying banners and flags, wearing orange or purple scarves, led by two bands who 'played a variety of stirring airs... and accompanied by large numbers of women' assembled at a local railway station, took a special train to Newton, gathered at the local Conservative hall, listened to political speeches, passed a resolution expressing loyalty to the Queen and condemning government concessions to Catholics, paraded through the village, took the train to Liverpool town centre and dispersed to their club houses for a meal. Heavy policing ensured no large-scale conflicts occurred though one newspaper noted 'some slight affrays... in which the Irish, as usual, were the offending parties' and in an editorial applauded the Order in perceptive terms:

> it possesses within itself materials not to be found elsewhere, binding in an indissoluble bond the upper, the middle, and the lower classes of Protestantism... with all classes of Protestantism, by whatever denomination they may be known, it loves to fraternise; against the enemies of the throne, the altar, and the constitution it presents an invisible front.[44]

The following year the celebration was confined to the town and passed off quietly with a procession and dinner.[45]

It is difficult to gauge the strength of the Orange movement at this point. One complication was the existence of the two competing organisations. From the late 1850s until the early 1860s the Association, under the bustling Squire Auty, may well have been the larger,[46] but a considerable number of the Liverpool lodges were affiliated to the LOI. Its constitution, adopted in 1842, made it clear that 'we admit none as members who are not strictly and devotedly Protestant, loyal and peaceable subjects'.[47] Some impression of numbers may be culled from local press reports on 12 July but must be used with caution because, as one newspaper admitted in 1859, 'no authentic returns to these [are] kept'.[48] Moreover, a distinction has to be made between estimates of those actually walking in the processions and those who were merely admiring crowds of relatives, supporters or simply spectators attracted by the spectacle. Some lodges did not participate in the processions, either because they felt they were too few in number, could not afford the expense of travel or did not possess suitable regalia. In 1859 it was reported that only 20 of the 68 lodges in the city participated.[49] Others, reflecting

---

[44] *Liverpool Courier*, 16 July 1845

[45] *Liverpool Courier*, 15 July 1846

[46] MacRaild, *Faith, Fraternity and Fighting*, p. 54

[47] *Laws and Ordnances of the Loyal Orange Institution of Great Britain. Liverpool.* Printed by Order of the Grand Lodge, 1842, p. v; LRO Town Clerk's Papers 352 CLE/460

[48] *Liverpool Daily Post*, 13 July 1859

[49] *Daily Post*, 13 July 1859

the puritan tradition discussed later and possibly unhappy at the violence and alcohol often associated with the processions, opted for private events. In 1871 some members organised a tea party on 12 July, a speaker regretting the growing number of Orange halls in which he feared dancing would take place during the day and 'God would not be glorified'.[50] Local newspapers seemed unaware until 1856 that two separate Orange organisations existed, but there is no further mention of this distinction until 1864, and even then reports are confused. It is also clear that Liverpool lodges were occasionally joined, as in 1851, by detachments from elsewhere in the north-west and 'some Irish lodges'.[51] Press coverage grew in length and detail from the late 1850s, possibly a realisation of the growing significance of the movement. In 1875, the last year before the merger, it was reported that the LOI numbered 'upwards of 10,000 members' in 90 lodges, of which 70 were represented in the 12 July procession, whilst at the separate Association event 3,000 members from 30 lodges walked.[52]

The 1876 demonstrations were the first to follow the amalgamation, resulting in 'an impressive exhibition of the forces of the united societies fused into one aggregated mass'.[53] The local press had clearly reached consensus on numbers, reporting 160 lodges with 7–8,000 in the procession, consisting of about 110 lodges of the LOI and 50 of the Association.[54] One source went so far as to try counting the numbers in each lodge, with limited success, suggesting that in 26 lodges the average number parading was 66 members.[55] The first annual report of the new Institution appeared in 1877, carrying statistics for the previous year. The Secretary was at pains to scold lodges that had not submitted returns. The report reveals that there were 536 lodges in England and Wales, organised into 7 Provinces, of which the largest was Manchester with 141 lodges, followed by Liverpool with 130. At this stage the Orange Order in Britain was overwhelmingly concentrated in the north-west, with 362 (68 per cent) of lodges in the Manchester, Liverpool and Lancaster Provinces.[56]

Conclusion

Throughout its history the Orange Order was marked by its Irish origins and its close association with the military, but by the 1870s it was clear that it had not merely survived transplantation, but put down deep local roots and proved

---

[50] *Liverpool Courier*, 13 July 1871
[51] *Liverpool Courier*, 16 July 1851
[52] *Liverpool Courier*, 13 July 1875
[53] *Liverpool Courier*, 13 July 1876
[54] *Daily Post*, 13 July 1876; *Evening Express*, 13 July 1876
[55] *Liverpool Courier*, 13 July 1876
[56] Loyal Orange Institution of England Report 1877

sufficiently robust to withstand official displeasure, formal dissolution and division. Contemporary observers remarked on the colourful 12 July events, the occasional sectarian clashes and strove to explain its presence. However, it was becoming abundantly clear that, whilst lodges were to be found amongst working-class people in many of the large industrial urban areas of northern England, in Liverpool 'conditions were increasingly proving to be unique'.[57]

---

[57] MacRaild, *Faith, Fraternity and Fighting*, p. 46

2

The Liverpool Context

This chapter will argue that the exceptional significance of the Order in Liverpool was the product of three interacting factors: first, a working class marked by an extraordinarily large casual element and closely bonded into an intense associational culture; second, large-scale immigration of Irish Catholics fleeing the Irish famine in the second half of the 1840s, reinforcing traditional Protestant fears and producing a strongly marked pattern of residential segregation and sporadic violent sectarian conflict in which the Order was an actor; finally, the articulation of those fears by a cadre of energetic, Irish-born, Anglican clergy, who articulated, justified and mobilised the atavistic fears of the Protestant working class and gave Liverpool Anglicanism and Conservatism a uniquely ardent proletarian and sectarian flavour.

The Liverpool labour market

In the nineteenth century Liverpool became the second largest city in the United Kingdom and the key commercial port of the expanding British empire.[1] From a population of 5,145 in 1700 the city grew to 55,732 in 1791, thanks to the steady expansion of its Irish Sea, north Atlantic, West Indies and notorious west Africa trade. Rapid economic expansion and extension of city boundaries saw a further increase from 77,653 in 1801 to 746,421 in 1911,[2] reflecting development of new trading links with South America, India and China. The total tonnage of shipping handled at its docks doubled between 1815 and 1830 and doubled again between 1830 and 1845. By 1914 the city had developed extensive trading with

---

[1] Tony Lane, *Liverpool: Gateway of Empire* London: Lawrence and Wishart, 1987; G. Milne, 'Maritime Liverpool', in J. Belchem (ed.) *Liverpool 800: Culture, Character and History* Liverpool: Liverpool University Press, 2006, chp. 4, pp. 257–309; Tristram Hunt, *Ten Cities That Made an Empire* Harmondsworth: Penguin, 2014, chp. 10: Liverpool

[2] J. Longmore, 'Civic Liverpool 1680–1800', in Belchem, *Liverpool 800*, chp. 2, pp. 113–69

the eastern Mediterranean and south-east Asia, handling 31 per cent of British visible imports and exports.[3]

Two features distinguished Liverpool's role as a port, namely the varied nature of its import and export trade and the extraordinary size of the casual element in its dockside labour force. The city has been described as 'the gateway between the world of raw material and that of manufacturing'.[4] Raw cotton for the Lancashire textile industry comprised 30 per cent of imports and finished cotton goods and 42 per cent of exports by value in 1914, but there were also imports of grain, sugar, palm oil, meat, dairy produce and livestock, much of which was processed at dockside mills and factories. Throughout the nineteenth and into the twentieth century the city was also a key transit point for departing emigrants, who have been estimated to number 9 million between the 1830s and the 1930s.[5] Thriving financial and commercial sectors also developed and prosperous merchants and shipowners marked their success with large villas, employment of servants and membership of a network of clubs and societies. The insuring of vessels and cargoes and administration of ships, cargoes, docks and harbours generated a wide range of clerking posts. Until the early twentieth century manufacturing was confined to shipbuilding, located at Cammell Laird in Birkenhead. Port-related activity was the keystone of the Liverpool economy.

The Mersey is notable for its large tidal range and, beginning with Old Dock in 1715, a string of enclosed docks nine kilometres long was excavated from the tidal mud, ending with Seaforth in 1972, signalling the containerisation revolution that rendered all its predecessors obsolete. Liverpool was probably at its peak as the prime port of the British domestic and imperial system during the period from the mid-nineteenth century to 1914. At that point it has been estimated that the docks and associated cartage, warehousing and processing trades may have employed 120,000 people.[6]

A distinctive feature of the Liverpool dock labour force was the high proportion employed on a casual basis. Dock work was always inherently variable but the Liverpool tidal range amplified the variability. Down to the early twentieth century much seaborne trade was carried in sailing vessels with time of arrival dependent on weather and wind. This meant lack of employment for dockworkers, drivers of vehicles waiting to carry the goods to warehouses and for workers waiting at mills and processing factories. There were also seasonal fluctuations in the flow of goods—raw cotton imports were at their height from October to May and migration traffic usually peaked in spring and early summer. Moreover, given the tidal range at Liverpool and the use of enclosed docks,

[3] Lane, *Liverpool*, p. 36
[4] Milne, 'Maritime Liverpool', p. 259
[5] Milne, 'Maritime Liverpool', p. 305
[6] Lane, *Liverpool*, p. 43

vessels had to queue in the river for dock space. It was difficult to estimate the size of the casual labour pool, but research suggests around 25,000 people were usually available on the dock estate and even at peak demand about 7,000 were surplus to requirement.[7]

The process of hiring varied between docks but the day normally began with men assembling at 'stands' on the quays where the foremen in charge would choose the number required. There was some jostling to catch his eye and according to folklore choice was influenced by family relationships, personal friendship or religious affiliation. In practice the nature of the work determined numbers and skills required, since there were fine distinctions between stevedores who loaded and unloaded, shipmen labourers who placed and distributed the goods, quay porters who sorted, weighed and marked the goods and passed them on for further transportation and 'casual casuals' who occasionally turned up on the chance of work. Foremen put a premium on gangs known for their ability to work as a skilled team. For employers Liverpool had the obvious advantage of a labour pool available when needed, with no obligation to provide support in slack times. The most skilled, experienced and best paid of the workforce liked the flexibility to choose where and when to work. Total abolition of the system was not achieved until 1967.[8]

In addition to the dangerous and physically demanding nature of the work, the casual system placed a great strain on the economy of dockland households and bore down particularly on women who had to plan weekly expenditure against a background of a totally unpredictable income, a point made by the redoubtable researcher, reformer, future councillor and MP Eleanor Rathbone. The result is illustrated by a member of Garston True Blues LOL 64 who, reminded that he was behind in payment of lodge dues, promised to pay 'if he got another day in at the docks'.[9] The struggle to cope had a wider impact on the social and cultural lives of working-class communities, restricting horizons to immediate material concerns and creating a fatalistic focus on mere survival and no sense of the potential for improvement.[10]

The system meant that to be on hand for news of work and able to report for selection as early as possible it was necessary to live close to the docks.

[7] Eric Taplin, 'Dock labour at Liverpool: occupational structure and working conditions in the late nineteenth century', *Transactions of the Historic Society of Lancashire and Cheshire*, 127, 1977, pp. 123–74; 'The history of dock labour, Liverpool', in S. Davies (ed.), *Dock Workers: International Explorations in Comparative Labour History*, vol. 2 Aldershot: Ashgate, 2000, chp. 21, pp. 442–70

[8] Susan Pedersen, *Eleanor Rathbone and The Politics of Conscience* New Haven, CT: Yale University Press, 2004, p. 103

[9] Garston True Blues LOL 64, 25 September 1922, Minute Book for 1921–23; held at Heald Street Orange Hall, Garston

[10] Taplin, 'Dock labour at Liverpool', p. 153

Consequently, on the other side of the road that ran north to south alongside the docks there developed a dense network of very basic residential housing inhabited almost entirely by dockworkers and those who serviced them in shops, cafes and pubs. It has been estimated that 75 per cent of Liverpool dockworkers lived within 1.6 km of their potential workplace and that those who lived over 2.4 km from the docks were people employed on a more regular basis.[11] Within these working-class streets there was a marked localism and awareness of the fine distinctions derived from the varieties of dock work, but this group work experience also created a strong awareness of the need for team work based on mutual trust and cooperation. Consequently, in both the strongly marked Protestant and Irish Catholic districts that will be described shortly there was a dense network of local organisations and associations, including mutual aid groups, often organised by dominant matriarchal figures, alongside a plethora of sporting, cultural or political activities. It was in this fertile ground that tightly bonded working-class communal life would generate an intense, localised, associational culture, in the Catholic areas often centred round the church and in the Protestant districts often based on Orange lodges.

Irish immigration, sectarian conflict and residential segregation

By the early seventeenth century Liverpool was the centre of a thriving two-way trade in linen yarn and finished cloth across the Irish Sea.[12] In the 1740s an increasing number of Irish names began to appear in local Catholic baptismal registers, indicating the presence of a permanently resident, Irish-born element in the city's population, along with migrant Scots and Welsh.[13] Connections were further boosted by the growing importation of foodstuffs from Ireland to feed the expanding population centres of urban industrial Britain. By the 1840s, thanks to the combination of regular Irish Sea crossings and the growing rail network, the greater part of the livestock and provisions sold at Manchester's markets was imported from Ireland via Liverpool.[14] Growth in trade and Irish immigration were further stimulated with the launch of a regular steamship service in 1824. By the 1840s there were links with 11 Irish ports and over 100 crossings per week for passengers and goods – competition between companies had reduced fares and journeys that once took days to as little as 14 hours, weather permitting.[15]

[11] Colin Pooley, 'Residential differentiation in Victorian cities: a reappraisal', *Transactions of the Institute of British Geographers* New Series, 19,2, 1984, pp. 131–44
[12] Busteed, *The Irish in Manchester*, p. 7
[13] Peter Doyle, *Mitres and Missions: The Roman Catholic Diocese of Liverpool 1850–2000* Liverpool: Bluecoat Press, 2005, p. 26
[14] Busteed, *The Irish in Manchester*, pp. 8–9
[15] Neal, *Sectarian Violence*, pp. 83–84; *Black '47: Britain and the Famine Irish* Basingstoke: Macmillan, 1998, p. 54 for sailing schedules and costs

The 1841 census, often regarded as the first fairly reliable count, found that London had the largest Irish population of any city in Great Britain (73,133 or 3.9 per cent), followed by Liverpool (49,636, 17.3 per cent), Glasgow (44,345, 16.1 per cent) and Manchester/Salford (33,490, 11.01 per cent). Clearly Liverpool, like all Britain's urban centres, had a well-established Irish-born population well before the famine influx of 1845–52.[16] It is also clear that a distinct pattern of residential segregation was emerging. Though there were some Irish in every part of the urban residential fabric, there was a distinct concentration in the north end of the city, particularly in the local government wards of Vauxhall, Exchange, Scotland and St George, though there were also clusters in Pitt Street, Great George district and Toxteth in the south.[17] The strong concentration in the north end was partly due to the fact that most Irish boats berthed at Clarence Dock, there were employment opportunities in the dock area and, as suggested earlier, it was important to live nearby to tap into information flows and be early at the stands. These wards, Vauxhall in particular, were to attract persistent attention during the nineteenth and early twentieth centuries from urban reformers gathering data on the notoriously poor housing and living conditions of its largely working-class and Irish population.

In 1842 the Liverpool Anti-Monopoly Association, supervised by the Anti-Corn Law League, set out to gather evidence supporting the argument that legislation restricting import of foreign corn kept the price of bread at an artificially high level, thus contributing to the distress of working people. They decided to carry out a survey in Vauxhall ward and present the results in support of their campaign. Vauxhall ward stretched inland from frontage on the Waterloo Road and Victoria and Waterloo docks to a short stretch on Scotland Road. It was found to have a population of 23,892. As for the area, '[i]ts character is manufacturing, consisting of iron foundries, soap, alkali, chemical and other manufactories all cheek by jowl with the homes of the Vauxhall inhabitants'.[18] One data collector noted '[a] very large proportion of the residents in this district depend chiefly upon being employed in discharging vessels and other business connected with the docks. These men complain that they can now scarcely get two days' work in the week...'[19] The investigators found that, of the total working-class labour force for which details were available, 1,737 (36.1 per cent) were unemployed, 1,490 (31 per cent) fully employed and 1,236 (25.7 per cent) employed for three days per week or fewer. Of the 4,834 families of the 'labouring class' 59.9 per cent were

---

[16] Neal, *Sectarian Violence*, p. 9

[17] J. Belchem and D. MacRaild, 'Cosmopolitan Liverpool' in Belchem, *Liverpool 800*, chp. 5, pp. 325–35

[18] *Statistics of Vauxhall Ward: The condition of the Working Class in Liverpool in 1842*. Comp. and ed. John Finch. A facsimile reprint, prepared and introduced by Harold Hikins. Liverpool: Toulouse Press, 1986, p. 9. LRO: H 331.83 FIN

[19] *Statistics of Vauxhall Ward*, p. 55

housed in 'bad, miserable or destitute conditions'.[20] The Irish were dominant—of the 4,977 heads of families of the 'labouring class' whose place of birth could be identified, 2,243 (45.6 per cent) were Irish, 'nearly the whole of whom are of the Catholic persuasion, mostly in indigent circumstances, and much needing education'.[21] Of the remainder, 1,326 (26.6 per cent) had been born in Liverpool, 367 in Lancashire (7.4 per cent) and 366 (7.4 per cent) in north Wales.[22] It was noted that there was a considerable Irish element in the outflow of migrants, with North America the favoured destination.[23] They were the precursors of an historic exodus.

By the early nineteenth century the economic resources of Ireland were unable to support the growing population which, by 1845, had reached about 8.5 million. One response had been increased planting of the potato, a notably nutritious food crop, and by the mid-1840s it was estimated that one-third of all tilled land in Ireland was under potatoes, its cultivation particularly notable in the small farm districts of the west and south-west.[24] A further option was emigration and with the advent of peace between Britain and France in 1815 and the steady fall in travel costs noted above this was an increasingly popular choice, hence the build-up of Irish communities in British towns and cities such as Liverpool.

Heavy dependence on a particular food crop brought obvious dangers and there were recurrent food shortages and occasional poor harvests between 1815 and the early 1840s. In late 1844 *phytophthora infestans* or 'the blight' as it was universally known appeared in North America and on 20 August 1845 it made its nervously anticipated arrival in Ireland. By November at least one-third of the potato crop had been destroyed, much of the seed crop had been eaten, little was available for planting in 1846 and 90 per cent of the yield was infected. By 'Black '47' the crop was tiny and more than 3 million people were dependent on private or official charity. From 1848 to 1851 the blight reappeared in sporadic form and by 1852 the famine was over.[25]

There has been academic debate over the precise number of 'excess deaths' during the famine period, settling at somewhere between 1.4 and 1.5 million.[26] Two-thirds of excess deaths may have been caused by the impact of typhus,

[20] *Statistics of Vauxhall Ward*, pp. 10–13, 45–47
[21] *Statistics of Vauxhall Ward*, p. 16
[22] *Statistics of Vauxhall Ward*, Table 11, p. 38
[23] *Statistics of Vauxhall Ward*, pp. 21–22
[24] Ciaran O'Murchadha, *The Great Famine: Ireland's Agony* London: Continuum, 2011, p. 7
[25] Christine Kinealy, *This Great Calamity: The Irish Famine 1845–52* Dublin: Gill and Macmillan, 1994
[26] James Donnelly jr., *The Great Irish Potato Famine* Stroud: Sutton Publishing, 2002, p. 171

typhoid, dysentery and diarrhoea on a grossly under-nourished population.[27] Movement of large numbers around the country, to search for food or relief works, crowding into workhouses or travelling towards ports with the intention of emigrating, meant widespread dissemination of measles, scurvy, scarlatina and tuberculosis.[28] During the period 1845–55 approximately 2.1 million people emigrated, of which the great majority went to North America, especially the USA, and 200,000 settled in Great Britain.[29] Liverpool was a major transit point for those bound for America. Approximately 580,000 Irish passed through the city at the height of famine migration, including over 300,000 in 1847 alone, of which 137,000 went on to the USA.[30] Of those who did not emigrate, some moved on elsewhere in Britain whilst others remained in Liverpool, either because they were too exhausted or impoverished to go any further or they had family already settled there.

The city's administrative structures for dealing with the poor and sick were overwhelmed. Legislation in 1842 had permitted councils to appoint a Medical Officer of Health and Dr William Henry Duncan was the first appointed in Britain. Initially employed on a part-time basis in 1846, he was made full-time in 1848 in view of the Irish influx. Born in Liverpool, he had attended the internationally renowned Edinburgh medical school from 1825–29. It is very likely that he was aware of the work of his fellow Edinburgh alumnus James Philips Kay, who had written up his experiences of the 1832 cholera epidemic in Manchester in a widely read book that gave Irish immigrants a key role in what he saw as the deterioration of working-class housing conditions and behaviour.[31] Duncan had already compiled reports on destitution in the areas between Vauxhall and Scotland Roads and he too presented the Irish as both victims and agents, acknowledging that poverty was closely associated with their situation but suggesting that their apathy, lack of education and poor personal cleanliness partly explained their situation and provided a bad role model for the native population.

It was an all too common outlook. The Liverpool Board of Guardians and the Select Vestry were responsible for relief of the poor. The Select Vestry quickly reorganised itself into 13 districts with 11 relieving officers who oversaw the vetting of applicants and distributed tickets entitling holders to receive 6 ounces of free bread and soup. Given the numbers and desperate state of the immigrants

[27] O'Murchadha, *The Great Famine*, p. 93

[28] W. P. McArthur, 'Medical history of the famine', in R.D. Edwards and T.D. Williams (eds), *The Great Famine: Studies in Irish History 1845–52* Dublin: Lilliput Press, 1994, chp. 5, pp. 262–315

[29] Donnelly, *The Great Irish Potato Famine*, p. 178

[30] Doyle, *Mitres and Missions*, p. 38; C. Pooley, 'Living in Liverpool', in Belchem, *Liverpool 800*, p. 187

[31] Busteed, *The Irish in Manchester*, pp. 23–28

some observers argued these measures were insufficient, but some ratepayers who financed the work of the Guardians contended that an excessive amount of the fast-growing budget was going to the Irish, that some did not qualify for support and others were defrauding the system. However, it has been argued that the cost of supporting the indigent Irish was significantly exaggerated, that they added considerably to the pool of labour available for employers and that this helped to hold down wages.[32] Nonetheless, the suspicions plus the sheer numbers arriving over a short period fed into the traditional anti-Irish and anti-Catholic sentiment which by then was a deeply entrenched feature of Protestant Liverpool's popular culture.

Outbreaks of disease reinforced these convictions. The infections which caused so many of the fatalities in Ireland also broke out in Great Britain, along with cholera in 1848. Legal responsibility for care of the indigent sick fell to the Boards of Guardians and there were special wards in the workhouse, but extraordinary measures were clearly required. Five temporary sheds were erected to provide additional beds, two ships in the Mersey were adapted to take patients and another to quarantine infected migrants. But the great majority of the sick were treated at home, where the crowded and insanitary conditions contributed to infection and fatalities. In 1847 alone it has been estimated that 17,280 people died in Liverpool from fever, dysentery and diarrhoea, of which 5,233 (30.3 per cent) were Irish-born. By February 1848 there were signs that the outbreaks of typhoid and typhus had passed their peak, though cholera did not abate until May 1849.[33] There was a common conviction that the responsibility for these infections lay largely with the Irish and the significant generic terms 'Famine Fever' or 'Irish Fever' passed into common parlance. The patterns of disease and fatalities reinforced popular prejudice. The fact that the highest levels were to be found in the wards of Vauxhall, Scotland and Exchange in the north end and Great George in the south end, already well known for their strongly Irish Catholic presence, reinforced popular prejudices.

By 1851 the Irish-born element in the city had risen to 83,813 or 22.3 per cent of the total population, the highest relative proportion in Great Britain. Irish immigration persisted throughout the century, though at a much lower rate until in 1891 the census recorded that 9.1 per cent of Liverpudlians were Irish-born.[34] By then there was a considerable number of second and subsequent generations in the Irish community and in absolute terms it has been estimated as 150,000 to 200,000 strong.[35] By far the largest part of the influx had sought out the widely known Irish neighbourhoods in the dense concentration of housing behind the

[32] Neal, *Sectarian Violence*, pp. 107–09; *Black '47*, p. 248
[33] Neal, *Black '47*, chp. 5: 'Liverpool and the Irish Fever'
[34] Pooley, 'Living in Liverpool', p. 249
[35] Belchem, *Irish, Catholic and Scouse*, p. 15

docks between Vauxhall and Scotland Roads. There they reinforced and extended the already intense, deeply rooted community life, creating a long-lived Irish enclave which can be seen as both a protective and a defensive measure.[36] Any tendency for the pattern of residential segregation to erode was checked by the periodic outbreaks of sectarian conflict which saw people in mixed areas move back into the safety and security of districts dominated by their coreligionists.[37]

But an additional factor in sustaining this residential pattern was the all-pervading associational culture. Up to the mid-nineteenth century this was dominated by locally based mutual aid societies, many organised on a street-by-street basis by female collectors, administrators and distributors. There was also a vibrant network based on local pubs, many owned by widows and deeply rooted in the clandestine, oath-bound lodges of the exclusively Catholic Ribbon movement, a proto-nationalist organisation in the Defender tradition with vague traditional aspirations towards an independent Ireland to be achieved by armed rebellion. By the 1820s the tradition had been carried over into the Irish settlements in Britain. There, in the hearty, male-dominated atmosphere of the pubs with their Irish iconography, newspapers, music and song, the lodges had taken on a strong ethos of group assistance, informally helping new arrivals to find accommodation and employment and more formally in mutual aid and burial societies. Clubs such as the Hibernian Benevolent Burial Society appealed because, unlike many others, they extended membership to part-time workers such as dockers and seasonal harvesters, giving them a reach deep into the Irish community.[38]

A further key element in the consolidation of that community was the Catholic church. By the early nineteenth century there were three chapels in the city, modest and discreet in site, size and appearance. In 1824 the significantly named St Patrick's on the south side of the city was opened for worship. French refugees had built a small chapel dedicated to St Anthony at the southern end of Scotland Road, which was later rebuilt, considerably extended and consecrated in 1833. By 1914 the city had been divided into 24 parishes, of which 16 were to be found in Vauxhall, Scotland and Everton districts.[39] Along with each church came the infrastructure of Catholic life, namely presbytery, parochial hall, school and cemetery. Church location both followed and consolidated religious and ethnic geography. Even for the significant number who had lapsed or were irregular in practice, the church was a familiar and comforting element in an

[36] J. Belchem, 'The Liverpool Irish enclave' in D. MacRaild (ed.), *The Great Famine and Beyond: Irish Migrants in Britain in the Nineteenth and Twentieth Centuries* Dublin: Irish Academic Press, 2000, chp. 5, pp. 128–46

[37] Neal, *Sectarian Violence*, p. 234

[38] John Belchem, *Merseypride: Essays in Liverpool Exceptionalism* Liverpool: Liverpool University Press, 2000, p. 67

[39] Belchem, *Merseypride*, pp. 109–10

otherwise bleak and sometimes hostile cultural landscape. Church authorities in Liverpool realised that, given the condition of the Irish arrivals, they needed to rethink the basis of their mission to deal not only with the spiritual needs of their congregations but also their deep-seated destitution, poor health and economic insecurity.

These were addressed through the creation of an associational culture built around parish-based organisations and associations, some locally inspired, others local branches of national organisations. Devotional fraternities were keenly encouraged alongside organisations with a more specifically philanthropic ethos. The approach had two additional advantages. First, it guarded against the danger of 'wastage' or falling off from the faith—in 1838 it had been noted that only 28.7 per cent of all baptisms and 10.3 per cent of marriages in the city had had been performed in Catholic churches.[40] In particular there was fear of 'souperism', proselytising Protestant missionaries offering food and monetary support in return for converting. But religion also diverted the faithful from the Ribbon-based organisations. This reflected the traditional church abhorrence of secret oath-bound organisations and nervousness at any groups with a hint of political subversion or violence in their philosophy. It also provided an alternative to the pub as a venue for meetings, as the need for temperance became a theme of church teaching. In their devoted attention to their flocks the Irish Catholic clergy became widely respected figures, 10 of the 24 in the city dying as a direct result of their ministrations during 1847 alone. The locally born, second-generation Irish priest Fr James Nugent focused on the problems of young children, organising night shelters, orphanages, industrial schools, temperance groups, concerts and emigration schemes.[41] Later in the century insurance clubs endorsed by the ecclesiastical authorities, such as the Irish National Foresters who set up their Liverpool District in 1889, and the rival Ancient Order of Hibernians, struck deep roots, often meeting in parochial halls with a priest as an officer.

The result was a densely interwoven network of philanthropy, associational support and pastoral provision which cared for the faithful from cradle to grave. It reached across cleavages of age, gender, class, faction and county origin and welded the Catholic Irish into a remarkably closely bonded community. This combination of residential segregation, community bonding and a well-developed interwoven network of lodges and clubs, with officers experienced in organisation and administration, made the north end a fertile ground for the organisation of an independent political grouping. A Protector Society and later a Catholic Club were organised in 1839 to counter recent mobilisation of Protestant voters

---

[40] Robert Walker, 'Religious changes in Liverpool in the nineteenth century', *Journal of Ecclesiastical History*, 19, 1968, p. 201

[41] John Furnival, *Children of the Second Spring: Father James Nugent and the Work of Child Care in Liverpool* Leominster: Gracewing, 2005

on educational issues. Catholic Liberals served as councillors for Exchange, St Paul's, Scotland and Vauxhall wards, and by the early 1870s, when the number of Irish voters was estimated to be about 10,000 in a total electorate of 58,000, it was felt that Liverpool was fertile ground for independent political representation through local branches of the increasingly confident Irish nationalist movement.[42]

Early local political leaders tended to be merchants and professional people who serviced their local fellow countrymen, in contrast to those whose interests were focused outwards to the Irish Sea trade or the expanding British empire. In 1875 an Irish National Party councillor was elected, the first of 48 who were to be returned down to 1922, mostly representing Vauxhall and Scotland wards. In time the community began to support candidates with intense face-to-face contact with their constituents such as shop keepers, publicans, insurance and club fee collectors and, alongside enduring interest in Irish affairs, there developed a constructive focus on material issues directly impacting on constituents such as housing and working conditions.[43] This same concentration of voters and networks enabled the election of Thomas Power ('Tay Pay') O'Connor as Nationalist MP for Scotland Road from 1885 to 1929.

However, this burgeoning Irish Catholic visibility, intensity of organisation, impressive community solidarity and political confidence fed into traditional anti-Catholic fears and contributed to the equally remarkable intensity of working-class Protestant self-identity and its expression through the Liverpool Orange Order and eventually the Conservative Party.[44]

Liverpool Protestantism

The peculiar strength and intensity of Liverpool Protestantism has long been noted by observers and analysts. To some extent it was merely a particularly strong regional manifestation of that traditional mix of anti-Catholic and anti-Irish sentiment that characterised historic English and later British popular nationalism. The fact that it should prove especially vehement and enduring in Liverpool was due to a combination of context, contingency and agency.

The north-west was one of the few regions of England where a significant number of people remained loyal to Catholicism despite the sixteenth-century Protestant Reformation. These recusant groups usually dwelt in remote rural areas under the quiet tutelage of landed families who had managed to retain

---

[42] Liam Brady, *T.P. O'Connor and the Liverpool Irish* London: Royal Historical Society, 1983

[43] Belchem and MacRaild, 'Cosmopolitan Liverpool', pp. 335–8

[44] Belchem, 'The Liverpool Irish enclave', pp. 142–43; Belchem and MacRaild, 'Cosmopolitan Liverpool', pp. 326–27

both faith and property. In the Liverpool area the most notable were the Norris family of Speke Hall and two families named Blundell around Crosby.[45] Their discreet quietism reflected the fact that for at least three centuries, Catholics were a suspect community subject to penal legislation and demonised as the great 'other' against which English and later British popular nationalism contested and defined itself.

Anti-Catholic sentiment has been described as 'probably the most ubiquitous, most eclectic and most adaptable ideology in the post reformation history of the British isles'.[46] At all levels in British Protestant society Catholicism was viewed as the epitome of everything Britain had escaped from at the Reformation. The more sophisticated regarded it as a demeaning peasant superstition typical of the credulous. At the popular level attitudes were much more visceral. Catholic clergy were characterised as tyrannical, intrusive and, in the confessional, pruriently inquisitive. Catholic lay people were looked upon with a mix of pity and mistrust, regarded as personally superstitious, credulous and subject to the demands of overbearing clergy. An historical narrative was crafted presenting Catholics as the perpetual enemy scheming to overthrow the British Protestant crown, church and constitution through foreign invasion such as the Spanish Armada of 1588 and domestic conspiracy such as the Gunpowder Plot 1605.

Popular prejudices and fears were constantly refreshed by sermons stressing that if the Protestant nature of the state was compromised the result would be persecution, slavery and foreign despotism. The message was also presented through pageants, processions and well lubricated dinners with celebratory toasts. Mass-produced almanacs, street ballads and later newspapers served to sustain these popular Protestant convictions. Mistreatment of their Protestant subjects by Catholic European powers was publicised as exemplifying what would happen if Catholicism were allowed to take root in Britain again. Over all was a flattering narrative of English and subsequently British history as a coherent 'island story' of a wise, sturdy, fortunate people free from clerical dictation and relatively prosperous, materially, thanks to their Protestant constitution, crown and church. In wartime this was a potent rallying cry in the raising of public support, troops and revenue.[47]

In the early nineteenth century circumstances converged to give these traditional fears and myths a new lease of life.[48] The religious landscape had

---

[45] Doyle, *Mitres and Missions*, p. 15
[46] David Hempton, *Religion and Popular Culture in Britain and Ireland from the Glorious Revolution to the Decline of Empire* Cambridge: Cambridge University Press, 1995, p. 45
[47] Linda Colley, *Britons: Forging the Nation 1707–1837* London: Pimlico, 1994
[48] John Wolffe, *The Protestant Crusade in Great Britain 1829–60* Oxford: Clarendon Press, 1991; David Hempton, 'Evangelicalism and eschatology', *Journal of Ecclesiastical History*, 31,2, 1980, pp. 179–84

been gradually changing in ways which some saw as a threat to the essentially Anglican nature of the British state. There was some concern at the growth of Methodism and nonconformity generally, but it was the growth and increased visibility of Catholicism that caused deepest alarm. In addition to the steady increase in the numbers and visibility of Catholic churches and clergy, events in Ireland, especially O'Connell's success in mobilising mass Catholic support for the emancipation campaign, was seen by some as the first stage in dismantling the providentially inspired British Protestant constitution. In the early 1820s these fears became particularly acute amongst Irish Protestants as the prophetic writings of 'Pastorini', the late Catholic Bishop Walmsley (1722–97), stirred excited expectations amongst the Catholic Irish peasantry. He claimed the book of Revelation predicted the year 1825 would see the collapse of Protestant power in Ireland and the return of all Irish property to the historic peasant owners. These hopes diffused widely and rapidly in a rural Ireland unsettled by the rising population and sporadic food shortages discussed earlier.[49] Irish Protestants were well aware of these rumours, reinforcing the chronic insecurity of the Anglo-Irish establishment.

Amongst those of a conservative world view these fears stoked a parallel sense of increasing apocalyptic doom amongst like-minded brethren in Great Britain. With the advent of peace in 1815 questions of parliamentary reform, working-class rights and economic distress came increasingly to the fore in British public affairs. Mass meetings were growing in size and frequency, and working-class leaders and orators were attracting large and enthusiastic audiences, culminating in the Peterloo incident noted earlier. For anxious traditionalists, with the 1789 French Revolution and its subsequent extremes still fresh in the mind, this was simply the most violent of many symptoms of incipient social disintegration.

This combination of existential religious and socio-political anxieties at home and in nearby Ireland led some of the devout to seek consolation and explanation in study of biblical passages that dwelt on times of drastic human upheaval in apocalyptic and eschatological terms. The result was that 'a more dogmatic millennial nationalist Protestantism came increasingly to the surface in the 1820s'.[50] These group anxieties were rooted in a Christian millenarian tradition that periodically erupted in periods of threatened radical disruption of established mores and structures. The phenomenon can occur within any social group who, convinced their status, values and very existence are under existential threat, experience a communal 'upsurge of fearful anxiety'.[51] In the disturbed

[49] G. Scott, 'The times are fast approaching', *Journal of Ecclesiastical History*, 36,4, 1985, pp. 591–604
[50] Wolffe, *The Protestant Crusade*, p. 30
[51] Myrtle Hill, *The Times of The End: Millenarian Beliefs in Ulster* Belfast: Belfast Society, 2001, p. 9

times of the early nineteenth century this was notable in both working-class communities and more sophisticated conservative circles as they struggled 'to find a meaningful explanation of events and to make sense of their baffling circumstances'.[52]

These widespread anxieties and expectations were particularly notable within the ranks of the devout and conservative wealthy. They led the prosperous, well-connected former MP Henry Drummond (1786–1860) to launch a series of annual gatherings at his home in Albury, Surrey, from 1826 to 1830. There the biblical passages on the second coming of Christ and their relationship to contemporary world events were subject to fervent analysis and debate. Drummond was patron of the Albury living and, having heard Hugh McNeile, minister of Stranorlar, county Donegal, preach in London, had appointed him rector in 1822. While Drummond convened the Albury conferences, McNeile chaired the proceedings. The gatherings usually numbered around 40, mostly Anglican clergy but with a significant number of laymen and women of other denominations. Meetings lasted over several days and their conclusions were to have an enduring impact on participants and indeed the worldwide evangelical movement.

They crystallised convictions that McNeile would hold throughout his life and, through him, would profoundly influence Liverpool Protestantism. McNeile had been born into minor gentry of Scottish descent near Ballycastle, county Antrim, educated at Trinity College Dublin and originally intended a career in law and possibly politics. However, he underwent a profound conversion experience which convinced him of a vocation to ministry in the Church of Ireland.[53] In 1820 he was appointed to Stranorlar, where he was a notable preacher and pastor. In this strongly Catholic region, he was appalled to discover that all local children attended schools at which the curriculum had been carefully crafted to avoid any bible passages likely to rouse controversy. He launched a highly successful fund-raising campaign in support of an alternative school network with a curriculum including instruction in Anglican catechism and liturgy based around assumptions of loyalty to Queen and country.[54] This conflation of evangelical Protestantism and Britishness was doubtless a reaction to the close bond between Catholicism and early Irish nationalism that he

[52] Eric Thompson, *The Making of the English Working Class* Harmondsworth: Penguin, 1968, pp. 127–30; John Harrison, *The Second Coming: Popular Millenarianism 1780–1850* London: Routledge and Kegan Paul, 1979; Malcolm B. Hamilton, 'Sociological aspects of Christian millenarianism' in S. Hunt (ed.), *Christian Millenarianism from the Early Church to Waco* London: Hurst and Co., 2001, pp. 12–25

[53] The Irish branch of the Anglican Communion; J.A. Wardle, 'The Life and Times of Hugh Boyd McNeile, BD, 1795–1879', MA dissertation, Department of Ecclesiastical History, Joule Library, University of Manchester

[54] *Liverpool Courier*, 10 July 1839

encountered in his Antrim home area and his Donegal parish. It was to be a defining element in his lifelong world view, because, as one admirer argued, 'he had seen Romanism on its worst side and had been proportionately impressed by its evils and dangers. He never lost an occasion of bearing his weighty testimony on the subject.'[55]

Participants at the Albury gatherings came to conclusions that became standard evangelical beliefs for many decades. They were convinced that the Antichrist of the bible was the Roman Catholic church and many believed that Great Britain, with its Protestant constitution and monarchy, was a key bulwark in opposition to Rome's insidious intentions. They also shared the belief that the world would end with severe judgment on church leaders, the Jews would return to Palestine and convert to Christianity and these events would be accompanied by 1,000 years of heavenly peace and justice, that Christ would return either before or after that millennium, and that the final phase of human history was at hand. This was a world view that formed the basis of McNeile's ministry throughout his life.[56] Given the social self-confidence and fervent sincerity of the participants internal schism was probably inevitable and the gatherings finished in 1830. For McNeile some of the ideas in circulation departed from Anglican orthodoxy and he parted theological company with Drummond. In 1834 his close Irish-born friend William Dalton, on the point of leaving his living at St Jude's Church, Liverpool, arranged for McNeile to be appointed his replacement.

Over the subsequent 34 years McNeile was to become 'in every respect, perhaps, one of the best known and most influential persons in the place'.[57] A major factor in the creation of this dominant role was his reputation as an outstanding public speaker. St Jude's congregations grew to the point that additional services were necessary. In 1848 McNeile moved to St Paul's, Prince's Park, built for him by supporters at a cost of £12,000. Amongst the qualities which made him so effective were his commanding, self-confident, personal presence and appearance,[58] and a widely admired voice deployed in a notably theatrical platform style.[59] The result was a charismatic populist who instinctively understood the visceral anxieties of his audiences. He attracted a following amongst whom his teachings resonated deeply, not least in the Orange lodges, some of whom, delighted to find such eloquent, biblically based justification of their fears and outlook depicted him on their banners. A hearer in Liverpool in

[55] C. Bullock, *Hugh McNeile and Reformation Truth* Publisher unknown, date probably 1881, pp. 24–25. LRO 920/MACN
[56] Donal H. Akenson, *Discovering the End Time: Irish Evangelicals in the Age of Daniel O'Connell* Montreal: McGill-Queens University Press, 2016, p. 359
[57] Bullock, 'Hugh McNeile', p. 21
[58] J. Evans, *Lancashire Authors and Orators* London: Houlston and Stoneman, 1850, pp. 185–6 LRO 920.1/EVA
[59] Evans, *Lancashire Authors*, p. 187

Figure 2.1   Statue of Hugh
McNeile, St George's Hall,
Liverpool. Unveiled December
1870 in an evening ceremony
attended by family and a small
number of invited guests.
Source: Author's collection

1850 confessed '[t]here is something indescribable in the majestic fervency that
is brought out in some of those grand and effective appeals, that characterise
the concluding efforts of his sermon'.[60]

For approximately two decades in the mid-nineteenth century McNeile was
the leading evangelical within the Church of England and he played a key role
in filling clerical vacancies in the city with clerics, often Irish-born, who shared
his world view. The result would have an enduring impact on the nature of
Liverpool Anglicanism and Protestantism. During the nineteenth century Trinity
College Dublin trained many clergy for the Church of Ireland who eventually
found their way into the Church of England.[61] In Liverpool the result was a large
group of clergy variously referred to as 'McNeile's Irish Brigade' and 'McNeile's
Thirty-Nine Articles'. Haldane Stewart, a regular attender at Albury, had already

---

[60] Evans, *Lancashire Authors*, p. 188

[61] A. McCormack, "'That ultra-Protestant nursery": Trinity College Dublin and the
supply of Anglican clergy to England', in T.P. Power (ed.), *A Flight of Parsons: The
Divinity Diaspora of Trinity College, Dublin* Eugene, OR: Pickwick Publications,
2018, chp. 8, pp. 143–61

been appointed to St Bride's in 1831. In May 1839, McNeile appointed Ulster-born William Falloon as his curate at St Jude's, then managed Falloon's appointment to a succession of city churches. In 1841 the new St Silas church was opened, one incumbent being Samuel Minton, whose daughter was to marry one of McNeile's sons. When McNeile left Liverpool to become Dean of Ripon in 1868 he was succeeded at St Paul's by another of his sons. Amongst the appointments he influenced were individuals who attained significant posts in the church hierarchy. One of the most significant was the Dublin-born W.F. Taylor, who later became Archdeacon of Liverpool. In 1861 McNeile influenced the appointment of Taylor to St Silas and by 1903 he had gained recognition in militant Protestant circles as 'one who, since the time that Dr Hugh McNeile was removed to the deanery of Ripon, has been the acknowledged leader of Protestants in the city of Liverpool'.[62]

One Irish appointment who influenced several clergy appointed to Liverpool parishes was Joseph Baylee. Born in 1807 into a prosperous family long active in the life of the Irish city of Limerick, he graduated from Trinity College and in 1842 was appointed first incumbent of Holy Trinity, Birkenhead, where he ministered until 1864. He was very much in the McNeile ultra-Protestant and anti-Catholic mould. A member of the Orange Order, he actively proselytised amongst Catholics in his parish and was noted for his readiness to indulge in public controversy.[63] The episode for which he became best known occurred in October 1862 as a result of the visit to Britain of the Italian nationalist leader Giuseppe Garibaldi, a hero to many of the British public but a hate figure to many Catholics for his conquest of the Papal States. When a debate in Birkenhead on the Italian question was cancelled out of respect for local Catholic feeling, Baylee held a gathering on 15 October with 300 Liverpool Orangemen in the audience. Several thousand Irish gathered and there were bitter clashes with the police. Yet another meeting was held on 23 October with a well-known former Catholic priest lecturing on 'Rome and Italy'. A large company of Liverpool Orangemen armed with cudgels attended and at the close of the event they marched in military order down to the ferry to the sound of pistol shots.[64]

Baylee's impact was much more enduring than a reputation for provocative trouble making. In September 1856 he opened St Aidan's College, Birkenhead as an Anglican training college. A skilled linguist and prolific writer, '[t]he course of instruction… was entirely of the Principal's own devising' including modules

[62] *Protestant Searchlight*, February 1903

[63] F.B. Heiser, *The Story of St Aidan's College 1847–1947* Chester: Phillipon and Golder, c.mid-1880s, pp. 31–2. Special Collections, Sydney Jones Library, University of Liverpool

[64] Sheridan Gilley, 'The Garibaldi riots of 1862', *The Historical Journal*, 16,4, 1973, pp. 697–732; Frank Neal, 'The Birkenhead Garibaldi riots of 1862', *Transactions of the Historic Society of Lancashire and Cheshire*, 131, 1982, pp. 87–112

on the Reformation, the apocalypse and prophecy and he undertook a significant part of the teaching.[65] His colleagues were fellow graduates of Trinity College, Dublin. He made it clear in the prospectus that 'students, in addition to the course of study, are required to visit such districts as may be assigned to them in Liverpool, Birkenhead and the neighbourhood, in connection with the clergy of the respective districts'.[66] By the early 1860s there was diocesan unease over alleged inefficiency and the increasingly apocalyptic tone of his publications. The college was closed in December 1868 and Baylee appointed to a living in Gloucestershire. In 1869 the college reopened with a Cambridge man as Principal and a revised curriculum with no mention of the apocalypse.

The large numbers who were attracted to the churches of McNeile and his associates, imbibed their apocalyptic anti-Catholicism and attended the public meetings in the campaigns described below, provoke questions on their social composition and the nature of the attraction. There are occasional glimpses in contemporary accounts. When McNeile arrived at St Jude's in the early 1830s the surrounding districts of Liverpool were inhabited by well-off professionals and this seems to have been maintained to the end of the century when T.J. Madden, county Antrim-born and St Aidan's trained, was appointed in 1889. By then it was noted that large numbers of men were regular attenders. When Taylor was appointed to St Chrysostom's in 1871, at first the parish and congregation were dominated by prosperous middle-class families.[67] Some hint of a skilled working-class element is contained in the description of the congregations at St John's, Haymarket, in the days of W.M. Falloon:

> every Tuesday evening... The working men, in their working clothes, came and filled every available spot in the building, placing the bags containing their tools under the benches... Filled by hundreds of working men and women... a true working men's church... such men constituted the greater proportion of Mr Falloon's flock...[68]

There are also indications of a less skilled working presence in some congregations. Taylor's parish of St Chrysostom's underwent change during his tenure, with the population growing to approximately 13,000, the middle-class element moving out to the suburbs to be replaced by predominantly working-class residents, but congregations remained large.[69]

[65] Heiser, *The Story of St Aidan's*, p. 47
[66] St Aidan's Theological College Birkenhead, Prospectus, p. 1. Special Collections, Sydney Jones Library, University of Liverpool D44/23/1
[67] *Protestant Searchlight*, February 1903
[68] Hugh Falloon, *Memoir of William Marcus Falloon* Liverpool: J.A. Thompson, 1893, pp. ix, 22, 25
[69] *Protestant Searchlight*, February 1903

A significant part of the attraction may have been the personal magnetic appeal of dominant personalities such as McNeile, Baylee and Taylor, plus the undoubtedly vivid nature of their preaching and speeches on the imminent second coming. Though the finer points of the precise timing of the rapture of the saints and the battle of Armageddon probably went far over the heads of most listeners, it was a thrilling, colourful, exciting narrative. Others were probably won over by the effective preaching style of a Falloon and the engaging personality of a Madden, a genial, sport-loving, 'muscular Christian'.[70] Still others may have been held by the high visibility of clergy who regularly visited parishioners at home. Taylor visited church members twice a year and every home in the parish once every twelve months.

But even more effective was the organisation of a network of church-based organisations and the mobilisation of lay members to take on administrative and leadership posts. A striking example was the work of Richard Hobson.[71] Born in modest circumstances in county Wicklow, he proselytised amongst Roman Catholics and gained a reputation as an ultra-Protestant, anti-Catholic controversialist. In January 1863 he began training at St Aidan's. Ordained in 1866 and serving as a curate in Birkenhead, he revealed a strong puritanical outlook, frowning on dancing, card games, the music hall and theatre, though 'open air recreations' such as football, cricket, tennis, skating and croquet were acceptable.[72] Part-way through his training he accepted the post of Vicar at St Nathaniel's, a new church still in the planning stage in the Windsor district on the south-eastern side of Liverpool.

It was 'a poor and ignorant district' with a population of approximately 5,000 that was 'emphatically... working class', the majority employed as casual labour. The housing was mostly of the 'small cottage' type, with a notable number of courts, 'mostly wretched specimens of decay and dilapidation to which in winter the sun rarely penetrates'.[73] Multi-occupation and infectious diseases were common. Approximately one-quarter of the population were Roman Catholic.[74] The church was consecrated in 1869. A survey taken on a Sunday 20 years later suggested that there were 3,404 people at services, the second highest attendance

---

[70] Peter Bell, *Liverpool and Birkenhead in the Twentieth Century: Contemporary Biographies* Brighton: publisher unknown, 1911, p. 111; *Liverpool Daily Post*, 27 November 1915

[71] M. Croft, 'Richard Hobson and the Anglican church in 19th century Liverpool', in J.A. Davies and J.E. Hollinshead (eds), *A Prominent Place: Studies in Merseyside History* Liverpool: Liverpool Hope Press, 1999, chp. 4, pp. 57–67

[72] Richard Hobson, *What God Hath Wrought* London, 1913; Banner of Truth reprint, 2003, pp. 35, 43–44, 244

[73] B.G. Orchard, 'Rev. Richard Hobson', in *Liverpool's Legion of Honour* Liverpool: Marples & Co., 1893, p. 383

[74] *Liverpool Mercury*, 1 March 1888

in the city, and 80 per cent of parish residents claimed to be Anglican, a
significant number working-class men.[75] Hobson was convinced that the way to
reach working men was through organisations centred round edifying pastimes.
He judged that in the parish the Orange Order was one of the most successful
in attracting members but,[76] though he recalled lodge meetings in his boyhood
home and acknowledged the Order's success in reaching working people, his
puritanism provoked reservations:

> A deputation waited on me to know whether I would allow an Orange Lodge
> to be formed in the parish? Whether I would join it? And whether it might
> be called St Nathaniel's Orange Lodge? To the first and last, I cordially
> replied in the affirmative, but to the second in the negative... I said that I
> would help them by all means in my power on the Protestant side of their
> programme. I do think the Evangelical clergy make a great mistake in not
> utilising, by appeal, instruction, and direction, the latent Protestantism of
> the masses; and in not taking Orangeism under their wing, which upholds
> the Bible and the Protestant Constitutional Settlement of 1688.

He concluded in prudish fashion '[t]hough this particular lodge did not come
up to my standard, it was a factor in the success of the church'.[77]

Hobson oversaw the development of a dense network of organisations, listing
10 clubs, both devotional and leisure-based, linked to his church and claiming
that the greater readiness of tenants to pay the rent, the ability of women to walk
the streets without molestation, the presence of 1,100 pledged total abstainers
and a total absence of brothels in the district bore out the moral transformation
achieved.[78] This was not brought about by personal charisma or elaborate forms
of service. One notably critical observer in early 1883 found Hobson to be quite
unremarkable in demeanour and preaching style, but granted him sincerity and
earnestness.[79] Services were notably plain and cheery, often led by lay persons,
popular hymns were sung and a short homily delivered on a familiar topic.
Another observer suggested that success was due to his gifts of 'sympathy and
adaptation'.[80] He too was a regular pastoral visitor, calling at up to 75 homes
each week.

But possibly even more effective, and with the potential to have an impact
on the wider civic life of the city, was his ability to mobilise lay members. A

---

[75] Hobson, *What God Hath Wrought*, p. 146
[76] Hobson, *What God Hath Wrought*, p. 224
[77] Hobson, *What God Hath Wrought*, pp. 77–78
[78] Hobson, *What God Hath Wrought*, pp. 109, 336
[79] *Liverpool Review*, 24 March 1883, pp. 4–5
[80] *Liverpool Mercury*, 1 March 1888

notably efficient administrator and organiser he delegated readily. After 20 years at the church he estimated that, aside from himself, a curate and a full-time scripture reader, there were 224 lay helpers.[81] He clearly had an eye for potential leaders amongst congregants, 'the more capable members of which were, in due time, drafted out to become, in their turn, teachers of others'.[82] Well aware that the skills and experience gained opened a route for working-class people into a wider world, he noted that from his congregation:

> [f]our have been from time to time elected members of the City Council, one is still a councillor [1903], two have become aldermen... All the four were downright staunch evangelicals. One of the two aldermen is a JP, and a decidedly strong Protestant, exercising, through the many thousand members of an association over which he presides, a powerful influence, in the interest of Protestantism, upon the municipal and Parliamentary elections in Liverpool.[83]

He was not unique. The end product was an intersecting network of organisations creating a close-knit, parish-based, associational culture deeply embedded within the community life of Protestant working-class districts and in many cases steeped in the traditional ultra-Protestant and anti-Catholic outlook of the clergy. Ironically, it mirrored the pattern in the Catholic neighbourhoods described earlier. It was to be reinforced and its members confirmed in their outlook and mobilised in its defence by a series of national events that bore particularly heavily on Liverpool and seemed to give the apocryphal warnings of McNeile, his associates and successors an urgent and prophetic local reality and the Conservative party a route to electoral revival.

Events 1835–50

As anti-Catholic sentiment gradually ebbed and penal legislation lapsed or was repealed, a plethora of ultra-Protestant groups appeared in nineteenth- and early twentieth-century Britain. Most faded within a few years, but they were noisy, theatrical and prolific in production of printed material. In May 1827 the steadily advancing campaign for Catholic emancipation led a group including William Dalton, McNeile's predecessor at St Jude's, to set up the Protestant Reformation Society. Some of the Albury group, including McNeile, were keen members, eagerly hoping for a 'second reformation' and eventual elimination of

---

[81] Hobson, *What God Hath Wrought,* p. 244
[82] Hobson, *What God Hath Wrought,* p. 167
[83] Hobson, *What God Hath Wrought,* pp. 249–50

Catholicism from Britain. By 1831 there were 39 local branches in England and Scotland.[84] They distributed bibles and organised events at which the errors of Romanism would be exposed and Catholics converted to Protestantism. Early meetings in Liverpool were quite well attended despite noisy interjections from groups of Catholic Irish. An observer described one such event in 1829 as 'a stormy and fruitless discussion of four hours continuance'.[85]

Within two months of his arrival McNeile made his first intervention in the public life of the city. Lord Melbourne's Whig administration struggled to reform the Church of Ireland's diocesan structures. In November 1834 King William IV reacted by dismissing the government and it was replaced by a shaky minority Tory administration, the last occasion on which a monarch took such an initiative. At a public meeting in late December, McNeile, angered by the Whig assault on Irish Anglicanism, spoke in favour of the royal initiative.[86] In October the following year he was a sponsor of the Liverpool Protestant Association dedicated to 'the diffusion of Protestant Information, and the maintenance of Protestant Principles'. The constitution significantly stated that as fees 'all persons among the poorer classes may subscribe to the collectors, one penny per week, for one year'. At the first annual meeting in November 1836, it was reported that 5,000 'persons of the utmost respectability' attended, including a notable number of women.[87] It was the first of a series of organisations that McNeile would set up with during his time in Liverpool, seeking to disseminate his outlook amongst the population, with an eye to the working class in particular.

Following the Municipal Reform Act of 1835, a new Liverpool council was formed and in the December elections that followed the Liberals returned 43 of the 48 councillors. In 1827 the previous council had set up two schools, one in the north and one in the south of the city. The curriculum was so dominated by Anglicanism that virtually no Catholic children attended. Since this ran counter to Liberal values, in July 1836 the council launched a new programme of religious instruction, strongly resembling the Irish system, using bible passages carefully selected to avoid giving offence to any group and on one day each week allowing clergy of all denominations access to the schools to give instruction to children of their faith.

The response was an outburst of fierce Protestant indignation brilliantly orchestrated by McNeile, doubtless fired by his experience in Donegal. A series of crowded and increasingly indignant public meetings climaxed in July 1836. This was advertised as a protest against the proposed new regulations for the schools

---

[84] Wolffe, *The Protestant Crusade*, pp. 33–36
[85] *Liverpool Mercury*, 17 July 1829
[86] Wardle, 'Life and Times', p. 105
[87] First Annual Report of the Liverpool Protestant Association 8 November 1836 Liverpool: Davenport, 1836 LRO 283.05 PRO

which, it was claimed, would 'virtually exclude the scriptures from practical use, and the clergy from effective superintendence' and invited attendance by 'advocates for the fundamental principle of Protestantism, the free use of the unmutilated Word of God'.[88] The meeting was attended by an estimated 4–5,000 people, 'of these the great majority, fully three fourths, were ladies'.[89] The speech by McNeile was described as 'undoubtedly the highlight',[90] provoking one speaker to refer to him as the new Luther. The meeting unanimously adopted a series of resolutions, first condemning the proposed new curriculum rules then another, seconded by McNeile, declaring that 'it is expedient to build and maintain Schools... in which the Scriptures shall be freely taught under the direction and superintendence of the Clergy of the Established Church' and finally forming a fund-raising committee on which the Anglican clergy, including McNeile, were joined by 30 lay members.[91]

The local Conservative party was quick to perceive a political opportunity. Since their electoral defeat in 1831 and the passing of the 1832 Reform Act the national party had been struggling to come to terms with the changing political landscape. In December 1834 party leader Sir Robert Peel had devised the 'Tamworth Manifesto' in which the party accepted the need for moderate reform. To the Liverpool Conservatives the education issue seemed the most promising weapon since it conflated traditional Protestantism, anti-Catholicism and patriotism. In July 1836 a correspondent to a liberally inclined newspaper discerned the new tactic, writing

> [t]he cloven foot of Toryism was distinctly visible, notwithstanding the efforts made to conceal it under the pretence of advancing the cause of religion and the education of the people. The municipal elections in November next, and the substitution of sixteen Tories for that number of Reformers, were the real objects which that meeting viewed in perspective.[92]

The tactic did indeed yield an enduring electoral harvest. Liberal support in municipal elections declined to the point where in 1841 Conservatives took control of the council. A new school curriculum was devised with only the 1611 version of the bible permitted. The result is demonstrated by attendance at the school in Vauxhall ward. In October 1841 there were 875 pupils, but in January 1842 there were only 301, a loss of two-thirds, largely due to the withdrawal of

---

[88] *Liverpool Courier*, 13 July 1836
[89] *Liverpool Mercury*, 15 July 1836
[90] Wardle, 'Life and Times', p. 115
[91] *Liverpool Courier*, 20 July 1836
[92] *Liverpool Courier*, 22 July 1836; Liberals campaigned as 'Reformers'

Catholic children.[93] The impact on Liverpool politics was even more dramatic. So successful was the Conservative appeal to working-class Protestants with this blend of Protestant patriotism, anti-Catholicism and subsequently anti-Irish sentiment that, from 1841 until 1955 with only a short break in the 1890s, the Conservatives controlled the city council and were almost equally successful at parliamentary level—henceforth Liverpool was 'Torytown'.

Following the 1832 Reform Act voters had to be registered to vote, leading parties to set up local associations to locate and register supporters. This was one motive behind the organisation of the Protestant Association in the city in October 1835 with McNeile as chair, and the Operative Protestant Association in 1838. A broader aim was to maintain the heightened sense of imminent Catholic threat amongst both middle-class and working-class Protestants, underlining the dangers of compromise by local Liberals in the face of Catholic demands and stressing Conservative readiness to uphold the traditional Protestant church and constitution. Regular meetings were addressed by McNeile and others, stressing the need for eternal vigilance. Such themes resonated powerfully with traditional Orange sentiment, leading to notable overlap in membership between these groups and the lodges.[94]

As discussed in Chapter One, official dissolution of the Order in 1835 did not mean abolition of Orangeism as a movement, but had seen the Order continue in more low-profile fashion, meeting in pubs and hotels for dinner, toasts and loyal speeches but without public parades. McNeile and company not merely restored the spirit and morale of the Orange lodges but in eloquent, vivid fashion now provided them with what they claimed to be a biblically based world view, giving their traditional outlook an air of religiosity, respectability and immediate local relevance. This underlined the need to be actively engaged in opposing the pretensions of the Catholic church and any effort to dilute the Protestant nature of the British state. Little wonder that McNeile, though never a member, was depicted on the banners of the Order in July 1855.[95]

Conservatives went on to capture both Liverpool seats in the 1837 general election and retain them in 1841. McNeile's rhetoric during the latter campaign vividly demonstrated the total conflation of ultra-Protestantism and British nationalist sentiment that henceforth was to be a feature of Liverpool Protestant working-class identity. In late June 1841 he addressed a meeting of the Protestant Operative Association, attacked the Anti-Corn Law League and set his opposition in the context of a paean of praise to English patriotism. He excoriated the outgoing Whig administration, praised Sir Robert Peel and asserted that 'the popish are in league with the anti-corn law leaguers', arguing that repeal would

---

[93] Finch, *Statistics of Vauxhall Ward*, pp. 15–16
[94] Neal, *Sectarian Violence*, pp. 46–53
[95] *Liverpool Courier*, 18 July 1855

lead to destruction of British agriculture, unemployment and resort to the workhouse. But he set the problem in a far wider context. Working up to his peroration, McNeile continued:

> I love the word England, including as it does the empire. Is it lawful to have a preference for England? Surely it is. A preference for everything English becomes an Englishman... English manufactures, English machinery, English commerce, English sailors, ready and prepared for every occasion and every enterprise alike of bravery and humanity, English navy, English army, English church... English constitution, securing the splendour and prerogatives of the crown, the dignity and possessions of the nobles, and the liberties and security of the people... be not deceived by the new-fashioned cant of cosmopolitan liberalism, as if patriotism had become a prejudice!... cultivate all that is dear to England—yes, and make the welkin ring with the cheers of honest hearts and tongues for old England—for OLD HOME-FED ENGLAND.[96]

A personal declaration of faith came a few days later: 'all the world is not one nation... nations are not artificial distinctions made by the caprice of man, but real permanent distinctions made by the hand of God himself; who, by confounding their languages, has stamped his own irresistible authority upon their separations.'[97] It is hardly surprising that he has been credited as one of the first to use the term 'nationalism'.[98]

But faith in the new Conservative government was soon shaken by an Irish issue. In 1796 the British government had supported the foundation of an Irish Catholic seminary at Maynooth in county Kildare with an annual parliamentary grant of £9,000, but by the early 1840s this was not meeting costs and in March 1845 Peel proposed a single payment of £30,000 for repairs and an annual grant of £25,000 automatically renewed without parliamentary vote.[99] There was an immediate noisy outburst of anti-Catholic campaigning with petitions, meetings and demonstrations throughout the country. In Liverpool McNeile and his fellow Irish clerics were well to the fore in a mass meeting on 7 April.[100] However, there were indications that the topic had limited appeal, possibly because the college was in distant Ireland and the issue did not touch families as closely as the education dispute. Three to four thousand were estimated to be in the audience

---

[96] *Liverpool Courier*, 18 July 1855; capitalisation as in original
[97] *Liverpool Courier*, Supplement 30 July 1841
[98] T. Kelly and L. Lunney, 'Hugh Boyd McNeile', in J. McGuire and J. Quinn (eds), *Dictionary of Irish Biography*, vol. 6 Cambridge: Cambridge University Press, 2009, p. 148
[99] Douglas Hurd, *Robert Peel: A Biography* London: Phoenix, 2008, pp. 323–26
[100] *Liverpool Chronicle*, 12 April 1845

with a notable proportion of women.[101] Though a large number of clergy were on the platform,[102] '[t]he rectors, and the most respectable and respected portion of the town and neighbourhood were absent...'[103] and '[t]he only Tories of any rank were... both of them... notorious for their ultra-religious dogmatism'.[104] McNeile ended the five-hour meeting with a peroration arguing that if the measure passed it opened the route to the extinction of Protestant England: 'And then what shall avail all her glory? What then shall avail her advance in science, her increase in commerce, her manufactures, her railroads...'[105] The composition on the platform party reveals some Conservative unease with a campaign against a policy urged by the Prime Minister, implying that the more staid and respectable middle class were distancing themselves from the ultra-Protestant working-class element in these campaigns.[106] The results of the 1847 general election in Liverpool confirm the impression of Tory disarray, since the incumbent Lord Sandon, a Peel supporter, stood down and the Tory candidates Mackworth and Manners were defeated by a Liberal and a Peelite.

Given the unparalleled and incomprehensible nature of the disaster which befell Ireland with the famine, it is hardly surprising that McNeile saw it as a literally apocalyptic event. The theme of his sermon at St Jude's on 28 February 1847 was 'the famine a rod of God', and he proceeded to argue that 'the famine and pestilence which are at present sweeping thousands of our fellow subjects into untimely graves, are punishments righteously inflicted by the hand of God for the sins of the nation'. However, when the sermon was published he added an appeal for donations towards relief of victims, noting that his congregation had pledged to miss one dinner per week and on one day this had raised £36.10s.4d.[107]

Such charitable feeling had evaporated by 1850 in the heat of popular reaction to the restoration of the Catholic hierarchy for England and Wales. Previously oversight of the Catholic community had been exercised by the Sacred Congregation of Propaganda, with the country divided into four vicaries or regions, each under a Vicar with episcopal rank. By the late 1840s it was clear that thoroughgoing revision was needed. In September 1850 a complete hierarchy was installed for England and Wales, with 12 sees, including a Liverpool diocese, under the newly created office of Archbishop of Westminster, the first incumbent being Nicholas Wiseman, who roused Protestant anger with a loudly triumphalist pastoral. This in turn provoked popular indignation at the 'Papal aggression' expressed in '[v]ast numbers of meetings... throughout the length

[101] *Liverpool Mercury*, 11 April 1845
[102] *Liverpool Times*, 8 April 1845, *Liverpool Courier*, 9 April 1845
[103] *Liverpool Mercury*, editorial, 11 April 1845
[104] *Liverpool Mercury*, 11 April 1845
[105] *Liverpool Courier*, 9 April 1845
[106] Wardle, 'Life and Times', p. 156
[107] *Liverpool Pamphlets 1797–1860 Religious No. 20* LRO G35.3, pp. 8–9

and breadth of the land... [which] fill to overflowing the columns of the press...'[108] Protestant Liverpool was particularly incensed that the first Bishop of Liverpool was Catholic, since an Anglican equivalent was not appointed until 1880. One newspaper editorialised in horrified tones: '[t]here is a Romish bishop of Liverpool appointed by the Pope'. Mention of the fact at public gatherings provoked '[l]oud cries of "No, no"'.[109]

It was decided there should be a full town meeting presided over by the mayor because citizens 'have witnessed with indignation the insolent and insidious attempt, on the part of the Pope of Rome, to ignore and overthrow that constitutional authority which is secured to the Sovereign by the law of the land'.[110] The official petition was signed by 'some of the principal merchants, clergy and gentry of the town'.[111] The local Orange Order devised an address to the Queen, expressing indignation at

> the stratagems of papal Rome, our glorious constitution now publicly assailed, and the dismemberment of the empire threatened by recent papal bulls and enactments... we humbly pray your majesty will put down... the late intolerable aggression of the Bishop of Rome and not only repel this wanton invasion of your majesty's supremacy but rebuke the insult offered to your majesty's loyal Protestant subjects...[112]

There was a note of civic pride at the fervour displayed at the meeting: 'as yet no Anti-Papal Demonstration in England at all approaches ours, either in numbers, or in influence' and it was noted that, with the exception of some of 'the poorer class of Irish' it was an overwhelmingly well-dressed male audience.[113] The five-and-a-half-hour meeting was addressed by McNeile and at least three of his Irish colleagues. In the final address he warned of the threat to the traditional religious and political liberties of England, because 'Popery slumbered like lava in the crater of a volcano, always burning, and ready to burst'.[114] His peroration blended religion and patriotism:

> Christian patriotism! The bold romance of sensibility and virtue!.... Englishmen up! Free-born Englishmen, be wise, be firm,... Deliver your

[108] *Liverpool Albion*, 25 November 1850; W. Ralls, 'The Papal Aggression of 1850: a study in Victorian anti-Catholicism', in G. Parsons (ed.), *Religion in Victorian Britain*, vol. 4: *Interpretations* Manchester: Manchester University Press, 1995, pp. 115–34

[109] *Liverpool Courier*, 20 November 1850

[110] *Liverpool Mail*, 16 November 1850

[111] *Liverpool Mercury*, 19 November 1850

[112] *Liverpool Mail*, 23 November 1850

[113] *Liverpool Mail*, 23 November 1850; *Liverpool Journal*, Supplement 23 November 1850

[114] *Liverpool Courier*, 20 November 1850

country, your beloved country, unequalled on the globe, O, deliver her, and keep her delivered, decidedly, and no mistake, from the despotic Antichrist, and from the iron chain of canon law.[115]

It was merely the most spectacular of a large number of fervent gatherings in the area along with rioting in Birkenhead.[116]

At the national level, Lord John Russell's government passed the Ecclesiastical Titles Act forbidding the Catholic church to duplicate Anglican titles when naming their dioceses and preventing the erection of steeples on Catholic churches. To avoid provocative public demonstrations the Party Processions Act of 1850 and the 1852 Party Emblems Act were passed. Russell went on to fight the 1852 general election on a strongly anti-Catholic ticket, whilst in Liverpool two Conservatives easily recaptured the seats on the strength of the ultra-Protestant surge. To maintain momentum McNeile organised the significantly named Liverpool Workingmen's Protestant Reformation Society in September 1853. Originally a branch of a national group, in October 1854 it was announced that 'after mature reflection, it has been determined to assume a more independent position, and will hereafter exist as a distinct organization for Liverpool'.[117] It aimed at evangelisation of Catholics by open-air meetings, literature distribution and lectures, including a talk on the alleged experiences of helpless young women 'in monkish prisons'.[118] Membership fees were collected through door-to-door visits, Baylee boasting '[e]veryone who is a collector is a Student of St Aidan's'.[119] McNeile took the chair at the first annual meeting when it was claimed there was a membership of about 800 'laborious and intelligent mechanics of Liverpool, her peaceful and intelligent operatives'.[120] The society expressed confidence in

the Right Hon. Benjamin Disraeli... to defend the Protestantism of England... believing that in proportion as Protestantism... is disseminated and upheld, will the institutions of our common country, unrivalled in the world's history for greatness and excellence, be guaranteed to our children and succeeding generations unimpaired.[121]

The events of the early 1850s were probably the peak of ultra-Protestant sentiment in England, from which the tide subsequently, if fitfully, declined. For McNeile it

[115] Wardle, 'Life and Times', pp. 258–59
[116] Neal, *Sectarian Violence,* pp. 131–33
[117] First Annual Report of the Liverpool Workingmen's Protestant Reformation Society 1853–4 LRO H 284.06 PRO, p. 6
[118] First Annual Report, LWPRS, pp. 16–17
[119] *Liverpool Mercury,* 25 April 1854
[120] First Annual Report, LWPRS, p. 16
[121] First Annual Report, LWPRS, pp. 13, 17

was something of an apotheosis, because there are indications he was mellowing, possibly because the second coming seemed to be incomprehensibly delayed, but also because of age and the impact of constant campaigning. In subsequent years his attacks on the progress of the Anglo-Catholic movement within the Anglican communion were as forceful and cogent as ever and he still drew large crowds, but the bitter vehemence of earlier days was absent.[122] In some respects, the torch was passing to the new generation of clergy and lay people who were the harvest of careful deployment of his powers of patronage, the campaigns he and his associates had mounted and the network of organisations and pressure groups they had planted.

Conclusion

The combination of a markedly casual labour market, the sudden influx of impoverished, often sickly and starving Catholic Irish refugees, reinforcement and extension of existing patterns of residential segregation, sectarian conflict and the mobilisation and electoral weaponisation of local working-class sentiment and loyalties created a unique socio-economic and political milieu in Liverpool. Within both communities a dense network of clubs, organisations and mutual aid associations developed, often based on local parishes, expressing and reinforcing loyalty to locality and community, mobilising unsuspected latent abilities amongst the populace, including gifts of administration and leadership. For a large section of the Liverpool Protestant working class the series of events from the 1830s to the early 1850s seemed to bear out the veracity of the lurid apocryphal warnings of McNeile and his 'Irish Brigade'. At a general level they resonated with that traditional ultra-Protestant anti-Catholicism which had long underlain popular English and British nationalism. For the Orange lodges they provided a deeply reassuring sense of providential justification for their ancient and contemporary fears and set them within a world view of the urgent need for the defence of Protestant Britain against the global wiles of the Catholic anti-Christ as revealed in their city.

From the 1830s onwards a succession of anti-Catholic organisations inspired by McNeile and his associates expressed these fears and give them enduring organisational and institutional form. Significantly, the strategic decision of the local Conservative party to annex popular Protestantism as a political rallying cry gave these existential anxieties a veneer of broader public respectability and a political voice. In 1879 one authority went so far as to observe that: 'Liverpool boasts of its Conservatism. It is well to remember that Hugh McNeile more

---

[122] Wardle, 'Life and Times', pp. 327–28; Disraeli appointed him Dean of Ripon, he retired in 1876 and died in 1879 at his home, Stranorlar House, Bournemouth

than any man created this political faith by basing it on the sure foundation of Protestantism.'[123] It is hardly surprising that his statue was placed in St George's Hall by 1870 (see Figure 2.1). This is the context within which the Orange Order was able to put down its deep local roots in Liverpool, survive formal dissolution in the 1830s and by the 1860s was to embark on a long period of flourishing popularity in working-class Protestant districts.

By no means all local observers were comfortable with the results, one commentator complaining that 'Liverpool has been long afflicted with a party of Protestant priests, who, reared in Ireland, and reeking from its orange hotbed, have planted themselves here, in a soil more congenial to their peculiar talent'.[124] This was because '[i]n many ways McNeile spent his life fighting the same battles he would have fought in Ireland, save he did it in England'.[125] After the controversy of 1850 anti-Catholicism as a political issue was increasingly marginal in British public life, but this was only true 'beyond the confines of Liverpool' and it was in this distinctive setting that Orange lodges became deeply embedded in the life of working-class Protestants in the city until well into the twentieth century.[126]

---

[123] *Liverpool Courier*, 20 January 1879
[124] *Liverpool Mercury*, 24 April 1865
[125] Akenson, *Discovering the End Time*, p. 351, n. 47
[126] D.G. Paz, *Popular Anti-Catholicism in Mid-Victorian England* Stanford, CA: Stanford University Press, 2004, p. 223

3

The Lodge: Structure, Ritual, Regalia
and Performance

Introduction

The Orange Order can be described as a private organisation with public manifestations in the form of parades and processions. This chapter will outline its structure, the nature of lodge meetings, the significance of ranks, ritual, regalia and etiquette, the status and work of the female and juvenile lodges, the significance of the increasingly elaborate 12 July festivities in lodge life and their potential for sparking community conflict.

Lodge meetings—terminology, ranks, gradations and behaviour

The basic unit in the Orange Order is the 'private lodge'. Lodges are grouped into Districts, Districts into Provinces and all come under the Grand Orange Lodge of England. The procedure for joining that emerges from the archives for the nineteenth and early twentieth centuries is that candidates were nominated by two existing members and interviewed to ensure that they were at least 17 years old, Protestant in religion, had never been a Catholic and were not married to a Catholic. If accepted by the lodge the candidate was then presented by their sponsors to the following month's meeting, where they took an oath of loyalty, heard a short lecture on the purpose and history of the movement and took their place amongst the assembled brethren.[1] Lodges normally met monthly, opened with a prayer and bible reading, sometimes a hymn, followed by perusal of minutes of the previous meeting, discussion of correspondence, a report from the Treasurer, collection of dues, initiation of new members, discussion of membership applications, sharing of news from committees, Juvenile Superintendents, District and Province. They then went on to discuss any resolutions brought by members on internal lodge or Orange Order affairs,

[1] Mervyn Jess, *The Orange Order* Dublin: O'Brien Press, 2007, p. 56

or broader public issues, shared plans for upcoming social events and closed with prayer and sometimes the national anthem. These formalities were occasionally followed by refreshments which might include alcohol, depending on the venue and lodge tradition.[2]

Aside from the devotional elements, these are the proceedings common to most organisations, but lodge workings could be carefully choreographed. Within the lodge there are degrees of membership; the basic category is the Orange. A member aspiring to a higher degree must pass an oral examination on biblical knowledge and aspects of the history and symbolism of the Order. After six months a member could graduate to the Purple degree and after twelve months to the Royal Arch Purple (R.A.P.). Of the 20 people listed as members of the Belfast Patriotic LOL 3 in 1954, 13, including the 5 key officers, were R.A.P. members.[3] R.A.P. members of more than three months' standing could then apply to join the Royal Black Institution, a sister organisation of the Order. A member's degree is indicated by slight modifications of the basic orange collarette. At a meeting of the Lady Stanley LLOL 97 on 10 August 1921, when the District Master gave out the new signs and passwords for the next 12 months, Orange degree members left the meeting for the R.A.P. members to receive their distinctive words and signs and returned when summoned.[4] As with the Freemasons, there were rumours about esoteric initiation rites. The Grand Lodge Report of 1958, which recommended revision of the rules and ordinances, carefully specified details of the correct ritual: '... Candidates shall be blindfolded and kneeling during initiation when Qualifications are read to them, and reading to be done by the most suitable person in the room, this being arranged by the W.M....' It also urged that '... horse-play in R.A.P. Degree be forbidden, this procedure being out-dated'.[5] Annual signs and passwords based on biblical references are devised by the Grand Lodge at its July meeting and passed down to Provinces, Districts and lodges.

At the annual general meeting, usually held in April or May and chaired by a District official, lodge members elect a full slate of officers and a Lodge Committee of at least five members for general oversight of lodge affairs, with the right to meet separately as required whilst referring all decisions to a lodge meeting. The leading officer is the 'Worshipful Master', (W.M.), who has the duty of calling the meeting to order, presiding over proceedings and ruling on points of procedure. Other posts elected are Worshipful Deputy Master, Chaplain,

[2] Ruth Dudley Edwards, *The Faithful Tribe: A Portrait of the Loyal Institutions* London: Collins, 2000, pp. 84–89 on details of Irish lodge proceedings
[3] List enclosed with Belfast Patriotic LOL 3 Minute Book LRO: 306.ORA/1/1/1; R.A.P. members were also known as 'two-and-a-half degree' members
[4] Lady Stanley LLOL 97 Minute Book 10 April 1921. LRO 306.ORA/5/1/2
[5] Loyal Orange Institution of England Report, 1958, pp. 28–29

Treasurer and Secretary. Two 'tylers' are elected with the duty of ensuring that all who wish to enter the room where the lodge meets are in fact members and enter in the prescribed manner. Two auditors are appointed. If the lodge is linked to a juvenile lodge a Male and a Female Supervisor are appointed. Other committees can be appointed where appropriate to deal with matters such as the banner, oversight of the mutual aid society run by many lodges, and a committee for care and maintenance of the Orange Hall, if the lodge owns its own premises. Ad hoc groups can be set up to deal with specific situations such as the Distress Committee organised by Garston True Blues LOL 64 in the early 1920s at a time of high unemployment. During a lodge meeting members must follow rules of debate and discussion, taking care to employ prescribed forms of address. Failure to conform can provoke a penalty, as in the meeting of Kirkdale's Glory LLOL 80 on 8 August 1905 when it was carried unanimously that 'Sister Bennett be fined 1d for calling a Sister by her Christian name'.[6] Traditional liturgy is important to the Order, the phrase 'in due and ancient form' constantly recurring in descriptions of the closing ceremony. But some flexibility was possible provided decencies were observed, as at the meeting of Pride of West Derby LOL 50 in September 1938 when the W.M. '... brought a suggestion that while the roll was being called, providing the Bible was closed, it would be quite all right for the meeting to adjourn for a few minutes, this would enable a Bro. to have a smoke or leave the room...' Members agreed.[7] At a meeting of Everett LOL 108 in February 1907 a member '... sang a most laughable song "The Wedding of Larry O'Shea" and was well applauded'.[8] But there were limits. The Secretary of Garston LOL 64 recorded that a member had not been admitted to a lodge meeting because '... he had no pass word and it was noted he had had drink and could not enter the lodge in the right way'.[9]

Five people can form a lodge provided they have received the permission of Grand Lodge and a warrant signed by the Grand Lodge Secretary. Motivation to start a lodge can simply be the enthusiasm of would-be members, but when a new lodge was opened in August 1955 the W.M. made the revealing remark that '[a]ll too often in times past a new lodge indicated a difference of opinion within a parent lodge' and expressed his pleasure that in this case the reason was simple enthusiasm for the loyalist cause.[10] Lodge loyalties were strong and the depth of feeling that could be involved in forming a breakaway lodge is revealed by the meeting of Lady Stanley LLOL 97 in 1908. As the meeting was about to close

---

[6] Kirkdale's Glory LLOL 80 Minute Book 8 August 1905 LRO 306.ORA/4/1/1
[7] Pride of West Derby LOL 5 Minute Book 20 September 1938 LRO 306.ORA/10/1/1
[8] Everett LOL 108 Minute Book 20 February 1907 LRO 306.ORA/1/1/3
[9] Garston True Blues LOL 64 Minute Book 1950–53: 12 February 1951; held at Heald Street Orange Hall, Garston
[10] Protestant Martyrs LOL 35 Minute Book 28 August 1955 LRO 306.ORA/15/1/1

the tyler announced the arrival of the District Secretary and it was agreed to prolong the meeting to hear him. He announced that a member of the lodge '... was going to open a new lodge at Aintree and he hoped that this Lodge would give her all the assistance they could'. The Treasurer pointed out that no member could found a new lodge until her transfer had been granted, that no transfer had been applied for and he '... commented very strongly upon the underhanded way [those] who were leaving this Lodge had gone about it instead of going about it in a straightforward manner'.[11] Figures on numbers attending lodge meetings are sparse. In a very small number of cases the Secretary noted numbers present, but this is a rare and sporadic practice. Lodges did keep records of those who paid dues on lodge night, but very few of these survive, some are illegible and they only indicate those able to pay on the night. Perhaps the most consistent indication is provided by a conscientious Secretary of Trevor LOL 820 who from December 1948 to 19 May 1956 noted numbers present on 25 occasions, giving a normal attendance of 7 or 8 members.[12]

Circumstances could lead to lodge closure. Over the years 1968 to 1977 the increasingly laconic minute books indicate that Protestant Martyrs LLOL 91 was struggling. There is no trace of lodge meetings between July and November 1968, the February 1969 meeting was cancelled due to '... bad weather and most of the sisters being unable to attend through sickness...', and several meetings closed early for lack of business. The August 1976 meeting was cancelled when only four people turned up. Finally, in March 1977 the District W.M. told the meeting it had been decided to withdraw the lodge warrant.[13] The local area was subject to slum clearance and redevelopment but it is also possible that the close links with the Protestant Reformers' Church were a factor, since the church was also declining in numbers, finally closing in the early 1980s.

Since the Order was an exclusively Protestant organisation with private meetings where carefully guarded signs and passwords were exchanged and internal matters discussed, venues were always a problem. From the earliest days a private room in a public house was a much-favoured locale, with refreshment easily available, and some pubs developed a reputation for favouring the Order and its members. The two Liverpool lodges with meeting places mentioned in the 1836 Parliamentary report both met in public houses. The 12 July celebrations in the years from the late 1830s to amalgamation in 1876 invariably finished with gatherings in pubs. Analysis of the venues used by the lodges of Liverpool Province in the period 1876–77 reveals that of the 128 venues listed the most frequently used were pubs or rooms in hotels (61, 47.7 per cent), followed by private houses (21, 16.4 per cent), Orange Halls or Protestant Clubs (20, 15.6 per

---

[11] Lady Stanley LLOL 97 Minute Book 12 February 1908 LRO 306.ORA/5/1/1
[12] Trevor LOL 820 Minute Book LRO 306.ORA/14/1/1
[13] Protestant Martyrs LLOL 91 Minute Book March 1977 LRO 306.ORA/15/1/3

cent), schools (10, 7.8 per cent, usually church schools), church or mission halls (6, 4.7 per cent), Conservative Clubs (3, 2.3 per cent) and 'Other' including the Cocoa Rooms in Birkenhead.[14] Pubs and hotel rooms had an obvious attraction, but there were problems with accidental intrusion by non-members and the unhappiness of temperance supporters.

The ideal venue was a hall owned and run by members, one Provincial secretary arguing that '... if more comfortable accommodation is provided no doubt the members will attend more frequently and new members would be more easily obtained'.[15] A hall was also a possible source of revenue when rented to other groups. Garston True Blues LOL 64 had traditionally met in private houses, hotel rooms and the local Conservative Club, but in November 1904 they launched a hall building committee which set about raising funds with concerts, street collections and private donations, including £25 from the local Conservative MP.[16] Eventually they settled on a site owned by the Rawlinsons, a prominent, local, Conservative, business family, and on 1 April 1907 the foundation stone was laid by Mrs Rawlinson. The occasion was something of an Orange pageant. A procession of 16 lodges and 12 bands from Birkenhead and Liverpool walked through the streets of Garston watched by a crowd estimated at 10,000 people.[17] The first speech at the site was given by the Irish-born 84 year-old William Touchstone, Secretary of the Grand Lodge of England, described by one of the platform party as '... the Grand Old Man of Orangeism', who praised the Garston project as a model for the Order.[18] He was followed by local worthies who joined in his condemnation of Irish home rule and praised the achievements of the lodge. Evening dinner and a concert followed.

The Order has always adorned its halls with significant iconography and the layout is designed with care. The lodge warrant, signed by the General Secretary, is normally on display, together with portraits of King William III and the current monarch. Occasionally the warrant would be draped in black for a recently deceased member.[19] Warrants are the basic documentation of a lodge's right to exist and were often carried in prominent positions in 12 July processions, age and fragility permitting.[20] Following the 1914–18 and 1939–45

---

[14] Loyal Orange Institution of England, Report, 1877, pp. 34–38
[15] Liverpool Provincial Grand Secretary's Report 1905, p. 4
[16] *A Glimpse Into 125 Years of History of Garston True Blues LOL 64;* privately published, 2001, p. 3
[17] *Garston and Woolton Reporter,* 5 April 1907
[18] M. Busteed, 'Irish Protestants in nineteenth century Manchester: the truly invisible minority' in S. Brewster and W. Huber (eds), *Ireland: Arrivals and Departures* Trier: Wissenschaftlicher Verlag, 2015, pp. 33–34
[19] Old Swan Arch Purple Heroes LOL 81 Minute Book February 1918 and 11 August 1920 LRO 306.ORA/8/1/1
[20] Sons of the Boyne LOL 28 Minute Book 9 July 1927 LRO 306.ORA/6/1/2

Figure 3.1   Lodge meeting room, Mill Street, Liverpool. Note the austere setting
and the prominence of bible (1611 version), war memorial and flags.
Source: Courtesy No. 7 District

wars some lodges erected a memorial engraved with the names of members who
had died in service. A bible and union flag are always on display and in some
cases banners. The 1958 report on revision of rules and ordinances presented a
model layout for a lodge room, insisting '... there shall be no over-elaboration
in Regard to Regalia or Emblems'.[21]

Certain artefacts were regarded as essential for the dignity of the Lodge,
including a specially made, usually purple, cloth with appropriate embroidered
symbols covering the table at which the W.M. sits wielding a decorated wooden
gavel. A small wooden arch, symbolising strength and durability, often sits on
the table. An official seal is necessary for every lodge, and it is significant that
after Trevor LOL 820 was founded in late October 1948, in December it moved
to request its own seal incorporating images of a crown and bible.[22] All official
correspondence must bear a lodge seal. In May 1906 Everett LOL 108 refused to
accept a letter requesting a transfer of a member '... on account of the seal not
being on it'.[23] Other items are occasionally donated by members, as in November
1890 when the W.M. and Deputy W.M. of Cromwell LOL 94 promised two

---

[21]   Loyal Orange Institution of England, Report 1958, p. 27
[22]   Trevor LOL 820 Minute Book 28 December 1948 LRO 306.ORA/14/1/1
[23]   Everett LOL 108 Minute Book May 1908 LRO 306.ORA/1/1/3

Figure 3.2   Table at Lodge meeting. Members sometimes present items to
embellish the presiding officers' table.
Source: Courtesy No. 7 District

dozen copies of a popular hymnbook in an effort to persuade their lodge to
open with a hymn.[24]

All voluntary organisations depend on members' willingness to attend
regularly and on some being willing to take on quite heavy, usually unpaid,
responsibility for organisation, administration, oversight and finance. Lodges
traditionally award long-serving members with testimonials or medals. On 19
August 1896 Everett LOL 108 presented two members with Certificates of Merit
and expressed happiness '... to see their homes decorated by the emblems of
the Loyal Orange Institution of England'.[25] Another sign of appreciation was
the award of a jewel. In April 1978 Grand Master Roberts and Ladies Grand
Mistress Williams presented a member of Rose of England LLOL 95 with a
50-year service bar and 25-year service jewels to 18 other members at an event
in Garston Orange Hall.[26]

Members take special care over personal adornment and regalia. Protestant
Martyrs LOL 35 was inaugurated in November 1959 and dress code was already

[24] Cromwell LOL 94 Minute Book 19 November 1890 LRO 306.ORA/2/1/2
[25] Everett LOL 108 Minute Book 19 August 1896 LRO 306.ORA/1/1/ and 20 March 1901
       LRO 306.ORA/1/1/2
[26] *A Glimpse Into 125 Years*, p. 24

on the agenda early in the new year, with decisions that in meetings members should wear white gloves and ties and orange ribbon be bought '... to be made up and worn as indoor regalia'.[27] The most distinctive item of regalia worn by members of the Order is the orange sash. Originally this was a long, broad, orange double ribbon usually mounted on the right shoulder, going across the chest and resting on the left hip, the ends held together with a bow of ribbon. However, as public parading became an increasingly significant feature of Orange culture, the presence of the material at the walker's side interfered with the military-style swinging of the arms. The result was a growing trend towards collarettes worn round the neck, resting on the chest and thereby freeing the arms not only for parading but also for carrying lodge emblems.

By the end of the nineteenth century these were standard, usually ordered from Belfast firms. Great care was taken over storage, handling and use, since they were regarded as symbolising lodge identity, smartness and discipline. When Everett LOL 108 received 57 new sashes in June 1901 and 24 existing sashes had been relined in satin the Secretary noted '... we now had a regalia next to none...' and there was a vote of thanks to a member '... for the handsome box he had made to hold the new Regalia'.[28] Some lodges insisted that collarettes be stored in the hall, signed for and a deposit paid when taken out. A member of Sons of the Boyne LOL 28 was fined 1 shilling in August 1924 for not returning regalia in time for lodge night.[29] Design details varied with office held and degrees taken, but emblems attached were strictly regulated, Daughters of Victory LLOL 11 warning members that '... no emblems must be worn on the regalia only what they were entitled to wear...'[30]

Wearing of regalia has always been strictly regulated. Collarettes have long been standard for public events such as 12 July, church parades and Remembrance Day, but special permission is required for other occasions. Old Swan Arch Purple Heroes LOL 810 agreed to appear in regalia at a reception for ex-servicemen in April 1920 but Kirby Defenders LOL 300 specified that for an open meeting in October 1965 regalia would not be worn.[31] Members could be rebuked for walking on parade without regalia[32] and threatened with punishment if they repeated the error.[33] Everett LOL 108 faced an embarrassing situation when the W.M. was accused not only of insulting the Secretary and revealing lodge business in

[27] Protestant Martyrs LOL 35 Minute Book 29 February 1956, 10 August and 9 October 1959 LRO 306.ORA/15/1/1
[28] Everett LOL 108 Minute Book 19 January 1901 LRO 306.ORA/1/1/2
[29] Sons of the Boyne LOL 28 Minute Book 9 August 1924 LRO 306.ORA/6/1/1
[30] Daughters of Victory LLOL 11 Minute Book 16 June 1924 LRO 306.ORA/9/1/1
[31] Old Swan Arch Purple Heroes LOL 810 Minute Book 14 April 1920 LRO 306.ORA/8/1/1; Kirby Defenders LOL 300 Minute Book 8 October 1965 LRO 306.ORA/16/1/1
[32] Everett LOL 108 Minute Book 19 October 1903 LRO 306.ORA/1/1/4
[33] Sons of the Boyne LOL 28 Minute Book July 1913 LRO 306.ORA/6/1/1

public but '... parading without colours'. When it was proposed he be expelled for '... conduct unbecoming an Orangeman... after a very careful consideration the motion was carried by a large majority'.[34]

Much more serious was the situation that required the presence of the District Master at a meeting of Ladies Stanley LLOL 97 on 19 November 1906. Lodge minutes record:

> Three charges were then brought against [a Sister]. 1st divulging the business of the Lodge outside the lodge room. 2nd. Disgracing the colours she wore by tearing them off her neck & throwing them on the table. 3rd By causing a disturbance at W. Mistress's house on November 5th & asking her out to fight & using obscene language not becoming an Orangewoman.

By a vote of seven to two it was agreed to expel the offending member and the subsequent meeting sent a request asking her to return her collarette.[35]

Female lodges: status and role

Female lodges have long been central to the smooth running of the Order, but their ambiguous status is summed up in the fact that strictly speaking they are 'associate lodges'.[36] Efforts to gain fuller recognition have encountered persistent opposition from male members and indeed many female members.

The dominant masculine ethos of the Order is rooted in its origins as a semi-secret male organisation, powerfully reinforced by the fact that so many early lodges were based in the military. This has been amplified by the attitudes of the largely working-class, socially traditionalist men who, as will be shown shortly, have always composed the greater part of the membership. There has been an automatic assumption, shared by significant numbers of women, that the appropriate role for female members is the extension into the life of the Order of traditional roles in the domestic space, namely home making, housekeeping, food preparation and the moral education of children. This attitude was well expressed by a speaker at a Liverpool meeting in late November 1869. The theme was 'What Does Orangeism Teach?' and in the course of his address he '... importuned the wives of Orangemen to teach their children truth and

---

[34] Everett LOL 108 Minute Book 19 October 1904 LRO 306.ORA/1/1/1

[35] Lady Stanley LLOL 97 Minute Book 19 November 1906 and 16 April 1907 LRO 306.1924 ORA/5/1/1

[36] Loyal Orange Institution of England, Report 1877, p. 109 lists the warrants for 'Female Orange Associated Lodges'. This was the first annual report of the newly amalgamated organisation

Figure 3.3
'The Hope of the
World'. The ideal
was a mother
who provided a
comfortable home
and biblically based
moral instruction for
a daughter.
*Source: Courtesy
LLOL 43*

sound morality, to give them a good education, and beyond all else to impart
to them the principles of pure Protestantism(applause)'.[37] Consequently, progress
in gaining official recognition for women within the movement was slow and
fitful, depending on local circumstances and the attitudes and personalities of
local leaders, male and female.[38]

From quite early on women demonstrated a keen interest in the anti-Catholic
campaigns that were such a feature of Liverpool civic life, as demonstrated
by their highly visible presence at the 1835 meetings against the council's

---

[37] *Liverpool Post*, 24 November 1869; the speaker was Edward Harper, future Grand
    Master of the amalgamated Order
[38] MacPherson, *Women and the Orange Order*, pp. 25–26; MacRaild, *Faith, Fraternity
    and Fighting*, p. 136

Figure 3.4
'A Mother's Sacrifice'.
The male role was to
make his way in the
outside world blessed
and equipped by
divine guidance
and maternal
self-sacrifice.
*Source: Courtesy
LLOL 95*

education reform plans. The earliest indication of their presence in a Liverpool Orange procession is in July 1845 and,[39] by the early 1850s, there were female lodges in some north Lancashire towns. In 1850, 22 are listed for the Grand Protestant Association, though none in Liverpool, where the Loyal Orange Institution held sway.[40] Women certainly participated in the 12 July parade of 1851 when a reporter particularly noticed the regalia: '[t]he Bible and Crown were the predominating emblems, and some of these were mounted on carts and other vehicles. Females, in some instances, were seated on the carts, as if

[39] *Liverpool Courier*, 16 July 1845
[40] MacPherson, *Women and the Orange Order*, pp. 25–26; List of Warrants of the Grand Protestant Association of Loyal Orangemen of Great Britain Chowbeat: 1850; Museum of Orange Heritage, Belfast, box 14 2 D

to protect the sacred emblems.'[41] When the Liverpool lodges rallied at Wigan for 12 July 1866 the procession:

> ... headed by a carriage and four bearing the regalia, began a march through the principal streets of the town... Every member wore an orange scarf; the women, of whom there was a great number, carried orange lilies or displayed the orthodox colour prominently in their dress.[42]

Women were clearly an integral element in the Liverpool processions from earliest times, but this was not universal practice. In some parts of west Cumbria during this period women were not permitted to parade with the men on 12 July and in Ireland they still do not take part unless specially invited by Grand Lodge and even then only a small number are involved.[43]

At the formation of the new Orange Grand Lodge of England in 1876 there were twelve 'Female Associated Lodges', two of which were in Liverpool.[44] At the 1885 Grand Lodge meeting the national total had grown to 23 lodges, including 5 in Liverpool. The meeting passed a resolution:

> That this Grand Lodge, convinced of the great influence wielded by women in the cause of God and truth, and conscious of the great work now being carried out on behalf of the Protestant religion and the liberties of England by the Female Orange Lodges, already established in connection with our Institution, deems it advisable to recommend that immediate action be taken to organise such lodges throughout the entire Order.[45]

The number of female lodges in England began to rise rapidly in the early twentieth century. In 1890 there were 8 in Liverpool, rising to 13 in in 1903, and 43 in 1914, faltering during the war years, resuming an upward trend in the early 1920s and levelling off in the 1930s.[46] In the period 1950–80 it fluctuated within the 40s and 50s. Despite Grand Lodge resolutions of encouragement, their official status remained one of subordination to the male lodges. This was vividly expressed in the fact that well into the twentieth century, of the five most important posts within Liverpool's female lodges, at least one and sometimes two were often occupied by men. In 1914, of the 37 Liverpool female lodges returning details of officer holders, 22 had male Secretaries;[47] and in 1938 the figure was

---

41 *Liverpool Mercury*, 15 July 1851
42 *Liverpool Courier*, 13 July 1866
43 MacRaild, *Culture, Conflict and Migration*, p. 148
44 Loyal Orange Institution of England, Report 1877, p. 109
45 Loyal Orange Institution of England, Report 1885, p. 14
46 McPherson, *Women and the Orange Order*, p. 29, Fig. 1.1
47 Loyal Orange Institution of England, Report 1914, pp. 26–44

22 of the 45 Secretaries of female lodges.[48] That this was accepted as normal by the female members is illustrated by the situation in April 1909 when Lady Stanley LLOL 97 elected men as Secretary, Treasurer and Chaplain, all proposed and seconded by women.[49] However, by 1950 only 9 of the 41 lodges had a male officer;[50] and by 1960 all posts in female lodges were filled by women.[51]

At times there were patronising and supercilious attitudes towards the female lodges, based on the assumption that women were apt to quarrel over trivia. In mid-1923 a dispute arose between Lady Stanley LLOL 97 and another female lodge and the interventions by the Secretary and Treasurer of Lady Stanley LLOL 97, both male, again reveal contemporary sexist assumptions, the Treasurer warning

> ... this gossip and jangle [sic] must cease as it was [sic] only bring discontent & ill filling [sic] amongst the members of the Lodge & if each member of this Lodge would only follow up their obligations & principles as Orangemen [sic] less mischief would be done.[52]

Male officers in female lodges often played a role well beyond their official positions, adjudicating on points of procedure as in late 1926 when one lodge commissioned a new warrant and when delivered at the June meeting 1927 it was the male Secretary who '... examined the new warrant & presented it to the Worthy Mistress'.[53]

At the highest ceremonial level there was verbal recognition of the value of the women's lodges, but it was extended in condescending fashion with little change in their constitutional position. In 1903 a precedent was set at the Grand Lodge dinner when there were three 'lady guests' and a toast to 'the ladies'.[54] The 1912 meeting agreed to set up a committee to devise new regulations for the female lodges and these were accepted in 1914 but no noticeable change followed.[55] Eleven women were present as 'Visitors' that year but the general opinion on what constituted the proper role of women was probably exemplified by General Secretary Louis Ewart in his report on fund raising: 'We have thousands of women members, why not ask them to use their needles in our cause? If every female in our order promised two articles every year, we could hold bazaars which could easily realise £500.'[56]

---

48   Loyal Orange Institution of England, Report 1938, pp. 31–45
49   Lady Stanley LLOL 97 Minute Book 20 April 1909 LRO 306.ORA/5/1/1
50   Loyal Orange Institution of England, Report 1950, pp. 22–35
51   Loyal Orange Institution of England, Report 1960, pp. 24–38
52   Lady Stanley LLOL 97 Minute Book 13 June 1923 LRO 306.ORA/5/1/2
53   Lady Stanley LLOL 97 Minute Book 8 June 1927 LRO 306.ORA/5/1/2
54   Loyal Orange Institution of England, Report 1903, p. 27
55   Loyal Orange Institution of England, Report 1912, p. 15
56   Loyal Orange Institution of England, Report 1914, p. 19

As early as 1914 a female lodge in Liverpool asked District to consider the possibility of female representation at its meetings, but the matter was 'left over', with no mention at the subsequent meeting and no effective action when the question resurfaced in late 1923 and early 1924.[57] A considerable number of female members simply did not question their status. At their May 1924 meeting Daughters of Victory LLOL 11 rejected a proposal for representation at District and they were of the same mind nine years later when '[a] suggestion from the District to form a special district for the Women Lodges of No. 3 was not received pleasantly by the sisters as it appeared to be the renewal of an agitation some years ago... when it was then turned down'.[58] Male lodges in Liverpool appear to have rarely discussed the status of women and when they did they generally opposed change. In 1920 Ivy LOL 783 unanimously rejected a proposal that women be allowed to be present at District and Province meetings.[59]

Possibly in response to their strenuous wartime efforts, which will be discussed below, there are indications of sporadic and contradictory rethinking on the position of the female lodges. At a special meeting of Liverpool District No. 3 in September 1919 it was noted that Grand Lodge had received notice of a motion that female members should be allowed to visit male lodges and male lodges to visit female lodges: '[t]he subject was well discussed and the W. Dis. Master asked everyone present to bring it before their own Lodge'. By its February meeting in 1920 the District had come to the firm conclusion '... that we use our efforts against these [measures] coming into effect'.[60] Surprisingly, at its meeting in 1921 described as '... historic in the annals of English Orangeism...', Grand Lodge passed a resolution '[t]hat female Lodges be allowed the same representation in District, Province, and Grand Lodge, as the Male Lodges, and that they pay the same dues'. But at the same meeting a female District Chaplain was ordered to stand down and was replaced by a man,[61] and the same action was taken in 1922, when an assistant District Secretary was disbarred.[62] A special committee was set up to discuss the status of women and bring recommendations to Grand Lodge. It concluded that no change was desired by members and this was put to a referendum of female members. The result was reported to the 1925 Grand Lodge : 70 per cent of female members had voted, of whom 53 per cent supported the status quo, 24 per cent supported equal representation and equal dues, 23 per cent supported establishment of a female Grand Lodge but there was no support

[57]   Enniskillen No. 5 District Minute Book 23 November 1923 and 21 February 1924 LRO 306.ORA/7/1/1
[58]   Daughters of Victory LLOL 11 Minute Book 17 August 1933 LRO 306.ORA/9/1/2
[59]   Ivy LOL 783, 100 Years of History, privately available on disc, p. 14
[60]   Liverpool No. 3 District Minute Book special meeting 27 November 1919 and quarterly meeting 17 February 1920 LRO 306.ORA/3/1/1
[61]   Loyal Orange Institution of England, Report 1921, pp. 9, 29, 10; emphasis in original
[62]   Loyal Orange Institution of England, Report 1922, p. 11

for female representation at the existing Grand Lodge.[63] A Ladies Imperial Grand Council was agreed in principle in 1930, but the ban on female attendance at District meetings was reinforced in 1937.[64]

More sterling wartime work by women members provoked hesitant rethinking, though the idea of a Grand Lodge for women was supported by Stuart McCoy Memorial LOL2 in 1949.[65] The Grand Lodge meeting that year set up a committee to examine the question.[66] It distributed a questionnaire to female members but reported to the 1950 meeting that it considered the responses 'too meagre to recommend any change at present' and the meeting decided to refer the report back for 'further consideration'.[67] The following year it was decided that female lodges could appoint two male representatives to Province.[68] However, male opinion at grass-roots level was still mixed. In April 1956 Garston True Blues LOL 64 voted by 31 votes to 3 against the idea of women selecting their own representative to District,[69] whilst in August Ivy LOL 783 was in favour.[70] The 1958 organisation and laws committee report took the initiative in suggesting consultation should take place between Grand Lodge and the private lodges; the following year a new constitution and laws were agreed, the draft was submitted to and 'granted' by Grand Lodge in 1960 and the first Ladies' Grand Committee was set up with its own officers.[71] Henceforth female representatives were admitted to Grand Lodge annual meetings and reports from the Ladies' Grand Committee were included in annual reports. In 1963 the first resolutions from female lodges were discussed at the Grand Lodge annual meeting.[72] But traditional attitudes lingered. In the very year when the Ladies Grand Committee was launched the official journal of the Order introduced 'The Ladies Own Page' and requested members to submit articles on such subjects as '... pet hints, recipes, anecdotes...' The first two items were advice on how to treat someone who had fainted and how to deal with ink stains on a carpet, in the hope that this would be '... a page of very real interest to the ladies'.[73]

[63] Loyal Orange Institution of England, Report 1925, p. 15
[64] Loyal Orange Institution of England, Report 1930, p. 12; 1937, p. 21
[65] Stuart Mccoy Memorial LOL 2 Minute Book 11 September 1949 LRO 306.ORA/12/1
[66] Loyal Orange Institution of England, Report 1949, p. 17
[67] Loyal Orange Institution of England, Report 1950, p. 13
[68] Loyal Orange Institution of England, Report 1951, pp. 13–14
[69] Garston True Blues LOL 64 Minute Book 1956–61: 9 April 1956; held at Heald Street Orange Hall, Garston
[70] Ivy LOL 783, *100 Years of History*, p. 35
[71] Loyal Orange Institution of England, Report 1958, p. 26; 1959, p. 22
[72] Loyal Orange Institution of England, Report 1963, pp. 19–20; subsequently each female lodge appointed representatives who, on invitation, could attend District and Province meetings with speaking but not voting rights
[73] *Orange Vision* No. 5, 1960, p. 13; author's collection

It should not be assumed that these traditionalist male attitudes stoked a long-lasting attitude of simmering discontent amongst the female lodges. On the contrary, as the referendum in 1922 demonstrated, on gender roles the majority of women members were quite deferential towards the male leadership pattern. When a member of Garston Rose of England LLOL 95 was thanked for her work on a planned social event, she '... ably responded remarking that the Females were only too pleased to give whatever assistance to the Garston lodges that lay in their power'.[74] Female lodges sometimes bought regalia for male lodges as in March 1925 when Sons of the Boyne LOL 28 sent a letter of thanks to '... our female lodge for our collarettes'.[75] But exasperation with male ineptitude occasionally surfaced, as in the joint meeting of 10 March 1952 when it was suggested that the men of LOL 64 could do more to raise funds;[76] and the following year the committee organising a flower day for the Orange Orphan Society noted that '... as a rule it was left to the women of LOL 95 to get things moving'.[77]

But male lodges did feel they could entrust care of regalia to the inherent talents of women. In public processions lodge members often carried the warrant, a bible and occasionally a model crown. Since the warrant was the lodge's founding document, particular care was taken over its public presentation. At the meeting of Everett LOL 108 on 20 July 1904 it was proposed '... that the best thanks of this lodge be given to Mrs Cook for the beautiful way [these two words in red ink] she had dressed the warrant reflecting on her good taste & skill the highest amount of credit which was carried unanimously & with acclamation'.[78]

Local male and female lodges could develop close relationships. In the 12 July procession of 1876 it was noted by one observer that '[t]he "female lodge" is very much admired and the members in their white dresses look very well, although they are apparently a little distressed with the weight of the banner and symbols and emblems which they carry amongst the rest'.[79] In fact female lodges usually sought help from a neighbouring male lodge. In 1922 Garston Rose of England LLOL 95 appointed two unemployed members of the local male lodge LOL 64 as banner carriers. Clearly there was mutual benefit in such working relationships.[80] Barely

---

[74] Garston True Blues LOL 64 Minute Book 1921–55 joint committee meeting 3 May 1923; held at Heald Street Orange Hall, Garston
[75] Sons of the Boyne LOL 28 Minute Book 14 March 1925 LRO 306.ORA/6/1/2; the possessive pronoun is notable
[76] Garston True Blues LOL 64 Minute Book 1950–53, 10 March 1952; held at Heald Street Orange Hall, Garston
[77] Garston True Blues LOL 64 Minute Book 1950–53, 11 May 1953; held at Heald Street Orange Hall, Garston
[78] Everett LOL 108 Minute Book 20 July 1904 LRO 306.ORA/1/1/3
[79] *Liverpool Daily Post*, 13 July 1876
[80] Garston True Blues LOL 64 Minute Book 1921–55, 4 July 1924; held at Heald Street Orange Hall, Garston

Figure 3.5   Early Members of Garston Rose of England LLOL 95.
Lodge founded *c.* 1904.
Source: Courtesy W.M., LLOL 95

six months after its foundation in August 1955, Protestant Martyrs LOL 35 had received an invitation from LLOL 109 to a forthcoming social evening in January 1956.[81] But a member of Stuart McCoy Memorial LOL 2 hinted at a further attraction when, at a meeting in 1951 in a discussion centred on the possibility of holding more social events, he '... stated that the idea of a social was good as we then met the ladies who are the mainstay of the LOL'.[82] Such encounters were a significant opportunity for Orange Lodge members to meet possible marriage partners who were 'safe' in terms of religion and general life outlook.

The eventual concession of official status was a belated recognition that the development and survival of the Orange Order was in large measure due to the tireless work behind the scenes of successive generations of women in the female lodges. This was particularly true of their efforts in catering, where it came to be assumed by male lodges that the purchase, preparation and serving of food and clearing up after events would 'naturally' fall to the female lodges. Following official dissolution in 1836 lodges continued to meet informally in pubs and, after 12 July processions, at sympathetic hotels for dinner, with the result that eating together became an increasingly important feature of lodge life. Following the 12 July parade in Liverpool in 1860 it was noted that lodges dispersed to

[81]   Protestant Martyrs LOL 35 Minute Book 29 January 1956 LRO 306.ORA/15/1/1
[82]   Stuart McCoy Memorial LOL 2 Minute Book 21 November 1951 LRO 306.ORA/12/1

various eating places '... where dinners and suppers were served'.[83] With the
gradual emergence of the Loyal Institution and the Protestant Association, and
their amalgamation in 1876, there was a growing tendency to replace pubs with
venues where they could conduct lodge business without fear of interruption by
non-members. This created a problem with catering since refreshments, meals
and social events had become central features of lodge life. The hotels and pubs
that had been used up to that point had the advantage of being able to provide
food, but even if the rooms and halls now being used had a kitchen, the food and
drink still had to be purchased, prepared, cooked and served. The transition is
illustrated by the sequence of meeting places used by Cromwell LOL 94. Records
show them meeting in Mrs Jones' Masonic Arms in Berry Street until March
1888 when they began using the vestry of St Mark's Church; from February 1890
onwards they gathered in the Orange Hall, Anne Street.[84]

The scale of the catering problem can be seen from the provisions ordered
by the Garston True Blues LOL 64 when 220 people were expected for the
gathering on 12 July 1890. Items listed were: 40 lbs beef, 50 lbs ham, 6 lbs tea, 12
lbs sugar, 50 lbs bread, 6 dozen ginger beer, 6 dozen lemonade, 25 lbs bunloaf,
25 lbs seed loaf, 7 dozen custard tarts, 7 dozen currant scones, 2 large bottles
pickles, 4 bottles Yorkshire relish and 20 quarts of milk.[85] One approach is
illustrated by the arrangements for the annual supper and smoking concert held
by Everett LOL 108 in February 1901. The venue was the Dingle Conservative
Association, negotiated by a lodge member who obtained '... not only the use of
the rooms and piano but also the use of the basement and also the use of the
cooking range... the company being waited upon by Sisters... the supper was in
every sense a success...'[86] It is equally clear that when things were going wrong
women members were expected, indeed instructed, to step into the breach. In
early March 1912 arrangements for a District fund-raising event broke down.
The solution was '... we do our own catering with the assistance of our female
lodges... W.M. LLOL59 be asked to take charge of the catering and that she
obtains the assistance of the Worthy Mistress of each of our four lodges and
that they then combined complete the arrangements for the Tea'.[87]

The women of the Order excelled as fund raisers. They were indefatigable
in the organisation of bazaars, rummage sales, bring and buy sales, sales of
work, tea and coffee parties, concerts and dances, with of course food also on
offer. Items for sale were given by members and prizes were donated for a draw.

[83] *Liverpool Courier*, 17 July 1860
[84] Cromwell LOL 94 Minute Book 15 January 1884 and 10 March 1885, 10 February
      1890 LRO 306.ORA/2/1/1
[85] *A Glimpse Into 125 Years*, p. 2
[86] Everett LOL 108 Minute Book 14 February 1901 LRO 306.ORA/1/1/2
[87] No. 3 District Minute Book March 1912 LRO 306.ORA/3/1/1

Amongst prizes listed are cakes, a doll, a ham, 50 cigarettes, a 10-shilling note, five hundredweight of coal, rabbits, a cockerel and canaries, but perhaps the most unusual offer came from the Treasurer of Daughters of Victory LLOL 11 in January 1926 who '... thought of having a draw for the Siberian wolf which was given towards the Bazaar in Sep. 1924 by one of the Sisters but up to now they had failed to dispose of it'.[88] Money raised went to a variety of causes, including the Orange Order Orphan Fund, Christmas breakfast for local children, support of ex-servicemen, purchase of regalia, construction and repair of Orange Halls, excursions and purchase and repair of banners. In May 1932 the Daughters of Victory LLOL 11 held a dance and draw to finance new uniforms for the band that would accompany them on 12 July, and proudly recorded that '[p]erhaps the special feature of our parade this year was the new uniform of [the] band who rendered some excellent music on the journeys to and from Southport... again a credit to the dear old lodge'.[89]

Women also flourished in committee work. In September 1952 the death of a member who had been W.M. of Rose of England LLOL 95 for 35 years led to the setting up of a temporary joint lodge committee of both men and women to make arrangements for the ceremonial surrounding an Orange Order funeral.[90] Other committees were longer-lived, with tasks such as alleviation of poverty amongst members and administration of mutual aid funds or the care and maintenance of Orange Halls. Examination of the changing membership of these groups demonstrates that at the grass roots women took their opportunities to demonstrate organisational and administrative skills but there were still some fine distinctions. In the booklet celebrating the 125th anniversary of the Garston True Blues LOL 64 there is a notable tribute: '[i]t must also be put on record that, if it were not for the stalwart persistence of the Ladies of LLOL 95, during the depression years, acting as unpaid caretakers, running dances and rummage sales to keep the Hall open, the picture we see today may have been an entirely different one'.[91] The lodge set up a Distress Fund which, between November 1921 and July 1923, distributed aid to members in difficulty. Female representatives were only invited to 2 of the 28 committee sessions and never to any of the meetings at which grants were discussed, but when it was decided to hold a fund-raising concert Sisters of LLOL 95 were to be asked to '... see to...' refreshments.[92]

---

[88] Daughters of Victory LLOL 11 Minute Book 21 January 1926 LRO 306.ORA/9/1/1; no takers recorded!

[89] Daughters of Victory LLOL 11 Minute Book July 1932 LRO 306.ORA/9/1/1

[90] Garston True Blues LOL 64 Minute Book 1956–61, 2 September 1957; held at Heald Street Orange Hall, Garston

[91] *A Glimpse Into 125 Years*, Acknowledgements

[92] Distress Fund Committee Minutes 12 April 1922; held at Heald Street Orange Hall, Garston

Women were notable in the oversight of Orange Halls. The records of the Kirby Defenders LLOL 300 Orange Hall Management Committee for June 1956 to June 1959 cover a period when the Order was edging towards formal acknowledgement of the position of women. Of the 17 members listed on 26 June 1956, 8 were male and 9 female, though the Chair and Secretary were invariably male and there are persistent indications of unease over female status. Rumours of plans for a reorganisation that would dilute the female roles, because of internal bickering, led to a meeting in September at which '... a rather heated discussion arose...' A male member '... paid tribute to the Sisters who had done a good job of work since the committee had first been formed, and readily agreed they always did their best'. The meeting was promptly closed.[93]

By the time the No. 6 District Hall Management Committee was operating the Women's Grand Committee of the Order had been established. The Hall Management Committee consisted of four male and four female members with the occasional female secretary, but there are persistent hints of traditional attitudes. Women are still notable as caretakers, cleaners, responsible for the first aid box, best equipped to comment on hall redecoration and organisers of social events—when it came to the preparations for Christmas 1962, it was remarked '... females usually give their services'. There are indications some women were far from inert under these attitudes. When in May 1963 it was reported that a male lodge had requested an additional representative on the Committee, a female member '... thought this should not be allowed as Brothers did not help like the Sisters...', but the appointment was made.[94]

The Liverpool Processions Committee had both male and female members throughout the period 24 July 1959 to 24 April 1973, but it is notable that the chief officers were all male though a woman closed the meeting in prayer in February 1964. In November 1959 permission was granted for a female member to lead a procession on horseback dressed as King William '... after some discussion...', and in September 1964 it was agreed that the speaker at the Juvenile gathering after a parade on 18 July the following year would be a woman. However, some attitudes clearly lingered—in November 1970 it was agreed that a decision on whether the Ladies Provincial Committee should be allowed to appoint its own marshals for its parades should be deferred for 12 months.[95]

Clearly the Orange Order was founded at a time when opportunities for female participation in public life were very restricted and this ethos of male

[93] Kirby Defenders LOL 300 Orange Hall Management Committee Minute Book 18 September and 16 October 1956 LRO 306.ORA/110/1/2

[94] Duke of York No. 6 District Management Committee Minute Book 15 October 1962, 4 and 5 February 1960, 20 May 1963 LRO 306.ORA/13/2/2

[95] Liverpool Province Processions Committee Minute Book 8 February and 27 November 1959, 25 September 1964, 27 November 1970 LRO 306.ORA/19/1/1

dominance was strongly reinforced by history and the traditionalist conservative social values of both male and female members. But when the need for female assistance emerged with the development of the strong social dimension of lodge life and the growing popularity of dining together as an inherent part of fund raising and for sheer social enjoyment, women in a sense worked their passage by proving their value in conservative male eyes, above all in wartime and times of economic stress. Even so, their progress towards formal recognition was slow and fitful, often dependent on the attitudes of leading men in the Institution at both local and national level and the determination and personality of individual women. Female members also proved their value to the Orange movement in their dedication to the work of the juvenile lodges, yet another extension of their traditional domestic roles.

Juvenile lodges

It is unclear when juvenile lodges were first organised. In Ireland it has been suggested that they appeared in 'the 1800s'[96] or the 'the 1880s',[97] whilst in Britain there is evidence of their existence in west Cumbria by 1878.[98] The earliest mention of their presence in Liverpool comes from a report of the 12 July celebrations of the Orange Association on the Wirral in 1875. Amongst the 25 Liverpool lodges there was '... a District Juvenile Lodge, with flag, accompanied by Lodges 20 and 141 (under the management of Brothers Kingston and Collins)'.[99] This clearly implies the lodges had been in existence for a few years. In the following year's procession '... the presence of young girls dressed in white, bearing beautiful-ly-covered Bibles between them, produced a very pleasing effect and elicited no little admiration...' and in the evening '... a number of the Orangemen of No. 7 lodge and juvenile lodge... assembled at the Major-street schoolroom and partook of a substantial tea'.[100]

From quite early Grand Lodge recognised the importance of these lodges for transmitting the values of the movement to the next generation. The 1887 annual report stressed the need for more female and juvenile lodges, because '[b]oth departments are of vital importance and ought to be encouraged', though only one juvenile lodge is listed.[101] However, by the early twentieth century numbers were growing, with six male and six female lodges in

[96] Jess, *The Orange Order*, p. 84
[97] Haddick-Flynn, *Orangeism*, p. 367
[98] MacRaild, *Culture, Conflict and Migration*, p. 149
[99] *Liverpool Courier*, 13 July 1875
[100] *Liverpool Courier*, 13 July 1876
[101] Loyal Orange Institution of England, Report 1887, p. 15

Liverpool in 1903.[102] In 1914 formal rules and regulations for women's and juvenile lodges were adopted by which time Liverpool had 32 male and 32 female juvenile lodges.[103]

Such growth must be seen against the contemporary development of organisations, often with a semi-military ethos, designed to instil discipline, patriotism and 'character' into British working-class children. Some were church-based and evangelistic, such as the Boys Brigade (1883) and the Girls Brigade (1893), others more secular but vaguely deist such as the Boy Scouts (1905) and the Girl Guides (1909). Many of the values of the juvenile lodges paralleled these organisations, but with the stress on their exclusively Protestant nature. Patriotism was reinforced by Grand Lodge approval of a resolution from Liverpool Province in 1965 introducing a new ritual for saluting the union flag.[104] It was also made clear that such patriotism went hand in hand with the Protestant religion. In 1969 a revised initiation ceremony for juvenile members contained the statement:

> ... this Lodge has been formed to promote the cause of Protestantism and loyalty to our Protestant Queen and Country; and to train youthful minds in that direction... You must never help that great enemy, which is known as the Roman Catholic Church, either by attending its idolatrous services, or by any other act... And while doing everything that we possibly can to counteract the evil influences of the Church of Rome, may we ever remember that the Bible teaches us to love those who despitefully use us and persecute us, and always pray that God may open their eyes.[105]

During meetings the young members were urged to attend church services and activities. Arrangements for harvest services were regularly announced and appeals made to join the church choir and support fund-raising events. However, at the meeting of Old Swan Star of the East Female Juvenile Lodge 105 in October 1957 an officer found it necessary to remind members of the need to attend church '... as they never seem to be there only on parade'.[106] In an effort to instruct juvenile members in biblical knowledge the Liverpool Province launched a Scripture Competition for its juvenile lodges in 1957, believing that '[a] sound knowledge of Holy Scripture is essential to our children... and will be a constant source of help, encouragement to them in later years'.[107] At lodge meetings superintendents distributed questions on biblical knowledge for

---

[102] Loyal Orange Institution of England, Report 1903, p. 24
[103] Loyal Orange Institution of England, Report 1914, pp. 23, 21
[104] Loyal Orange Institution of England, Report 1965, pp. 22–23
[105] Loyal Orange Institution of England, Report 1969, pp. 12–13
[106] Old Swan Star of the East Female Juvenile Lodge LOL 105 Minute Book 24 October 1957 LRO 306.ORA/17/1/1
[107] Loyal Orange Institution of England, Report 1958, p. 19

members to report on at the next meeting and encouraged participation in the competition. Response was variable—there were six candidates from Pride of West Derby mixed lodge in April 1965, none in February 1967 but another six in April 1970.[108]

Juvenile members were aged from 5 to 16 years old, by which time it was hoped they would graduate into adult lodges. Each juvenile lodge was attached to an adult lodge, which appointed the Superintendent and Treasurer from amongst its members, ensuring that they were '… in good standing of the Loyal Orange Institution…' Juvenile members aged between 11 and 16 could be lodge officers. Any breach of regulations or '… conduct unworthy of an Orangeman on the part of an Adult Officer of the Juvenile lodge…' was dealt with under Grand Lodge regulations, clearly implying further legal action.[109] Meetings were modelled on those of adult lodges with amendments allowing for age. Instruction on the ritual and liturgy of the institution was an integral part of proceedings. The annual meeting took place in April or May, electing officers on the adult model. Monthly meetings opened with prayer and a bible reading by the Chaplain, the flag was saluted and the minutes of the previous meeting presented and voted on. Members repeated 'The Protestant Declaration': 'I am a Protestant because I love the Lord Jesus Christ most of all. He is my only advocate and mediator between God the Father, whose words were contained in the Holy Bible, my rule of Faith, and guide unto salvation.'[110] They also went through a series of set questions and answers known as the Juvenile Orange Lecture:

> What are you? A Brother/Sister
> Of Whom? King William III
> How came you to be a Brother/Sister of King William III? By being a True and Faithful Protestant
> Have you a Number? I have
> What is your Number? One
> Why One? Because of the Lord Jesus Who died for our Sins and rose again in justification
> Have you a sign? I have
> What is your sign? Put left hand over left breast
> Why do you take that to be your Sign? To show that I bear a true heart to my fellow Juvenile
> Have you a Pass Word? I have

---

[108] Pride of West Derby Juvenile Lodges LOL 11 and 12 Minute Book 12 April 1965, 15 February 1967, 15 April 1970 LRO 306.ORA/10/3/2

[109] Regulations and Ceremonies of the Juvenile Branch; enclosed with Garston True Blues LOL 64 Minute Book 1957–59; held at Heald Street Orange Hall, Garston

[110] Loyal Orange Institution of England, Report 1964, p. 16

What is your password? I have

(Questioner and respondent then say the following in turn: Jesus said suffer little children to come unto me).[111]

The meeting then proceeded to general business, which followed practice in adult lodges, including acceptance of new members, transfers, correspondence and lodge news. When a member of the mixed Pride of West Derby LOL 11 and 12 was about to enter hospital for surgery it was noted that '... all Juveniles would be thinking of her and praying for her...' and a member declared she would visit the hospital.[112] Forthcoming activities were publicised, together with details of arrangements for outings, dues were collected and the meeting closed with prayer and the singing of a hymn or the national anthem.

Considerable care was taken over the moral and physical welfare of the juvenile members. In 1935 the Grand Master reported he had sent 10,000 copies of a booklet on Sunday observance to the Liverpool Juvenile Superintendent,[113] and in 1965 concern was expressed at the rumoured extent of gambling in the life of Orange lodges and its possible impact on juvenile members.[114] In April 1967 some members of Protestant Martyrs LLOL 91 expressed dismay that a Provincial meeting had discussed the possibility of an alcohol licence, suggesting this was inappropriate since juvenile members met in the hall.[115] The Processions Committee was clearly alarmed at a report that some juvenile members wearing regalia had entered public houses and sat at tables in July 1971 and agreed the matter be taken up with the Juvenile Superintendent.[116] Physical safety on outings was a concern. When Old Swan Star of The East LOL 105 were discussing arrangements for the Whit Monday procession in 1958, there were repeated warnings from a male officer that '... all Juveniles would take care getting on the buses... he hopes nobody would rush on the buses and nobody would hang out of the windows... all sisters had to be very careful on the buses'.[117]

Juvenile lodges mirrored their adult counterpoints in their enthusiasm for fund raising, though their methods were somewhat different. These included

---

[111] Enclosed with Garston True Blues LOL 64 Minute Book 1953–55; held at Heald Street Orange Hall, Garston; probably used when admitting new members

[112] Pride of West Derby LOL 11 and 12 Minute Book 19 November 1966 LRO 306. ORA/10/3/2

[113] Loyal Orange Institution of England, Report 1935, p. 14

[114] Loyal Orange Institution of England, Report 1965, p. 22

[115] Protestant Martyrs LLOL 91 Minute Book April 1967 LRO 306.ORA/15/1/3

[116] Liverpool Province Processions Committee Minute Book 23 July 1971 LRO 306. ORA/19/1/1

[117] Old Swan Star of The East Juvenile Lodge 105 Minute Book 27 March, 24 April, 22 May 1958 LRO 306.ORA//17/1/1

collecting silver paper, halfpennies, jam jars and making cards and calendars for sale at Christmas and New Year. The aim was not only to finance a Christmas party but also to support local charities. In 1968 it was reported to Grand Lodge that Liverpool Province juvenile members had raised £1,000 in halfpennies, had endowed a second cot for Alder Hey children's hospital and were now raising funds for a third.[118] Lodge meetings were occasionally varied with games and 'half-pound' nights, when members brought a half-pound weight of edibles, and Christmas parties were a regular feature. Swimming galas and football teams were organised and in the late 1960s and early 1970s there were visits to Northern Ireland to play junior teams in the lodges there. Outings, camping trips, visits to the pantomime, Blackpool illuminations, Southport and cruises on the *Royal Iris* Mersey ferry were popular. In 1979 and 1980 the juvenile lodges took part in the Lord Mayor's Parade, winning prizes in the 'Special Float' section.[119]

The ideal arrangement was a close working relationship between a local adult lodge and a juvenile lodge, but it was automatically assumed that women would take the lead. This was made explicit by Grand Secretary Touchstone in 1909 when he welcomed the growth in both the female and the juvenile lodges and argued that '[i]f we could get a Juvenile, or better still, a women's lodge also, connected with every orthodox Protestant church, it would do much to meet and put down many evils which now affect society'.[120]

The minute books for the Old Swan Arch Purple Heroes LOL 810 for the period March 1914 to June 1922 suggest how this could work. The adult lodge kept in regular contact, receiving reports on local juvenile activity, accepting former juvenile members into full membership of the adult lodge, agreeing several donations towards the cost of juvenile activities and supporting the idea of a levy on every adult member to support a juvenile lodge.[121] Material from other male lodges reveal less involvement. Between 1884 and 1905 the records of Cromwell LOL 94 contain no reference to juvenile work and the same is true of Everett LOL 108 between 1882 and 1913, a period of notable increase in juvenile lodges. Other lodge records reveal desultory rather than regular connections. These are generally responses, not always positive, to requests for financial aid. Sons of the Boyne LOL 28 actually requested formation of a juvenile lodge in September 1917 and promised assistance, but little proved forthcoming. The opening of the lodge was reported in November but there is no further mention until August 1918.[122] Former juvenile members were accepted into membership in December

---

[118] Loyal Orange Institution of England, Report 1968, p. 21

[119] Loyal Orange Institution of England, Report 1979, pp. 2 and 7; Report 1980, pp. 6 and 10

[120] Loyal Orange Institution of England, Report 1909, p. 22

[121] Old Swan Arch Purple Heroes LOL 810 Minute Book LRO 306.ORA/8/1/1

[122] Sons of the Boyne LOL 28 Minute Book September and November 1917, August 1918 LRO 306.ORA/6/1/1

1920 and June 1923 and there were occasional donations towards events such as 10 shillings towards the cost of the juvenile lodge Christmas party and tree in November 1926,[123] but the appeal in April 1927 for assistance with an Empire Day event was rejected.[124]

Female lodges and superintendents displayed a much more consistent interest. Lady Stanley LLOL 97 received a new member from a juvenile lodge as early as 30 July 1907, agreed to finance the purchase of 200 certificates for juvenile lodges in February 1909 and received a further two members in February 1910.[125] There was some disruption of activity during the 1914–18 war, with no further mention of any juvenile activity until August 1919 when regular interaction was resumed. The lodge was particularly generous in financial support. There were grants for outings, collarettes were bought for a juvenile lodge, there was a fund-raising carnival and a bazaar and the W.M. gave quite regular reports of activities. Lodge records for 1940–52 are missing, but when they resume they again contain regular reports of juvenile activities, with plans for presentation of a Coronation memento in September 1952 and a party in May 1953 with each member urged to '... bring something on the Juveniles['] next Lodge night and give the Juveniles a bit of a party for the Coronation'.[126]

It was in preparation of the juvenile lodges for public events that the female members excelled themselves. Much time and effort went into ensuring the youngsters were smartly turned out and well behaved. By the early nineteenth century there was a tradition of public parades by the members of the various Christian churches on Whit Monday, with Sunday school classes, teachers and clergy processing in best clothes, and displaying emblems of faith and loyalty.[127] From July onwards members of Pride of West Derby LOL 11 and 12 were encouraged to begin saving towards the cost of dress material[128] and in Old Swan Star of the East LOL 105 all money was to be in hand by the following April.[129] The material, almost invariably white, was decided on quite

---

[123] Sons of the Boyne LOL 28 Minute Book December 1920, 9 June 1923, November 1926 LRO 306.ORA/6/1/2

[124] Sons of the Boyne LOL 28 Minute Book 9 April, 14 May and 10 December 1927 LRO 306.ORA/6/1/2

[125] Lady Stanley LLOL 97 Minute Book 30 July 1907, 10 February 1909, 1 February 1910 LRO 306.ORA/5/1/1

[126] Lady Stanley LLOL 97 Minute Book 13 August 1919, 13 May 1925, 12 June 1925, 13 June 1928, September 1952 LRO 306.ORA/5/1/2

[127] A.R. Wright and T.E. Lones, *British Calendar Customs: England* London: Folk Lore Society, 1936

[128] Pride of West Derby Male and Female Lodges LOL 11 and 12 Minute Book 20 July 1966 LRO 306.ORA/10/3/2

[129] Old Swan Star of the East Female Juvenile Lodge LOL 105 Minute Book 27 March 1958 LRO 306.ORA/17/1/1/1

early in the year, ordered from a local shop, the children measured up and the dresses hand-made,[130] though occasionally clothes from the previous year were reused.[131] The processions were a public pageant with '... walking tableaux...'[132] Considerable effort was devoted to presenting the patriotic credentials of the Order, with the selection each year of lodge members to dress up in 'national costumes' representing John Bull, Miss Wales, Miss Ireland, Scotland and Britannia. The staging of such events clearly required considerable help from adult lodges. Kirkdale's Glory LLOL 80 acknowledged this at their meeting in June 1921 when they expressed thanks for the loan of a team of horses and a wagon for the local juvenile lodge and to the person who had painted the wagon.[133] Lady Stanley LLOL 97 records carry regular news of juvenile participation in the parades, the event of May 1933 being described as '... a great success'.[134] The 1937 Grand Lodge Report even mentioned the Liverpool entry.[135] When the Grand Lodge met in Liverpool in July 1947 a juvenile parade was reviewed by G.M. the Reverend Harry Dixon Longbottom, Protestant Party leader, city alderman and minister of the City Temple church. The Annual Report was ecstatic:

> It is difficult to write in anything like adequate terms. The Grand Master took the salute, standing with the other Grand Lodge officers. District after District marched past, each with their band, and passed into the Picton Hall, which was crowded mostly with juveniles... It is estimated that over 2,000 were present... Altogether a scene was witnessed which will live in our memories.[136]

Clearly the great burden of work with these lodges was carried by the female members, possibly because male members regarded this as ' women's work'. Contacts between male lodges and juvenile lodges were sporadic and infrequent compared with the close relationships developed by female lodges. The female superintendents in particular not only oversaw lodge meetings, but supervised a vast range of activities and took the responsibility for the organisation of juvenile participation in public events. In the process latent skills of organisation, administration and leadership were discovered and some notably strong

---

[130] Old Swan Star of the East Female Juvenile Lodge LOL 105 Minute Book 22 August 1957 LRO 306.ORA/17/1/1/1
[131] Pride of West Derby Male and Female Lodges LOL 11 and 12 Minute Book 18 May 1966 LRO 306.ORA/10/3/2
[132] Old Swan Star of the East Female Juvenile Lodge LOL 105 Minute Book 27 March 1958 LRO 306.ORA/17/1/1/1
[133] Kirkdale's Glory LLOL 80 Minute Book 13 June 1921 LRO 306.ORA/4/1/1
[134] Lady Stanley LLOL 97 Minute Book 9 August 1944 LRO 306.ORA/5/1/2
[135] Loyal Orange Institution of England, Report 1937, p. 20
[136] Loyal Orange Institution of England, Report 1947, p. 24

personalities emerged within the niche that women were allowed to occupy in the Order. But when it came to celebration of the highpoint of the Orange year both men and women were actively involved.

The 'Twelfth'

Following a 12 July riot in 1851, the liberally inclined *Liverpool Mercury* struggled to understand the appeal of the demonstrations to the largely working-class participants and followers:

> Processions... are costly pageants, interesting to childhood and to adolescents, but a nuisance and an absurdity to men of sense... To make them worth seeing, even to the rudest on-lookers, requires an expenditure of money which may be said to be enormous for poor men. In order that some two or three thousands of persons, under the impulse of vanity or the compulsion of circumstances, may march for an hour or two through hail, rain, sleet, and mud, or through a cloud of blinding dust and under a scorching sun, thousands of pounds are most willingly expended or sacrificed! Of all the follies of the working classes, the maddest and saddest is the folly of spending yearly a weeks hard-earned wages in buying gilt sticks, tinsel, frippery, painted daubs, tin swords, glaring emblems, symbols and devices, in order that they may trudge through the filthy streets in their barbaric finery, like troops of merry-andrews going to a fair. The money expended on one such flashy display would educate for a year the children of the whole body of mummers, or give to them and their families a pleasant rural excursion and a feast that would make their hearts glad.[137]

But for Orange Order members the 12 July was the climax of their year. During the second half of the nineteenth century it evolved into a multi-dimensional day-long event that not only celebrated the history, principles and outlook of the Orange Order but also took on something of a family folk festival, albeit with provocative sectarian aspects which a significant section of the Liverpool population found deeply offensive.

The actual day of the processions was variable. If the 12th fell on a Sunday, sabbatarianism required the procession be held on the following Monday.[138] If it fell on a Friday or a Saturday, it might also be postponed since many lodge members were dock workers whose wages were paid at the end of the week. In 1878 it was decided that '... as the men receive their wages on the Saturday, it

[137] *Liverpool Mercury*, 18 July 1851
[138] *Liverpool Courier*, 13 July 1885

was deemed advisable for these and other reasons to postpone the gathering until the beginning of the week'.[139] After the processions there were often dinners with dancing until late in the evening. At St George's Hall in July 1884

> ... there was an immense gathering of the brethren and their friends. An efficient quadrille band was provided for the occasion and the enjoyment of the company was fully equal to what had been anticipated. Similar gatherings were also held at the Great George-street Assembly-rooms, the Skelmersdale Masonic-hall, Westminster-road, the Oddfellows-hall, St Anne-street; and at the Marlborough-hall, Tuebrook, at each of which there was a good attendance.[140]

But in terms of public interest and spectacle the procession of the lodges to and from a specially arranged rallying point was the dominant feature.

The growing size and elaboration of the event can be seen against a broader European background.[141] With the rise of the nation state, governments devised a calendar of official events with specified dates on which leading personages, attired in regalia and often accompanied by designated officials carrying iconic implements and banners, proceeded along prescribed routes and converged on gathering points where carefully devised ceremonies were enacted. The carefully structured liturgical sequence of movement, spoken words, music and orchestrated silences created a sense of liminality well beyond the everyday concerns of the participants.[142] Amongst spectators, the combined multi-sensory appeal of colour, movement, music, symbols of national identity and representations of national heroes and victories provoked an excited sense of involvement and pride.

In Britain there is a long tradition of public processions by governing bodies, the armed services, faith groups, trade organisations and supporters and opponents of various causes. Along with riots, public meetings, petitions and broadside ballads they were a means by which those excluded from the political class could express their views on public issues. The period from the outbreak of the French Revolution to the mid-nineteenth century was notable for lively conflict between the forces of government and loyalism and burgeoning radical and working-class elements.[143] However, from that point onwards there is evidence of progress towards a more ordered, or possibly

[139] *Liverpool Courier*, 16 July 1878

[140] *Liverpool Courier*, 15 July 1884

[141] M. Busteed, 'Nationalism: historical geography of', in R. Kitchen and N. Thrift (eds), *International Encyclopaedia of Human Geography*, vol. 7 Oxford: Elsevier, 2009, pp. 255–60

[142] Martin Forker, 'Ritual and metaphor in the Orange Order', *Journal of Irish Studies*, 28, 2013, pp. 68–77

[143] Katrina Navickas, *Loyalism and Radicalism in Lancashire 1798–1815* Oxford: Oxford

a more restrained, society. Amongst the factors at work were the gradual broadening of the local government and Parliamentary franchise providing a peaceful route for political expression. But ideas on what constituted acceptable behaviour in public spaces were evolving. From 1835 onwards British cities were authorised to recruit a full-time professional police force that could be used to enforce public order.[144] The new force bore down on traditional aspects of working-class street life such as card playing and dog fighting and groups loitering in what was regarded as a suspicious fashion were 'moved along'. By the second half of the nineteenth century there was almost a set of rules on what constituted acceptable behaviour, deportment and dress in a public procession, with considerable efforts by both local authorities and organisers to ensure that nothing untoward would arise. In nineteenth- and early-twentieth-century Liverpool these assumptions and police efforts to enforce them were frequently challenged.

One reason for this challenge was the importation into the city of two Irish parading traditions. The origins of processions in Ireland generally followed the European model with its roots in Catholic and trade guild parades, but the Irish model took a distinctive curve because of the country's history. Within the Protestant tradition there were two strands, official and popular. By the early eighteenth century there was an official calendar of processions devised by the ruling Anglo-Irish minority elite.[145] But from the mid-1790s onwards there was also a growing tradition of Orange Order processions whose sometimes rowdy anti-Catholic demonstrations frequently provoked clashes with the local Catholic population.[146] Wherever Orange Order members migrated they took with them the tradition of public parading on 12 July.

Whilst there was a strong tradition of popular religious processions amongst the Catholic population, particularly the Corpus Christi processions in early June each year, within Irish nationalism the custom of political procession developed

University Press, 2009; *Protest and the Politics of Space and Place 1789–1848* Manchester: Manchester University Press, 2016

[144] Miles Ogborn, 'Ordering the city: surveillance and the reform of urban policing in England 1835–56', *Political Geography*, 12,6, 1993, pp. 505–22; R.D. Storch, 'The policeman as domestic missionary: urban discipline and popular culture in Northern England 1850–80', *Journal of Social History*, 9, 1975, pp. 481–509

[145] Toby Barnard, 'The uses of 23 October 1641 and Irish Protestant celebrations', *English Historical Review*, cvi, 1991, pp. 889–920; Jacqueline Hill, 'National festivals, the state and Protestant ascendancy in Ireland, 1790–1829', *Irish Historical Studies*, 24, 1984, pp. 30–51; J. Kelly, 'The emergence of political parading 1600–1800', in T.G. Fraser (ed.), *The Irish Parading Tradition: Following the Drum* London: Macmillan, 2000, chp. 1, pp. 9–26

[146] Dominic Bryan, *Orange Parades: The Politics of Ritual, Tradition and Control* London: Pluto Press, 2000

rather later and research, particularly within the diaspora, is a relatively recent phenomenon.[147] Some of the agrarian secret societies of late-eighteenth-century Ireland, motivated by a hazy mix of economic grievance and Catholic revanchism, ventured on public demonstration, but the earliest explicitly political processions were organised by the Ribbon societies. These were a movement strongest amongst the lower-class elements of Dublin city and eastern Ireland, with considerable support in the Irish migrant communities in British cities.[148] By the early nineteenth century they had captured the popular celebration of St Patrick's Day and the tradition of parading on 17 March. In Ireland the Orange Order strongly opposed such demonstrations and in the 1820s and 1830s there were recurrent clashes over routes and territory, particularly in Ulster. The occasional fatalities were followed by funerals attended by numerous supporters, providing further opportunities for parading and conflict and launching the tradition of the political funeral.[149] But it was the campaigns of Daniel O'Connell for Catholic emancipation in the late 1820s and repeal of the union in the early 1840s that firmly established the custom of the elaborate nationalist parade with green sashes, numerous flags, banners and tableaux converging on a rallying point to acclaim popular leaders and hear rousing speeches. As with the demonstrations of the Orange Order, the custom of parading was retained wherever an Irish Catholic migrant community was established.

In both cases the processions were a performance: '... a widespread if not universal ritual used by groups in all sorts of contexts to ensure their existence is both remembered and taken into account'.[150] Such events are '... not only a moving assemblage but a manifestation of speech that expresses the claims and identity of the group who is parading'.[151] For participants there is the satisfaction of taking part in an affirming event with people of like mind. For followers who accompany the processions because they are relatives or simply sympathetic in outlook, there is a sense of participation without the effort of preparation. For the wider public the spectacle, colour, bustle and noise are attractive. But for organisers there is a deeper intent. The numbers of people united in public affirmation of a single purpose and proceeding in a disciplined, organised fashion

[147] J. Bradley, 'Wearing the green: a history of nationalist demonstrations among the diaspora in Glasgow' in Fraser, *The Irish Parading Tradition*, chp. 7, pp. 111–28

[148] K. Hughes and Don MacRaild, *Ribbon Societies in Nineteenth-Century Ireland and Its Diaspora: The Persistence of Tradition* Liverpool: Liverpool University Press, 2018

[149] Neil Jarman and Dominic Bryan, *From Rights to Riots: Nationalist Parades in the North of Ireland* Coleraine: Centre for the Study of Conflict, University of Ulster, 1998

[150] S. Dunn and V. Morgan, 'Series editors' preface' in Fraser, *The Irish Parading Tradition*, pp. vii–viii

[151] S. Marston, 'Space, culture, state: uneven development in political geography', *Political Geography*, 23,1, 2004, pp. 1–16

are designed to convey a message of serious-minded, determined purpose. For the Orange Order this is expressed not merely by the numbers involved but by sober respectable dress, disciplined behaviour and the careful self-monitoring of regalia, implements carried and conduct on what was the key public event on the most significant day in the Orange calendar.

The importance of making an impressive show is demonstrated by the Daughters of Victory LLOL 11 as they reported to their lodge meeting on the 12 July processions of the 1930s. Particular attention was paid to the physical appearance and behaviour of participants, especially from the juvenile lodges, and the likely impact on the general public. In 1934 it was felt:

> [t]he day passed over very well... all was quite satisfied that we had again created a good impression by the excellent way in which we all helped to make our part of the demonstration a success... special thanks are due... for the excellent manner in which the Juveniles turned out... [and the following year]... there was a very good turnout of the Juveniles whom [sic] were all very neatly dressed and the behaviour was splendid...[152]

This striving for effect is to be seen in the evolving structure of the Liverpool processions and the increasing efforts from the early 1850s to combine the striking visual impact of the parades with inclusiveness and discipline. In terms of inclusiveness, it has already been noted that the Liverpool Orange lodges have been remarkable for the presence of women from at least the early 1850s and juvenile lodges from at least 1875. The result is a message of engaging, winsome inclusiveness and peaceable intent, which also boosts the numbers.

From the early 1850s the 12 July processions became increasingly elaborate. In 1851 lodge officers were noted as carrying wands, swords, bibles and model crowns, sometimes in special carriages, and it was noted that members '... were generally well dressed, and were decorated with Orange scarves and rosettes... The procession, viewing it as a display, may be said to have been a brilliant success, and it was the most imposing which the brotherhood have had in Liverpool'.[153] The 1859 procession was even more elaborate. The Grand Master of England and other officers travelled in an open carriage drawn by four grey horses, escorted by outriders and preceded by a file of members carrying swords. Their carriage displayed a massive silver bust of King William III and a Grand Master's silver mace. It was reported '[m]any of the other insignia were equally interesting and

---

[152] Daughters of Victory LLOL 11 Minute Book 19 July 1934, 18 July 1935 LRO 306. ORA/9/4/2

[153] *Liverpool Daily Post*, 15 July 1851

imposing and appeared to be looked upon with no small degree of respect by the members of the order'.[154] As for the rank and file:

> [g]ay and expensive scarves were donned, swords drawn, pikes elevated, battle-axes thrown over the shoulder, emblems of church and state placed on cushions to be carried with reverential dignity, together with banners and all the paraphernalia which go to make illustrious the several lodges... some of these arms were decorated with ribbons, or surmounted with orange lilies, to show that their object was more for ornament and peace than cruel work... A further 60 spring carts filled with women and children brought up the rear.[155]

In the years following the First World War decorated maypoles became a feature of the procession, the guide ropes and orange streamers carried by female juvenile members, preceded by others carrying baskets of flowers. Another distinctive Liverpool feature were male juvenile members dressed as King William, accompanied by female juvenile members as Queen Mary. In 1932

> ... a royal atmosphere was imparted to the parade by the presence of numerous King Williams and Queen Marys. Five of the Kings rode on horseback, rather more anxiously than regally... Every King William had his top-boots, lace cravat, silk breeches, plumed hat and gleaming sword.[156]

But the item carried by parading members which has always attracted most attention is the banner. The earliest mention in Liverpool comes in July 1820, but there is no further reference until regular processions are resumed in 1845, when it is noted that there were two flags and '... a very considerable number of orange and blue banners'.[157] Subsequently they were a regular and much remarked feature. Hung from a pole framework, requiring special 'carrying belts', with at least four guide ropes held by lodge members, they are difficult to carry in procession, especially in windy, wet or hot weather.[158] Expensive, fragile, woven, stitched and painted by hand, they were ordered from firms in Liverpool, London or Belfast. A new banner for Everett LOL 108 in January 1900 cost approximately £18, a considerable sum for an overwhelmingly working-class organisation.[159] The wording, scenes and personalities to be depicted are carefully

[154] *Liverpool Courier*, 13 July 1859
[155] *Liverpool Daily Post*, 13 July 1859
[156] *Liverpool Daily Post*, 13 July 1932
[157] *Liverpool Mercury*, 14 July 1820; *Liverpool Courier*, 16 July 1845
[158] Cromwell LOL 94 Minute Book 12 August 1884 LRO 306.ORA/2/1/1
[159] Everett LOL 108 Minute Book 16 January 1900 LRO 306.ORA/1/1/1

Figure 3.6
King William III at
the Battle of the
Boyne, 1690.
Enduring hero and icon.
*Source: Courtesy
LOL 94*

chosen. Each banner bears the lodge title and depicts personalities and incidents significant for the Order. The individual most often depicted is King William III on a white horse crossing the Boyne in July 1690. Religious belief is expressed by biblical characters and scenes. Protestantism is often portrayed by mid-six-teenth-century Protestant martyrs being burned at the stake for their faith. Living members are not depicted but deceased past masters and personalities do feature.

Given their cost and iconic significance for a lodge, banners are carefully tended. In July 1928 Daughters of Victory LLOL 11 noticed '... that the banner after several small repairs would have to be attended to before another turnout... it was [agreed] that we ask for voluntary contributions each month towards the cost and that we send it away about February 1929'. By then a fund-raising dance had been arranged, but an anxious secretary noted that the banner would have to be sent off as soon as possible if it were to be carried on 12 July and he '... drew attention to the finance required to meet this expense... and he appealed for them all to do their best to make the Dance on April 17th a great success'.

By May the repairs were under way, the banner arrived in time and there was considerable satisfaction when it was reported on 18 July that at the recent demonstration '[t]he Banner was floated... and looked very well', but there was dismay when it was noted that '... there was a tear in the blue silk near one of the brass fastenings...' and the August meeting was informed that the total cost had been £11.17s.7d.[160] In July 1933 the banner had again suffered damage on 12 July and a replacement was necessary. By the following April the new banner was ready for dispatch and a 'Committee of Officers with Sisters' was set up to make arrangements for ceremonial unfurling.[161]

The significance of the banner in lodge life and the emotions aroused by such ceremonies are well conveyed by events in Garston in November 1954. Both the male and female lodges had new banners and the female lodge was celebrating 50 years of life. It was decided that a special joint church parade was appropriate '... to make it a rare heyday for the history of the Garston Lodges'.[162] The event was held at the local parish church, the choir sang, bells were rung and there was a procession through local streets with the new banners. The secretary's not entirely coherent report held nothing back:

> ... I myself was amaised [sic] at the tremendous turnout of the members more so members of LOL 64. For my part I shall always remember it as the most outstanding parade in Garston in my twenty years as an Orangeman. The dedecation [sic] of the banners was the most wonderful sight I have ever witness... the welcome in the church was the warmest homely welcome given us by the Vicar of our church, using his own words. After the parade... the W.M. thanking all present for their presence at the service & parade, more so the members of Lodge LOL 64 who volunteer to carry the banners on the occasion of the dedication. I am sure they must have been the proudest members on parade, more so when taking them down the isle [sic] for the dedication and unfurling.[163]

With the passage of time the July demonstrations underwent significant changes. Up to the mid-1830s they were small-scale affairs consisting of processions with flags and banners which then broke up as lodges adjourned to favourite pubs and hotels for dinner and carousing. After formal dissolution in 1835 celebrations

---

[160] Daughters of Victory LLOL 11 Minute Book 19 July 1928, 21 February, 16 May, 18 July, 15 August 1929 LRO 306.ORA/9/1/1
[161] Daughters of Victory LLOL 11 Minute Book 20 July 1933, 19 April 1934 LRO 306. ORA/9/1/1
[162] Garston True Blues LOL 64 Minute Bool 1953–55, joint meeting with Rose of England LLOL 95, 21 October 1954; held at Heald Street Orange Hall, Garston
[163] Garston True Blues LOL 64 Minute Book 1953–55, 4 November 1954; held at Heald Street Orange Hall, Garston

were much more modest and less public, but from 1845 onwards there are occasional reports of processions. However, the sectarian conflicts of 1851 led the city council to ban party processions and the display of party emblems within the borough boundary and some rethinking was necessary. From 1852 to 1861 members assembled just outside the council boundary, donned regalia, walked in procession to a local rallying point, heard speeches, reformed and paraded back to the boundary where they removed regalia and dispersed. In 1859 they assembled at Dingle where '[l]arge flags were unfurled... Gay and expensive scarfs were donned...' On the return from the rally,

> [a]rriving at Wavertree Bridge, the boundary of the borough, a band played 'God Save the Queen', the flags were furled, the swords were sheathed, or, where there was no scabbard, as was the case in many instances, folded in a handkerchief or newspaper and thrust down the trouser leg and the procession broke up, the members and their friends returning to their respective lodge rooms to spend the evening in festivity.[164]

The rally itself gradually became more elaborate. By the late 1850s lodge officers were making a regular practice of gathering at local hotels for an extended lunch with toasts and speeches before reforming the procession and dispersing at the boundary. In 1859 comes the first mention of refreshment for the rank and file as local businessmen saw an opportunity.

> The day was excessively hot, and on arriving at Wavertree, the procession, after marching round the village, separated for refreshment. The village was crowded in every part, and although some of the shops had shuttered up... the scene altogether was like a fair, with stalls crowding some of the streets. The public houses and beer houses soon became crowded like hives, and bakers' shops were nearly emptied of their contents.[165]

In 1861 regulations had been relaxed and the main assembly was within the city boundary, but this resulted in bitter sectarian clashes. It may well have been in reaction to this that in 1862 the rally was held well beyond the environs of Liverpool, at Ruabon, north Wales, on the estate of the local MP. Considerable hospitality had been laid on. Following greetings from the host:

> ... a general dispersion took place for the purpose of obtaining refreshments, which were supplied at various tents erected on the ground... the long walk

---

[164] *Liverpool Post*, 13 July 1859
[165] *Liverpool Daily Post*, 13 July 1859

provoked a keen appetite, and a speedy clearance was soon effected of everything in the shape of provisions...[166]

In 1864 the two organisations held separate rallies, the members of the Loyal Orange Institution travelling to Wigan whilst the Grand Protestant Association rallied at Wavertree, where an observer noted that nothing official seemed to have been arranged:

> ... British enterprise had, however, erected one or two shooting galleries, weighing machines, respirating machines, and other examples of the muscular amusements to which the national character inclines, which met with a fair amount of support. There were also three bands on the ground... and to the music some of the younger persons commenced dancing on the grass. Of course, the various taps at Wavertree received an immense amount of attention...[167]

Such popular entertainments gradually became an established feature. At Birkenhead in 1874 there is the first mention of games, when '[f]oot races and other forms of amusement were watched by the visitors until about 5 o'clock'.[168] The following year the rally took place in Lord Derby's estate grounds. A local report headlined it as 'The Gala at Knowsley Park' and noted '[o]n entering the park the carriage containing the Grand Master and other prominent members of the order was received with loud cheers. Refreshment tents (the caterer being Mr. Thompson of Brunswick-road) had been provided, the bands supplied music to those inclined to dance, and various sports were improvised.'[169] The year 1876 saw the first 12 July demonstration of the newly amalgamated Loyal Orange Institution of England and was clearly well planned. The rally, again at Knowsley, was a ticketed affair with '... refreshments of a substantial character...'[170] Near the park lake the refreshment tents were '... besieged and taken by storm. Here there are a great number of amusements, in character not unlike those to be found at a race meeting... and large numbers of the visitors are allured by the attractions of the dancing, the kiss-in-the-ring and the refreshments.'[171] The speeches on political and religious matters attracted '... the older portion of the throng'.[172]

By the early 1880s refreshments, dancing, various forms of 'amusements' and 'recreation' were standard but when there was a delay in reforming the

---

[166] *Liverpool Courier*, 16 July 1862
[167] *Liverpool Daily Post*, Supplement 13 July 1864
[168] *Liverpool Courier*, 14 July 1874
[169] *Liverpool Courier*, 13 July 1875
[170] *Liverpool Evening Express*, 13 July 1876
[171] *Liverpool Daily Post*, 13 July 1876
[172] *Liverpool Courier*, 13 July 1876

procession at Birkenhead in 1883 many were '... "slipping round the corner", presumably to fortify the inner man and strengthen their loyalty and devotion to Protestantism...'[173] At Farnworth near Widnes in 1889 competitive games were organised, '... including flat racing, obstacle racing, tugs of war between the different lodges... and old English games...'[174] which, along with the 30 prizes, proved '... a source of much pleasure during the afternoon'.[175] Some form of sporting activity with prizes also became an integral part of the day. At Southport in 1906 there were 100-yard handicap flat races for girls and for boys of 16 and under, a 100-yards ladies' thread-needle race, a 100-yard flat race for married ladies, a tug of war, a 100-yard sack–hurdle race and an 800-yard obstacle race.[176] Success in such events was applauded. In 1905 the local Garston newspaper reported '[a]mongst the athletic successes secured by the Garston members was the first prize in the one-mile bicycle race... a prize in one of the juvenile races... and the third prize in the egg and spoon race for ladies'.[177] By 1905 the Provincial Secretary was reporting that the Order had gained 12 new lodges and hailed the previous year's Twelfth celebrations as the largest and most impressive for years.[178]

The July events had developed to the point where the *Courier*, stalwart supporter of everything Conservative and Orange, was convinced they had taken on the flavour of an enjoyable day out for all ages and offered a risible analysis of the contemporary state of civic relations:

> The glorious 'Twelfth' of July is not now so 'lively' as it used to be in times gone by. Most of the bellicose element which once characterised its worshippers has been eliminated or transformed into a more ethical force... it is quite certain that all those profoundly bitter feelings aroused in the minds of both parties on this historical anniversary are kept under firmer control... The celebration of the 'Twelfth' nowadays is nothing more or less than a great political and religious picnic... the participants anticipate a day of pleasure at a bright holiday resort, amid surroundings that are more likely to elicit their admiration for the marvels of nature, than to incite that combative instinct which lies latent in most members

---

[173] *Liverpool Echo*, 12 July 1883
[174] *Liverpool Courier*, 13 July 1889
[175] *Liverpool Courier*, 16 July 1889
[176] *Liverpool Courier*, 14 July 1904
[177] *Garston and Woolton Reporter*, 15 July 1905; Elaine McFarland noted similar trends at Scottish celebrations in 'Marching from the margins: twelfth July parades in Scotland 1820–1914' in Fraser, *The Irish Parading Tradition*, chp. 4, pp. 60–77
[178] Provincial Grand Secretary's Report 1905, p. 4; archives section, Museum of Orange Heritage, Belfast

of partizan organisations... under the hot rays of the sun, the day was happily whiled away with joyous games.[179]

But from 1909 onwards, as will be described later, more serious religious and political matters had come to the fore with the result that reportage increasingly dwelt on speeches by the leaders of the movement and much less on games and refreshments.

Processions were suspended during the First World War but, when they resumed in 1919, it is clear that the reverse was now happening: the much-diminished overall coverage devoted little space to official speeches and much more to description of the colour and pageantry of the processions. Recreational activities were still a significant dimension, with regular, if brief, reference to '... games and various forms of recreation'.[180] By 1939 a reporter was somewhat carried away: '... bands and processions converging on the station represented as near an approach to the continental fiesta as the English ever get'.[181] The processions were again suspended in wartime, but when they resumed in 1949 it is clear that these social and recreational aspects remained key features, even as lodge and procession numbers began to decline from the early 1960s onwards.[182]

As well as displaying their beliefs through regalia and banners, members adorned their houses and streets for the Twelfth thereby marking out what they regarded as their home spaces and territory. From the early 1870s observers had noted that in certain streets off Scotland Road in the north end, '... where the residents are almost all Catholics, the children were decorated in green ribbons [and] sprigs of shamrock...' whilst in nearby streets '[t]he party emblems were orange and blue... and not only were the inhabitants of the streets extensively decked with these colours, but strings of flags were hung across the street and fastened to the chimney stacks...'[183] Houses were decorated. In one case '... an industrious carpenter had carved a representation of Prince William of Nassau on horseback, with drawn sword in hand, which he hung out of one of his windows'.[184] Others displayed flags, portraits of King William III, bunches of the ubiquitous orange lilies and decorated trellis arches around their doorways. Streets tried to outdo each other, with prizes for the most elaborate.[185] In 1910 a journalist waxed lyrical on the slopes of Everton:

---

[179] *Liverpool Courier*, 16 July 1901
[180] *Liverpool Courier*, 13 July 1922
[181] *Liverpool Daily Post*, 13 July 1939
[182] Roberts, *Liverpool Sectarianism*, pp. 85–96
[183] *Liverpool Courier*, 13 July 1871
[184] *Liverpool Courier*, 13 July 1872
[185] Oliver Bullough, '"Remember the Boyne": Liverpool Orange Processions 1919–1939', MA dissertation, Department of British and American History, University of Warwick, 1990; copy Liverpool Record Office, pp. 39–40

> ... the loyalty to 'King Billy' was exuberant in all directions. Not only streamers, but heavy garlands and festoons turned an otherwise indelectable thoroughfare into a forest of beauty... Looking down from the hilltop... the spectacle was like a fairy scene from a pantomime.[186]

Close to, the reality was somewhat more visceral, though not without a touch of mischievous farce. In both communities there was a tradition of making effigies of the heroes of the other side. These often '... consisted of a suit of old clothes, stitched together, and filled either with shavings or with paper. The face was represented by a stiff paper mask, and frequently decorated with a pipe.' Knowing what was intended, the police made great efforts to confiscate effigies, with the result that in 1888 a local police station ended up with '... a grotesquely interesting exhibition of them, numbering in all about twenty...'[187] In Protestant-dominated streets the effigies were of the Pope, while in Catholic areas they were of 'King Billy'. One particularly elaborate creation

> ... was dressed in light coloured coat and trousers and a dark vest, the head was surmounted with a white hat on which was a black band, and one or two orange lilies were attached to various parts of the clothing. In order that there might be no mistake as to whom the figure represented a large label was pinned to the breast bearing the inscription, 'King William'.[188]

Children went from door to door asking for money to buy oil, which would be poured on the effigies. They then suspended the figures from wires, the ends of which were strung across the street, attached to local houses. The effigies were set alight and the wires pulled taut to dangle above the street. Children enjoyed standing on the roofs of the houses to which the wires were attached, swinging the effigy back and forth to stoke the flames until the figure disintegrated, to the applause of cheering crowds. The police went to great pains to remove the wires by throwing a length of rope tied to a brick across them and pulling them down, but for the spectators, especially the children, this merely added to the fun.[189] In 1890 one reporter came across '... fires round which children danced and sang. In the centre of the flames a rude effigy, dressed in old clothes, represented the Orange hero. "Who are you burning sonny?" met with the inevitable reply, "King Billy" in a gleeful, mischievous tone.'[190] By the 1920s the

[186] *Liverpool Daily Post*, 13 July 1910
[187] *Liverpool Courier*, 13 July 1888
[188] *Liverpool Courier*, 13 July 1872
[189] *Liverpool Courier*, 13 July 1871
[190] *Liverpool Daily Post*, 13 July 1890

tradition of burning effigies had died out, though house and street decorations and bonfires remained a feature.[191]

By the late 1850s it is clear that the Order was giving serious thought to the maintenance of order and discipline during the processions, possibly in response to the outbreak of 1851 and the new by-laws. The ban on party colours and processions within the city meant careful instruction and organisation were needed to ensure lodges were carefully briefed on orderly behaviour and the time and place of assembly. By 1858 a procession committee had distributed a code of conduct to the lodges. Amongst the new rules were the warning that '[p]ersons who were found discharging firearms in the public street, road, lane or other thoroughfare, were to be fined 10s. Parties smoking in procession, or getting tipsy, were liable to a similar fine; and each member of a lodge was held strictly responsible for the good conduct of his members.' It was reported that

> [o]n the whole, everything was done which was likely in any degree to be subservient to the wishes of the constituted authorities, both within and without the boundary. [It was noted that]... some days previously the magistrates and police, both in town and country, were made acquainted with the route of the procession, and the utmost good feeling and unanimity existed between them and the procession committee. [Consequently when marchers returning from the rally reached the city boundary]... the procession halted, the music ceased to play, the banners were furled for twelve months more, and the members, under the direction of the Procession Committee, divested themselves of their regalia and quietly dispersed.[192]

Regulations were revised in the light of experience. The ban on firearms had to be constantly re-emphasised and in 1869 the ban on smoking was reinforced with a 1-shilling fine, those on parade were forbidden to break ranks and District committee members were appointed to stand at doors of pubs whilst their lodges passed to ensure that temptation was resisted.[193] By the 1870s reporters were regularly remarking on the good order in the processions.[194] In 1876 the procession committee membership had swollen to 60, with its chair promoted to ride with officials in the leading carriage.[195] But constant monitoring was necessary—in 1882 it was restated that '[a]ny member breaking the ranks or smoking in the procession to be fined one shilling. Any member allowing a female to take his arm on procession to be fined one shilling. Any member using

[191] *Liverpool Courier*, 13 July 1928
[192] *Liverpool Courier*, 17 July 1858
[193] *Liverpool Daily Post*, 13 July 1869
[194] *Liverpool Courier*, 13 July 1871
[195] *Liverpool Courier*, 13 July 1876

firearms during the procession or on the grounds to be fined 2/6d.' Excepting those carrying flags, banners or regalia, no cart or vehicle was allowed to join the procession.[196] But personal behaviour was a perpetual problem. In the 1960s and 1970s meetings of the procession committee were still preoccupied with breaches of the ban on smoking in processions, punctuality at the railway station and the overall need for '... dignity on parades'.[197]

Particular anxiety was caused by the behaviour of some banner carriers and band members who, overcome by the excitement of the day, would dance as they paraded. In 1927, '[o]ld and young danced jigs to the airs played by the band, drum-majors twirled their staffs jauntily and even the big-drummers pranced light heartedly'.[198] In 1961 the Procession Committee noted that the Chief Constable '... had asked that the members carrying banners must walk straight and there must be no dancing along the roads...' and a subsequent meeting also heard objections to dancing with bass drums.[199] Enthusiastic visiting Scottish bands were a particular problem. In June 1968 a Glasgow flute band had been allowed to join the parade, but following complaints about their fighting and disturbing neighbours at 5 am it was decided to ban them from future processions and requests to take part in Liverpool parades would in future be dealt with by the Grand Masters concerned.[200]

In 1894 one observer of Liverpool's 12 July demonstrations declared that '[t]he essentials to a successful demonstration are good weather, organising tact on the part of the leaders, obedience from the rank and file to their instructions, and enthusiastic interest in the proceedings' and concluded that in this case '[e]xcellent arrangements had been made by the procession committee'.[201] By that date the task had extended well beyond merely monitoring the behaviour of those in the procession. As the numbers of those who actually formed up and paraded in Liverpool processions grew, there was a parallel increase in accompanying family members and supporters and, as has been shown, the rallies developed into large-scale outings with food, refreshment and entertainment. When the rallying point was far removed from the outskirts of the city transport had to be arranged for the thousands involved. In 1904 the rally was at Southport. This involved organising not only the lodge members but

> ... women and children who are close adherents of the Order, numbering altogether something like 9,000... No fewer than eight special trains were requisitioned to convey this small army of demonstrators to their

[196] *Liverpool Courier*, 13 July 1882
[197] Liverpool Procession Committee Minute Book 25 October 1969 LRO 306.ORA/19/1/1
[198] *Liverpool Daily Post*, 13 July 1927
[199] Liverpool Processions Committee Minute Book May 1961 LRO 306.ORA/19/1/1
[200] Liverpool Processions Committee Minute Book 28 June, 23 August, 27 September 1968, 25 April 1969 LRO 306.ORA/19/1/1
[201] *Liverpool Courier*, 13 July 1894

destination, the first being despatched before nine o'clock. It was a tax on the railway officials to get the trains away up to the scheduled time, and all things considered the heavily-laden trains were sent on their way with despatch.[202]

The fact that the organisers coped is witness to the considerable administrative and organisational talent within the Order.[203]

The dark side of 12 July was the sectarian violence that erupted all too frequently. Until party processions were banned within the city boundaries, there had been a problem in the 1840s and early 1850s as lodges assembled early in the morning. Individual lodges drifted into the city centre in haphazard fashion and the exchange of banter with opponents could easily escalate. In July 1851 it had been arranged that lodges would assemble at 9 am at a monument in London Road:

> Owing, however, to the difficulty of getting so many different lodges together simultaneously... it unfortunately happened that at the appointed time but a few stragglers had arrived. A small lodge, No. 24, was the first on the ground... scarce had the little band mustered than a crowd of Irish... were seen and it was evident they meant business... for the assailants seemed to have chosen the very time for their attack—owing to the absence of the police force and the paucity of their opponents. A volley of stones and other destructive missiles was soon thrown... the report of fire-arms, and the flashing here and there of a sabre among the parties assembled, gave unmistakable indications of a vigorous resistance... the Orangemen having mustered together about a dozen swordsmen, they charged in gallant style, and the mob quickly gave way...[204]

It was the first stage in a day-long conflict resulting in two fatalities.

The subsequent city ban on party processions and colours went a considerable way to solving the problem of slow and erratic assembly of the lodges. It not merely shifted the gathering of vividly dressed lodge members from the crowded and intense streets of the city but it imposed on the Order the discipline of careful organisation discussed earlier. The need for tight organisation was reinforced when railway companies offered cheap group travel on specially ordered trains.[205] Once the lodges began to choose distant rallying places such

---

[202] *Liverpool Courier*, 13 July 1904

[203] McFarland, 'Marching From the Margins', p. 68

[204] *Liverpool Courier*, 15 July 1851

[205] S. Major, 'New crowds in new spaces: railway excursions for the working classes in north west England in the mid-nineteenth century', *Transactions of the Historic Society of Lancashire and Cheshire*, 166, pp. 120–35

as Southport they had to ensure that each member had a ticket and arrived on time for the specified train. This in turn required prompt and orderly assembly and parading to the station with no delays or diversions.

A further source of conflict arose from the highly developed sense of local territorial awareness in the residentially segregated districts. As noted in Chapter Two, in the north end streets off Scotland Road were dominated by Irish Catholics and the streets off nearby Netherfield Road in Everton were equally strongly Protestant. A similar pattern of residential segregation existed on a lesser scale in the south end in parts of Toxteth and Garston. Certain thoroughfares were widely accepted as boundary lines and the mere threat or rumour of trespassing was enough to mobilise large crowds to defend 'their' territory.[206] Some idea of the dynamics involved is conveyed on a minor scale by an incident in Toxteth in July 1854. It started when a Mr Haley from predominantly Catholic Albert Street was accused of having thrown dirt at an individual from Protestant Northumberland Road, who then attacked him, whereupon:

> ... immediately a number of women endeavoured to protect him [Haley], and the outbreak then became general. The Orangemen of Northumberland-street assembled their forces and, armed with sticks, stones, bricks &c., marched into Albert street, where the Irish turned out in hundreds, and were also prepared with weapons to meet their opponents. Showers of stones and bricks flew from one body to another... a section of police-con-stables... succeeded in driving the Irish into their houses in Albert street. The mob then commenced throwing stones and bricks from the windows, but ultimately the police restored order.[207]

Considerable care had to be taken on 12 July to avoid lodges venturing into the 'wrong' areas, though this was more of a problem at the end of the day than at the outset. An obvious solution was to plan procession routes that avoided historic trouble spots and consultation with the authorities became routine. As noted earlier there had been consultations with police and local magistrates before the 1858 processions. The following year rumours circulated that the lodges would parade through the village of Old Swan, which had a notable Catholic population. Lodge officers reassured local magistrates that their committee had striven to ensure '... they avoided every chance of coming to a collision with parties of antagonistic views... [and] so planned their route as to avoid this'. They clearly succeeded since '[t]he manner in which the whole of the persons connected directly or indirectly with the proceedings conducted themselves was highly creditable to the members

---

[206] *Liverpool Courier*, 15 July 1835; *Liverpool Mercury*, 17 July 1835
[207] *Liverpool Courier*, 13 July 1854

of the order…'[208] This tactic of calculated avoidance proved very necessary in July 1927 when railway authorities suddenly realised that the twelve special trains hired by the returning Orange lodges were going to pull into Lime Street station at the same time in the early evening as three trains bringing back pilgrims from the Catholic pilgrimage site of Lourdes. However, this '… awkward sectarian meeting was tactfully averted… by taking the Protestant trains into Lime-street after a wait, and sending the three Roman Catholic trains via Wigan to Exchange Station'.[209]

Deviation from traditional routes was highly dangerous. For the 1877 demonstration it had been decided '… to extend the procession to the northern end of the town, where the Irish residents of the lower order principally abound'. Bootle, which was chosen as the rallying point, was then in the throes of a large-scale dock extension scheme employing an estimated 3,000 navvies '… in a great part Irishmen and Roman Catholics'. A local observer reported '… it would appear that a strong feeling of resentment was awakened amongst this class by the course taken by the Orangemen in extending their celebration to the northern district of Liverpool'. On the Twelfth the celebrations passed off peacefully, the procession dispersed and the police held in reserve were stood down. A large force of navvies quickly emerged and began to parade around the town. The police were recalled and a four-hour riot developed in which slings were used and stones and bricks were thrown.[210]

The most frequent clashes took place when the lodges returned from the rally by train. Family, friends, supporters and spectators gathered at the station to greet returning members and walk alongside as they paraded back to their dispersal points. By the end of the day a considerable amount of alcohol had been taken. Catholic crowds would gather to ensure that traditional territorial boundaries were respected. Mutual taunting and provocation were customary, degenerating into fights, with the danger of escalation. Conflict sometimes centred around the station itself. In 1903 trains arrived between 7 and 9.20 pm to find that crowds had gathered to greet the arrivals with cheers and Orange songs, or boos, waving of green decorations, a rendering of 'God Bless the Pope' and occasional surges of the contending crowds towards each other, only separated by police tactics. Stones were thrown and at least one sword put to more than ceremonial use, but police averted a wider conflict.[211] Tension could also build when lodges paraded through the city to dispersal points with banners flying and bands playing. In July 1901 feelings were running high because of a sectarian clash the previous Sunday in which two Catholic priests had been injured. As the returning lodges processed, singing patriotic songs, '… several counter processions on a small scale were organised, mostly by women and boys,

[208] *Liverpool Courier*, 13 July 1859
[209] *Liverpool Courier*, 13 July 1927
[210] *Liverpool Daily Post*, 14 July 1877
[211] *Liverpool Courier*, 14 July 1903

who sang... airs... but no serious accidents have been reported to the police... who kept the turbulent spirits in check'.[212] It was a mix of sectarian passions, territorial defence, provocative coat-trailing and sheer mischief-making.

By the early 1920s the *Courier* noted that '[w]ith the passage of years the bitterness and the provocation of sectarian convictions have assumed a quieter tone, a less aggressive intensity. These convictions are no less deep seated and real.'[213] Whilst it is true that the large-scale conflicts of the late nineteenth and early twentieth centuries were no more, 12 July was not trouble-free. The reports by Daughters of Victory LLOL 11 on the returning processions in the late 1920s and early 1930s contain recurring references to the 'hostile' behaviour of a section of the crowds who gathered at the station and along the routes to dispersal. In 1926 outside Exchange Station '[a] crowd of "the opposition" was gathered singing Irish Nationalist songs' but '[n]o serious disorder occurred in any part of the city, though there were several minor disturbances and some half dozen arrests were made'.[214] The numbers and intensity involved were slowly ebbing. However, there were still sensitive areas, most notably at what was described in 1931 as the 'No Man's Land' of Great Homer Street, one side of which was patrolled by 'Orange parties' and the other by '... the opposite faction' until late in the evening, but overall the situation was simply described as involving '... some disorder...'[215] Two years later a magistrate hearing a minor incident remarked '... he was glad that Liverpool had not had disturbances of this kind... for what seemed now a considerable time'.[216] In the years following 1945 such incidents had passed into history and the most frequent derogatory remarks were on the occasional drunkenness of bandsmen and their tendency to dance whilst playing.

Two factors which helped mitigate the scale and intensity of community conflict were the spatial awareness of the local population and the evolution of the consultation process discussed earlier. The populations of the most sensitive areas developed a finely nuanced knowledge of respective territories and strove to keep the peace by careful observation of traditional boundaries and practices, especially around 12 July, though some did transgress out of pure mischief. Pat O'Mara, author of an intriguing memoir of his upbringing as a Liverpool Irish Catholic, recalled how on the Twelfth he and his mates ventured '... down toward Netherfield Road to witness the Orangeman's parade and... do our bit toward making it a failure...' but he also noted that '... the parade very discreetly kept away from Scotland Road, executing a nice turn at London Road...'[217]

---

[212] *Liverpool Courier*, 16 July 1901
[213] *Liverpool Courier*, 13 July 1922
[214] *Liverpool Daily Post*, 13 July 1926
[215] *Liverpool Daily Post*, 13 July 1931
[216] *Liverpool Daily Post*, 13 July 1933
[217] Pat O'Mara, *The Autobiography of a Liverpool Slummy* New York: Vanguard Press,

Other sources bear out that locals had an acute awareness of the intricacies of local social geography. St Anthony's Church on Scotland Road was in many ways the mother church of the Liverpool Catholic Irish. In pastoral visitation the clergy had to develop keen sensitivity to the fine detail of territorial bounding. One cleric who served from 1952 to 1964 recalled that, when travelling around the parish:

> ... we couldn't do the Hillside—Great Homer Street to Netherfield Road—because of the long-standing agreement that no Catholic processions could go beyond the bottom lamp posts of the streets leading to Great Homer Street... and the Orange processions would never come past the bottom lamp posts on the other side of Great Homer Street and that neither side would walk along Great Homer Street.

Another found that it was possible to enter that district though not at certain times of the year: '... we never made collections on the Sunday before or after 12 July'.[218]

Despite such precautions chance encounters could lead to problems. The sight of Catholic clerical garb seemed to provoke peculiar Protestant ire. In March 1958 the Catholic Archbishop Heenan was stoned while making a pastoral visit to a Catholic home in largely Protestant Robsart Street, but this was widely condemned.[219] Another cleric, who served in the parish from 1963 to 1968, recalled that '... around the 12 July you had to be careful...', with the significant rider '... but it was more about memories than current practice'.[220] It was careful respect of such local spatial niceties that helped keep the peace.

Perhaps the most effective measure was the further development of the process of consultation with local authorities. By the early twentieth century formal application to the Council watch committee was needed for permission to hold a procession, with details of proposed date, times, routes and numbers, music to be played, emblems to be carried and literature to be circulated.[221] By the second half of the century the Liverpool Province processions committee and the city council watch committee met regularly to review recent experience and discuss future plans. Analysis of discussion during the period 1959–63 reveals almost no mention of sectarian conflict, the topics most frequently discussed being the need to avoid

---

1933, p. 33; McFarland noted similar spatial sensitivities in Scottish urban areas: 'Marching From the Margins', p. 70

[218] Michael O'Neill, *St Anthony's Scotland Road, Liverpool* Leominster: Gracewing Press, 2010, p. 262; 'collections' involved visitations to collect money for parish work and charities

[219] Roberts, *Liverpool Sectarianism*, p. 127

[220] O'Neill, *St Anthony's*, p. 290

[221] Bullough, 'Remember the Boyne', pp. 30–32

traffic congestion together with occasional comment on personal behaviour during the processions. Clearly the Order and the authorities had developed a close and quite amicable working relationship. As early as July 1935 the Daughters of Victory LLOL 11 agreed to the proposal of their Secretary who '... wished to send a letter to the Chief Constable of Wallasey thanking him the officers and men for the great manner in which they had helped them on the route to New Brighton on the 15th'.[222] There were annual meetings with the Chief Constable and relations had developed to the point where the Provincial processions committee sent a letter of good wishes to the retiring Chief Constable in 1964.[223]

Conclusion

Clearly the 'private lodge' with its carefully devised and strictly observed internal degrees, ritual, liturgy, regalia, code of conduct, dress codes and specialist committees was the core of the Order. It is equally clear that with the passage of time female members grew in numbers and came to play a central role, though official recognition of their centrality was long contested. The need for a juvenile branch to transmit the values of the Institution was recognised quite early but again progress slow and it is also clear that female members were notably more conscientious in oversight of juvenile lodges.

With the passage of time public performance of Orangeism in procession became much more carefully organised and regulated until 12 July became an enjoyable, multi-dimensional occasion, displaying numerical strength, conviction, respectability, sociability and sheer enjoyment. The inclusion of women and juvenile members in the processions from quite early on was a unique feature of the Liverpool parades. But there was also a dark side in that all too often, especially at the end of the day, the processions provided opportunities for provocation, coat-trailing and sectarian violence at group and individual levels. Such conflicts served to underline not only the convictions of the contending groups, but also what they considered to be their respective spaces and boundaries. But local-group spatial awareness and informal mutual respect plus consultation with local authorities lessened the opportunities for collision. Participation in such public performance and community conflict helped bond the participants to fellow members, their lodges and their beliefs, but as will now be shown, they were also bonded by broadly similar social origins.

---

[222] Daughters of Victory LLOL 11 Minute Book 18 July 1935 LRO 306.ORA/9/1/2
[223] Liverpool Province Procession Committee Minute Book 23 October 1964 LRO 306. ORA/19/1/2

4

Class, Origin, Sociability and Mutuality

Introduction

Analysis of the class basis, origins and long-term survival of the Orange Order has long been inhibited by lack of access to lodge records, and even when available these can be limited in the detail they convey. The picture has been further complicated by some aspects of the history of the Order, but the trend towards increased openness discussed in the Introduction and the availability of some lodge documentation have opened up the possibility for analysis of the class background of the members and the social and material benefits of lodge life.

Socio-economic patterns of membership

Discussion of the social basis of the Orange Order has been complicated by the fact that at various stages in its history middle-class elements and even members of the landed aristocracy and royal family have flirted with the institution when politically convenient. As discussed in Chapter Two, in the somewhat fevered debates of the two decades leading up to Catholic emancipation in 1829, some ultra-Tory aristocratic elements and royal dukes found the Order a useful vehicle for mobilising traditional anti-Catholic sentiment and became members and significant office holders. With the passing of the act these elements quickly fell away, setting the pattern for the flirting, on–off relationship which was to last into the twentieth century. The Conservative party followed a similar pattern, looking favourably on the movement when politically convenient, but distancing themselves when it proved embarrassing.

A second problem has been the very limited access to lodge records until recently and the limited nature of those that have become available. Home addresses were necessary for posting out notice of lodge meetings, but there was no reason for secretaries to have details of the occupation or place of birth of members. Payment of lodge dues was recorded, but records merely listed member names. Where home addresses do emerge, they can be checked against census returns but only if dates of compilation coincide, however roughly.

In this section it is proposed to examine the reports of the Grand Lodge of England for opinions on the socio-economic nature of their membership, discuss the extant academic literature and then proceed to an analysis of the evidence on social class in the Liverpool lodges which can be culled from newspaper reportage on 12 July processions, the rule books of three mutual aid societies from the 1840s, private lodge records and some material from lodge LOL 64 in the Garston area.

Grand Lodge reports have generally focused on the state of the Order and concern with the politics of state and church, making little reference to social and economic context. However, in the mid-1930s it was recognised that a significant part of the membership was feeling the impact of successive economic crises. In 1933 it was noted that conditions

> are bearing more hardly on our members, especially in the North and North Western Provinces, where shipbuilding has been practically at a standstill, and the other heavy industries being almost as bad, with the result that many of our brethren and sisters are still out of work... This lack of employment has to a considerable extent affected our membership, as a number of our brethren and sisters have resigned... they being unable to meet their dues.[1]

The following year it was reported that the secretary of one District 'informed me that half the town is unemployed, consequently their membership is not so large as it would be under the circumstances; this applies to several districts'.[2]

Academic work on the socio-economic basis of the Order was sparse until recently. Pioneering research on the Order in Northern Ireland in 1997 found 40 per cent in manual occupations, 22 per cent in white collar jobs and 22 per cent farmers, and questionnaire analysis conducted over the period 2006–08 certainly confirmed the long-held conviction of a strongly working-class base, with 56 per cent of respondents self-identifying as working class, 17 per cent as middle class and 25 per cent not identifying with any class.[3]

Early work on the Order in Britain asserted that members were 'largely urban labourers... plebeian',[4] and this became a widely accepted truism, together with

[1] Loyal Orange Institution of England Report 1933, p. 16
[2] Loyal Orange Institution of England Report 1934, p. 14
[3] Eric Kaufmann, *The Orange Order: A Contemporary Northern Irish History* (Oxford: Oxford University Press, 2007), p. 4; James W. McAuley, Jonathan Tonge and Andrew Mycock, *Loyal to the Core? Orangeism and Britishness in Northern Ireland* (Dublin: Irish Academic Press, 2011), p. 58
[4] Senior, *Orangeism*, pp. 158 and 283

the assertion that the membership was to be found concentrated in the urban industrial slums of northern England and Scotland and to consist of 'working class Irish Protestants and English anti-Catholic workers'.[5] In Scotland it was also asserted that the Order was essentially working class but with a notable middle-class element in its early days.[6] Subsequent work utilising newspapers, pamphlets, electoral registers and directories analysing the occupations of lodge officers in Greenock, Paisley, Glasgow and rural parts of Lanarkshire and Ayrshire found that while unskilled and casual labourers were the largest group, there was also some skilled working-class element and some petty bourgeois members, relative proportions depending on local socio-economic structure.[7]

Work on the Irish in Victorian Cumbria broadly reinforced these conclusions.[8] Subsequent access to lodge records in the north-east together with census material enabled the same author to reconstruct the occupational profile of lodge leadership cadres in northern England in 1881 and 1901. This confirmed the overwhelmingly working-class nature of lodge officers. In 1881 the unskilled made up 51 per cent of officers, closely followed by the semi-manual and well-paid at 42.9 per cent, with only 5.1 per cent non-manual; in 1901 the respective figures were 36.8 per cent, 55.9 per cent and 7.4 per cent, a reinforcement of the semi-skilled element but still underlining the working-class nature of the leadership. Clearly 'Orangeism was resolutely and overwhelmingly a movement staffed by ordinary men and women... slightly more skilled than unskilled'.[9] Work on the leadership of past female lodges, deducing the socio-economic status of members from the occupation of the head of household, found the leadership cadre to be overwhelmingly working class along with some middle-class officers, relative numbers again varying with local economic structure.[10]

[5] Gray, *The Orange Order*, p. 83

[6] Steve Bruce, *No Pope of Rome: Militant Protestantism in Modern Scotland* (Edinburgh: Edinburgh Publishing Company, 1985), p. 150; Tom Gallagher, *The Uneasy Peace* (Manchester: Manchester University Press, 1987), p. 25

[7] Elaine MacFarland, *Protestants First: Orangeism in 19th Century Scotland* (Edinburgh: Edinburgh University Press, 1990); see also G. Walker, 'The Protestant Irish in Scotland' in T. Devine (ed.), *Irish Immigrants and Scottish Society in the Nineteenth and Twentieth Centuries* (Edinburgh: John Donald, 1991), pp. 44–66; William Marshall, *The Billy Boys: A Concise History of Orangeism in Scotland* (Edinburgh: Mercat Press, 1996)

[8] MacRaild, *Culture, Conflict and Migration*, pp. 150 and 155

[9] MacRaild, *Faith, Fraternity and Fighting*, pp. 127–28, 122 and 220

[10] MacPherson, *Women and the Orange Order*, pp. 52–55

The Liverpool membership

In the case of Liverpool, the widespread assumption has been that here too the membership was 'overwhelmingly working-class... most participants seem to have been English working men'.[11] It was possible to discern some hint of the social class of members from newspaper reports of court cases following riots and from local directories. The clash in 1819 revealed that amongst those giving evidence for the prosecution were a cooper, a shoemaker, a ropemaker and a shipwright, described as 'the trades that were subsequently to provide the mainstay of Liverpool Orangeism'.[12] Liverpool newspaper references to the class composition of lodges are few and far between, but there are occasional asides. In 1820, when it was estimated that about 90 people took part in the 12 July procession, it was noted that 'their dress was that of a very inferior class of society'.[13] A quarter-century later, as the movement was gradually emerging from the 1836 ban and the first 12 July procession for many years was held, the local, pro-Conservative, newspaper praised the Order for 'binding in an indissoluble bond the upper, the middle and the lower classes of Protestants'.[14] But 30 years later it was somewhat more perceptive when it congratulated the Order for the July turnout by 'the Protestant working men of Liverpool'.[15] By the late 1880s the entrenched presence of the working-class Orange Order element within Liverpool Conservative ranks was celebrated by the same source with the remark that '[f]or the most part the brethren belong to the artisan class and are active workers in the Conservative cause'.[16]

In the mid-1840s Grand Lodge reports and local directories revealed the presence in the Liverpool leadership cadre of a bookbinder and a stationer, a marine stores dealer, a stationer and printer, a partner in a clerical and scholastic agency, a warehouse owner, a small brewer and an auctioneer and estate agent, suggesting a notable, skilled working-class element.[17] Eight years later the pattern was confirmed by the occupations of those arrested for defying a ban on parading, though a distinction is discerned between this leadership and the generality of the membership.[18] Of the four Liverpool delegates listed as attending a half-yearly meeting of the Grand Protestant Association in February 1864, two were shoemakers, one a coppersmith and the last a merchant.[19]

---

11 Lowe, *The Irish in Mid-Victorian Lancashire*, p. 153
12 Neal, *Sectarian Violence*, p. 40
13 *Liverpool Mercury*, 14 July 1820
14 *Liverpool Courier*, 16 July 1845
15 *Liverpool Courier*, 13 July 1872
16 *Liverpool Courier*, 13 July 1887
17 Neal, *Sectarian Violence*, p. 71
18 Neal, *Sectarian Violence*, pp. 170–71
19 Grand Protestant Association of Loyal Orangemen of England, Half Yearly Meeting, 3 February 1864, Appendix 5, p. 23; private collection

Lodge records suggest the possibility of unemployment was a perpetual anxiety. The Everett LOL 108 minute book for the period March 1882 to June 1898 opens with a note on the inside cover stating that where '[a]ny Bro. has been out of work or ill we the Brethren do exempt them for such time that they may be out of work or are not able to follow there [sic] employment be so exempt from paying there [sic] dues for such time should notified [sic] the Secretary's of such illness or want of work'.[20] This chronic anxiety is reflected in the arrangements the lodge made for the 12 July processions in 1905. They appointed five banner carriers, who would be paid 4s. each, one to be a reserve and 'it was agreed should any of the [appointed] be in work & a Bro. out of work turn out the former should stand down so as to give the latter the place'.[21] Efforts were made to ensure that officer duties did not involve personal expense. In 1932 it was noted by members of Lady Stanley LLOL 97 that the female Superintendent of the juvenile lodge was out of pocket because of her efforts and it was decided 'through so much unemployment' to organise an event to make up the costs.[22]

The great majority of members were employees subject to the demands and the dangers of the work routine and the vicissitudes of the trade cycle, because they were, as one minute book put it in an extremely rare reference to personal social background, 'only working men'.[23] There are frequent apologies from members for unpunctuality or for missing meetings due to work commitments. In June 1892 the Secretary of Cromwell LOL 94 was reported unable to attend a lodge meeting because he was 'working all night'[24] and on 27 June 1950 the Chaplain of District No. 6 Duke of York explained his late arrival as due to 'working'.[25] In some cases officers explained they had to resign their post because of work demands as in the case of the Treasurer of No. 3 District in August 1903.[26] Other members had to refuse election to officer posts because of work commitments, as the sitting Deputy Master of Everett LOL 108 explained to their annual meeting in July 1904.[27] Members employed in the merchant service found regular attendance a problem and some lodges stretched a point. The Sons of the Boyne LOL 28 held a special meeting in March 1924 to initiate 'a seagoing member' in the presence of his father.[28] Port workers suffered from the high accident rate in the workplace. In November 1919 Lady Stanley LLOL 97

[20]   Everett LOL 108 Minute Book 1882–98 LRO 306.ORA/1/1/1
[21]   Everett LOL 108 Minute Book 21 June 1905 LRO 306.ORA/1/1/3
[22]   Lady Stanley LLOL 97 Minute Book 16 February 1933 LRO 306.ORA/5/1/2
[23]   Garston True Blues LOL 64 Hall Committee Minute Book 1921–25, 22 August 1922; held at Heald Street Orange Hall, Garston
[24]   Cromwell LOL 94 Minute Book 28 June 1892 LRO 306.ORA/13/1/1
[25]   Duke of York No. 6 District Minute Book 27 June 1950 LRO 306.ORA/13/1/1
[26]   No. 3 District Minute Book 18 August 1903 LRO 306.ORA/3/1/1
[27]   Everett LOL 108 Minute Book 20 July 1904 LRO 306.ORA/1/1/3
[28]   Sons of the Boyne LOL 28 Minute Book 8 March 1924 LRO 306.ORA/7/1/1

were informed that their Secretary was 'at present in hospital owing to a nasty accident received at his work'.[29] In 1936 the Grand Lodge report carried the news that '[d]ue to a very sad accident at the Docks, our esteemed Bro. A.E. Coates was suddenly called to higher service. He served the Cheshire and North Wales Province well for many years as Provincial Grand Secretary.'[30] The occasional postponement of 12 July events for work reasons has already been noted. The precarious domestic economy of the majority of members is well illustrated when, in 1935, the Bootle lodges paraded on 14 July because 'most of the men could not afford to come until they had drawn their unemployment pay. About 500 were kept back until the early afternoon because their clearance money at the docks was not paid until midday.'[31]

The loss of even a day's pay was a serious blow. In 1843 rule 14 of lodge no. 14 of the Loyal Orange Benefit Society, whose workings will be discussed shortly, stated '[t]hat officers or members called off in working hours on society's business, shall be paid at the rate of four shillings per day'.[32] Over 60 years later in 1904 Everett LOL 108 agreed that 'any member of [the band] attending funeral on weekday be paid 3/- for loss of time provided there is funds'.[33] Nearly 50 years later the same anxiety emerges. When a special Lodge Committee meeting was held by Garston True Blues LOL 64 to discuss arrangements for a member's funeral 'it was decide [sic] that the band and bearers received expenses for time lost at work'.[34]

The available lodge archives have almost no information on the job titles of lodge members. Very occasionally there are lists of members recording their payment (or non-payment) of dues and sometimes these include home addresses that can be compared with other sources. The records for the Garston True Blues lodge LOL 64 are unusual in that they contain a listing of all lodge members' names and almost all addresses for the period January to June 1903, possibly in preparation for an application for renewal of the lodge warrant in 1905. The lodge strength is given as 246, of whom 236 had an address. These were cross-referenced against data on occupation and birthplace from the 1901 census. It proved possible to recover data on occupation for 100 members. The 'unskilled' numbered 50, of whom 38 were returned as 'labourer', by far the largest single category in the membership. Those who may be considered as semi-skilled

[29] Lady Stanley LLOL 97 Minute Book 12 November 1919 LRO 306.ORA/5/1/2
[30] Loyal Orange Institution of England, Grand Secretary's Report 1936, p. 15
[31] *Liverpool Post*, 15 July 1935
[32] *Rules and Regulations to be observed by the Members of the Loyal Orange Benefit Society Lodge No. 14. Held at Liverpool.* (Liverpool: Reston, 1843). LRO Town Clerk's Papers 352.CLE/460
[33] Everett LOL 108 Minute Book 2 November 1904 LRO 306.ORA/1/1/3
[34] Garston True Blues LOL 64 Minute Book 1950–53: 6 September 1953; held at Heald Street Orange Hall, Garston

numbered 45, 4 were in clerical employment and 1 a professional (photographer). Of the 15 officers and committee members listed, 9 had traceable addresses and occupations: two mariners, two foremen, one each of salesman, painter, porter, carter and boiler riveter.[35] The pattern reflected an economy heavily dependent on employment on the local docks, the railway network, at saw mills, iron and copper works, tannery, gasworks and bobbin manufacturers.[36] This strongly endorses the pattern discerned in the literature of an overwhelmingly working-class membership, a majority unskilled, a notable minority semi-skilled or reasonably well paid and a tiny clerical and professional element.

A significant theme in the literature is the assertion that Ulster immigrants played a key role in both importing the Order and sustaining its membership in Scotland,[37] and that in northern England both Ulster and Scots migrants were a key component of the lodges,[38] though it was also widely recognised that Liverpool was an exceptional place where the Order 'recruited strongly among Protestant workers… with no Ulster or Irish connections'.[39] The data from Garston True Blues LOL 64 in 1903 bears out this assertion. Lodge documentation that year contained details of 84 members whose place of birth can be discerned from the 1901 census. This reveals that 48 (57.1 per cent) of members were born in Liverpool or Birkenhead, and a further 14 in Lancashire or Cheshire, giving a grand total of 62 or 73.8 per cent born in north-west England. Of the remainder only three (3.6 per cent) were born in Ireland and none in Scotland.[40] A similar pattern emerges in data culled from the records of other lodges for a variety of periods. For the years 1909–10 Everett LOL 108 listed the names and addresses of 24 members, all in the Liverpool region;[41] for Belfast Patriotic LOL 3 only 2 of the 49 people listed as members at various points in the mid-1950s gave Irish addresses;[42] for Trevor LOL 820 none of the 16 new members admitted between 1948 and 1954 originated from Ireland;[43] and when the Protestant Martyrs Lodge

[35] List of members and addresses of Garston True Blues LOL 64; held at Heald Street Orange Hall, Garston
[36] *Garston News*, September 2002
[37] McFarland, *Protestants First*, pp. 50, 65
[38] MacRaild, *Faith, Fraternity and Fighting*, pp. 142–46; Donald MacRaild, 'The Irish and Scots in the English Orange Order in the later nineteenth century' in L. Kennedy and R.J. Morris (eds), *Order and Disorder: Ireland and Scotland, 1600–2001*. (East Linton: John Donald, 2005). chp. 5, pp. 120–35
[39] Belchem, 'The Liverpool Irish enclave', p. 142
[40] List of members and addresses of Garston True Blues LOL 64; held at Heald Street Orange Hall, Garston
[41] Everett LOL 108 Minute Book 1909–10 LRO 306.ORA/1/1/4
[42] Belfast Patriotic LOL 3 Minute Book LRO 306.ORA/11/1
[43] Trevor LOL 820 Minute Book 1948–54 LRO 306.ORA/14/1/1

was launched in August 1955 there were no Irish addresses amongst the 21 founding members.[44] Clearly, in every sense these were Liverpool lodges.

This is not to argue that there were no people of Irish origin or descent within the Liverpool lodges. Transfers from Ireland emerge sporadically from the records. In March 1914 the Old Swan Arch Purple Heroes LOL 810 admitted a member from LOL 1189 based in Sandy Row, west Belfast, one of the most fervently loyalist areas of that city.[45] Some idea of the administrative work involved comes from the meeting of Everett LOL 108 on 21 September 1898 when the secretary 'asked permission to rite [sic] to Ireland for 2 brethren which were both young and respectable men and he the secretary had seen letters of recommendation from there [sic] Ministers in Ireland as been attendents [sic] at church and bible classes'.[46] Such incomers could rise to officer positions. Everett LOL 108 had a long-term member in the Belfast-born John Long, owner of a business in the middle-class Lark Lane area of the city, a Mason and member of the local Conservative party, who occupied every office in the lodge.[47] William Watson went even further, serving as local Conservative councillor, Lord Mayor 1902–03, MP for Edge Hill constituency and Grand Master of the Orange Order 1912–15. In 1914 he declared his vehement opposition to Irish home rule was due to the fact that 'he was sprung from the Ulster race'.[48] Clearly, as will be discussed later, the special relationship with Ireland persisted, but it is equally clear that the Order had become a distinctly Liverpool phenomenon in the depth of its roots and the strength of its appeal within the city's Protestant working class.

Localism

If the private lodges were the backbone of the Order, it is also true to say that its members 'were men of localities... it was in the localities that, so far as the foot-soldiers were concerned, its main work was done'.[49] Lodge titles such as 'Garston True Blues', 'Lily of Toxteth', 'Rising Star of Wavertree', 'Kirkdale's Glory' and 'Old Swan Royal Arch Purple Heroes' emphasised local identity. It is significant that the two privately published lodge histories to hand—by Garston True Blues LOL 64 and Ivy LOL 783—feature hand-drawn maps of the

---

44 Protestant Martyrs LOL 35 Minute Book—list of founding members in August 1955 LRO 306.ORA/15/1/1
45 Old Swan Arch Purple Heroes LOL 810 Minute Book March 1914 LRO 306.ORA/8/1/1; Catherine Hirst, *Religion, Politics and Violence in Nineteenth-Century Belfast: The Pound and Sandy Row* (Dublin: Four Courts Press, 2002)
46 Everett LOL 108 Minute book 21 September 1898 LRO 306.ORA/1/1/2
47 Everett LOL 108 Minute Book 15 December 1897 LRO 306.ORA/111
48 Loyal Orange Institution of England Report 1914, p. 17
49 MacRaild, *Faith, Fraternity and Fighting*, p. 76

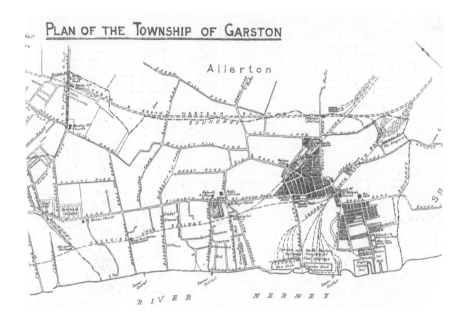

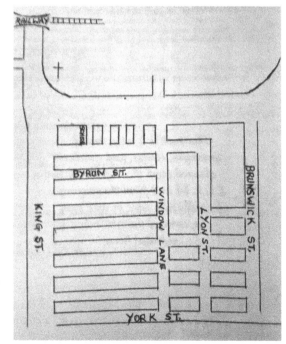

Figure 4.1 Mapping localism: the heartland of the Garston lodges. *Source: Courtesy Garston LOL 64*

Figure 4.2　Mapping localism: the Everton core area of Ivy LOL 83.
Source:　Author's collection

areas from which the authors clearly believed their lodge drew the core of its membership. In the Garston case, the map actually focuses on the area 'under the bridge' south of the railway line that transects the district, where, in 1904, 40 per cent of the total membership lived.[50]

Documentation bears out the extent to which lodges were embedded in locality. The three surviving minute books of the proceedings of Orange Hall management committees demonstrate extensive use of the premises by local community groups as well as lodges. Hiring charges were a valued source of income, but significant distinctions were made in the charges with a preference for events linked to lodges or their members and what were clearly considered respectably married couples. In March 1959 Kirby Defenders LOL 300 charged £3.3s. for lodge events but £4 for non-member wedding receptions,[51] while in

---

[50]　*A Glimpse Into 125 Years*, Introduction, p. 4; Ivy LOL 783, *100 Years of History*, p. 15
[51]　Kirby Defenders Orange Hall Management Committee Minute Book 20 March 1959 LRO 306.ORA/110/1/2

June 1959 No. 6 District Hall was available for wedding receptions at £5.5s. for those married in church but £10.10s. for others.[52] Groups and individuals associated with the Order clearly had priority. In November 1962 the Garston Hall Committee Secretary noted that the current weekly pattern was for a room to be booked every weekday evening by lodges or their bands.[53] Members made bookings for private events such as wedding receptions and birthday parties, sometimes at favourable rates—in early 1963 the fee was waived when a member held a 21st birthday party for his daughter.[54] The halls were also quite frequently hired by local churches for church council meetings, Sunday school parties, bible classes, evangelistic meetings, meetings of the Protestant Truth Society and scripture examinations. The Garston hall was frequently used by the Conservative Party. In January 1922, November 1923 and January 1925 it was hired by the Ladies Conservative Club social for a whist drive,[55] in July 1955 for a Young Conservative rummage sale and the following year for a dance. In October 1922 it was used for a political meeting and on election day December 1923 and July 1945 it was hired for a fee of £15.12s., presumably as a campaign committee room. But, doubtless with an eye to the fees involved, the rooms were also hired out to the Transport Workers Union, the Amalgamated Engineering Union and the National Union of Railwaymen, though there was consternation in October 1960 when it was discovered that the NUR had used the premises for a strike meeting.[56]

A great variety of local groups made use of the halls, including football, cricket, archery and pigeon-racing clubs, keep fit, tap, ballet and old-time dancing and sewing classes. The Garston Hall was used in early 1923 'for recreation etc. afternoon for unemployed',[57] the Co-operative Society held quarterly meetings there and in February 1940 took a four-day booking to distribute members' dividend.[58] Other groups to use the halls included the Ladies Zionist League, the Boy Scouts, the Girls Friendly Society, a Meccano club, a tenants' association, St John's Ambulance, dog show organisers and local tontines. The records for all three halls note occasions when they were unable to accommodate any further

---

52 No. 6 District Hall Management Committee 19 June 1961 LRO 306.ORA/13/2/1
53 Garston Orange Hall Committee Minute Book 1954–62: 7 November 1962; held at Heald Street Orange Hall, Garston
54 No. 6 District Hall Management Committee Minute Book 18 February 1962 LRO 306.ORA/13/2/2
55 Garston Orange Hall Management Committee Minute Book 1921–25: 3 January 1922, 21 November 1923, 14 January 1925; held at Heald Street Orange Hall, Garston
56 Garston Orange Hall Committee Minute Book 1954–62: 12 October 1960; held at Heald Street Orange Hall, Garston
57 Garston Hall Committee Minute Book December 1921–October 1925: 6 March 1923; held at Heald Street Orange Hall, Garston
58 Garston Hall Committee 27 February 1940 Minute Book April 1939–June 1954: 27 February 1940; held at Heald Street Orange Hall, Garston

lettings. Despite the high esteem in which the armed forces were held, in 1958 Kirby Defenders LOL 300 had to refuse a booking by the local branch of the British Legion because there were no free nights available.[59]

A final factor which embedded lodges deeply in both community and personal life was the entrenchment of a tradition of lodge membership within families. On the rare occasions when lodge members are listed, family groups emerge. In July 1919 Sons of the Boyne LOL 28 accepted a father and son into membership at the same meeting;[60] when Protestant Martyrs LOL 35 was founded in August 1955, 23 members were listed of whom 9 were from 3 families;[61] and a listing of the members of Belfast Patriotic LOL 3 in the same period reveals that 12 came from 5 families.[62]

Clearly Orange lodges could be deeply embedded in community life and could become a key component of local social capital, not merely by their active presence but through use of their premises by a broad sweep of local organisations and associations, thereby enabling a lodge and its parades and activities to become an accepted part of local normality. But whilst the lodge and its activities can be regarded as significant for the ebb and flow of community life, they were also significant for particular families who established a tradition of membership and at the personal level the links developed between lodge members could generate quite close social bonding.

Sociability—having a good time

A key attraction of the Order was the intensity of lodge social life. One of the many forms this took was the organisation of outings. Amongst the destinations mentioned are Llangollen, Frodsham, Cumberland and Blackpool. In September 1924 Daughters of Victory LLOL 11 decided on a 'charabanc' trip to Southport, costing 6s.9d. each for fare, dinner and tea. It was reported that 'everything passed off very successful and all those who took part appeared to have enjoyed themselves'. Some idea of the organisational logistics is conveyed by the Secretary who 'sincerely thanked the [organiser] for the efficient manner in which she had taken charge of same'.[63]

In September 1904 a member of Everett LOL 108 suggested that 'we should have a pleasant evening once a month free from toil and business...',[64] the purpose being, as members of another lodge put it, 'so that all the members can

---

[59] Kirby Defenders Orange Hall Management Committee Minute Book 4 March 1958 LRO 306.ORA/110/1/2
[60] Sons of the Boyne LOL 28 Minute Book 15 July 1919 LRO 306.ORA/6/1/1
[61] Protestant Martyrs LOL 35 Minute Book 28 August 1955 LRO 306.ORA/15/1/1
[62] Belfast Patriotic LOL 3 Minute Book LRO 306.ORA/11/1
[63] Daughters of Victory LLOL 11 Minute Book 18 September 1924 LRO 306.ORA/9/1/1
[64] Everett LOL 108 Minute Book 21 September 1904 LRO 306.ORA/1/1/2

be together'.[65] Whilst members seemed quite happy with the ritual and routine of monthly lodge meetings, with phrases such as 'altogether the evening was spent in a very pleasant manner' constantly recurring,[66] it is equally clear that a strong social dimension developed around these meetings. When formal business had closed some lodges adopted the same practice as Lady Stanley LLOL 97 where 'the members... held a social gathering for about an hour and partook of tea and cakes and an all-round conversation and a very nice evening was spent'.[67] Though suspended during the First World War, the practice was resumed in December 1919.[68] In some lodges it was institutionalised in the form of a 'pound night' to which members brought along a pound (in weight) of eatables, usually cake and biscuits. In some lodges this occurred at regular intervals, but in others it was triggered by a formal resolution.

Gatherings could take on a more elaborate form, usually to mark a special personal occasion or an event in the life of the lodge. In August 1930 the W.M. of Lady Stanley LLOL 97 treated fellow members to tea and cakes to celebrate her 60th birthday, provoking 'expressions of joy and best wishes... from all the sisters... a small present was handed over...'.[69] In December 1924 Daughters of Victory LLOL 11 held a special pound night with tea and cakes at which their long-standing male secretary was presented with a 'double gold Albert'.[70] This lodge had been formed in July 1876 and celebrated its jubilee with dinner, games and entertainment on 3 July 1926.[71] Male lodges clearly preferred a hot meal, with 'hotpot supper' a favourite, and one such was enjoyed by Everett LOL 108 in December 1900 at a local hotel for 1s.3d. per head.[72] Participation was by no means confined to lodge members. In September 1907 Lady Stanley LLOL 97 closed their meeting and then 'the members of the lodge and visiting Sisters to the number of about 40 sat down to a substantial tea provided by the Sisters of this lodge and visiting Sisters'.[73] Although 12 July was the high point of lodge life, throughout the year there was a perpetual buzz of social activity within and between lodges, with invitations to dinners, 'smokers', coffee suppers, tea parties, socials and concerts constantly circulating. Entertainment, singing and dancing as well as food were often features of such events. Music was sometimes provided by the bands which accompanied the lodges on 12 July but other groups were on offer, such as the 'Southern Coons Minstrel Troupe', a form of entertainment

[65] Protestant Martyrs LLOL 91 Minute Book January 1968 LRO 306.ORA/15/1/3
[66] Lady Stanley LLOL 97 Minute Book 15 February 1935 LRO 306.ORA/5/1/2
[67] Lady Stanley LLOL 97 Minute Book 13 November 1912 LRO 306.ORA/5/1/1
[68] Lady Stanley LLOL 97 Minute Book 10 December 1919 LRO 306.ORA/5/1/2
[69] Lady Stanley LLOL 97 Minute Book 21 August 1930 LRO 306.ORA/5/1/2
[70] Daughters of Victory LLOL 11 Minute Book 18 December 1924 LRO 306.ORA/9/1/1
[71] Daughters of Victory LLOL 11 Minute Book 15 July 1926 LRO 306.ORA/9/1/1
[72] Everett LOL 108 Minute Book 19 December 1900 LRO 306.ORA/1/1/2
[73] Lady Stanley LLOL 97 Minute Book 16 September 1907 LRO 306.ORA/5/1/1

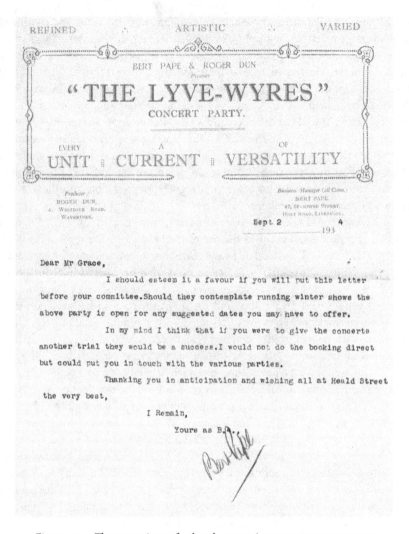

Figure 4.3　The organiser of a local entertainment group reassures
Garston True Blues LOL 64 that they offer a respectable family show.
Source:　LRO

notably popular well into the twentieth century.[74] The 'Live-Wyres' concert group,
who were advertised to Garston True Blues LOL 64 as being 'Refined, Artistic,

---

[74]　Belchem, *Irish, Catholic and Scouse*, pp. 324–26 for the popularity and cultural significance of such groups amongst Irish migrants, especially in North America

Varied, Well Dressed, Clean', were recommended by the Lodge's Secretary as being 'a good clean show'.[75]

Perhaps the atmosphere at lodge dinners is best conveyed by the account of the 'Annual Supper and Smoking Concert' of Everett LOL 108 held in February 1901:

> Bro. Clarke kindly enlivened the supper with the gramfone [sic] which the company thoroughly appreciated... when the refreshments were brought in and the company supplied with smoking appurtenances the Worthy Chairman Ald. Roberts gave a pleasant speech... Bro. Arthur Evans then sang a song and received tremendous applause he was followed by Bro. Walter Mercer with a most humorous song... Bro. Wise gave a speech... Bro. Arthur Evans & friends then sang the brethren thoroughly enjoying the singing although it was very trying to the singers with the smoke they all sang with gusto he's a jolly fellow... Bro. W. Coslett followed with an address... [although] he has spoken before a great many audiences he never let his warmth of feeling be seen to such advantage before thus showing that a brother's heart is always warmer to a brother Orangeman than to anybody else... The meeting was brought to a close by singing the national anthem.[76]

Presence at such events served to bind members not merely to the lodge and the Order but to each other in a sense of shared, warm, fraternal, good-humoured, hearty enjoyment in the company of like-minded people. The result was that a member's entire social life could consist of 'lodge night' plus all the intensely hectic activities organised by lodge, District and Province. If a member was also an officer the degree of involvement was even stronger.

The intense bonding that resulted was spontaneously testified by several members. In July 1900 an Everett lodge member remarked 'he was proud to boast of being a member and always looked forward with pleasure to the Lodge night which he always enjoyed'.[77] When a member had to leave the city it was quite a wrench. In March 1901 lodge Chaplain Reverend Barnhill, about to take up a curacy in Yorkshire, addressed the lodge and 'spoke of the pleasure and benefit he had derived since he had become an Orangeman... though so many miles separated them still in his sympathy he would always be with the brethren of 108'.[78] The departure could be felt equally keenly by the lodge. In October 1919 a member informed Old Swan Arch Purple Heroes LOL 810 that he was about to emigrate: 'it would be his last visit to any Lodge in Liverpool before his departure

---

[75] Document enclosed with Garston True Blues LOL 64 Minute Book of Hall Committee January 1926–March 1933; held at Heald Street Orange Hall, Garston

[76] Everett LOL 108 Minute Book 14 February 1901 LRO 306.ORA/1/1/2

[77] Everett LOL 108 Minute Book 18 July 1900 LRO 306.ORA/1/1/2

[78] Everett LOL 108 Minute Book 20 March 1901 LRO 306.ORA/1/1/2

for America in which [a Brother] gave a very helpful address & had prayer with him in which all the brethren stood up & sang the first verse of "God be With You Till We Meet Again"'.[79] This deep sense of mutual bonding was expressed when a new member of Trevor LOL 820 explained why he transferred in: 'he was pleased to be a member of our Lodge as he liked the members and the way we got on with one another. He said that it was the reason he did not wish to join any other lodge in his own District'.[80] From the earliest days of the Order this sense of bonding took concrete shape not only in verbal support and occasional gifts in times of distress but also in organised institutional form.

Mutuality

The concentration by commentators and analysts on the vivid regalia, banners, noisy bands and occasional violent clashes with Irish nationalist opponents on 12 July have overshadowed the long tradition of mutuality within the Orange Institution.[81] Lodge records contain regular reports on the welfare of members, with messages of goodwill and gifts sent to those in difficulties. In November 1958 it was reported that a member of Garston True Blues LOL 64 was in hospital and suggested that 'if anyone was going in, they could take him a bottle of beer'.[82] This clearly became accepted practice, because early the following year another member informed the lodge meeting that he had taken the patient 'extra cigs and drinks'.[83] Members with money problems could receive a gift, the amount varying with lodge resources, the seriousness of the applicant's situation and their standing with the lodge. Some lodges seem to have debated each grant. In May 1902 Everett LOL 108 received an application: '[t]he worshipful master then informed the Brethren that [a member] had been laid up with a serious illness for some weeks and spoke of his general character and willingness for this Lodge and the Institution in general'. A gift of £1.10s. was unanimously agreed.[84]

Since members were subject to the vagaries of the economic cycle, there were quite frequent applications for help in times of heavy unemployment. In March 1885 Cromwell LOL 94 agreed grants of 10s., 4s. and 1s.3d. to three men in difficulties 'through... slackness of work'.[85] Grants were also given to members

[79] Old Swan Arch Purple Heroes LOL 810 October 1919 LRO 306.ORA/8/1/1
[80] Trevor LOL 820 Minute Book 4 February 1959 LRO 306.ORA/14/1/2
[81] MacRaild, *Faith, Fraternity and Fighting*, pp. 200–05
[82] Garston True Blues LOL 64 Minute Book 1956–61: 10 November 1958; held at Heald Street Orange Hall, Garston
[83] Garston True Blues LOL 64 Minute Book 1956–61: 9 February 1959; held at Heald Street Orange Hall, Garston
[84] Everett LOL 108 Minute Book 21 May 1902 LRO 306.ORA/1/1/2
[85] Cromwell LOL 94 Minute Book 24 March 1885 LRO 306.ORA/2/1/1

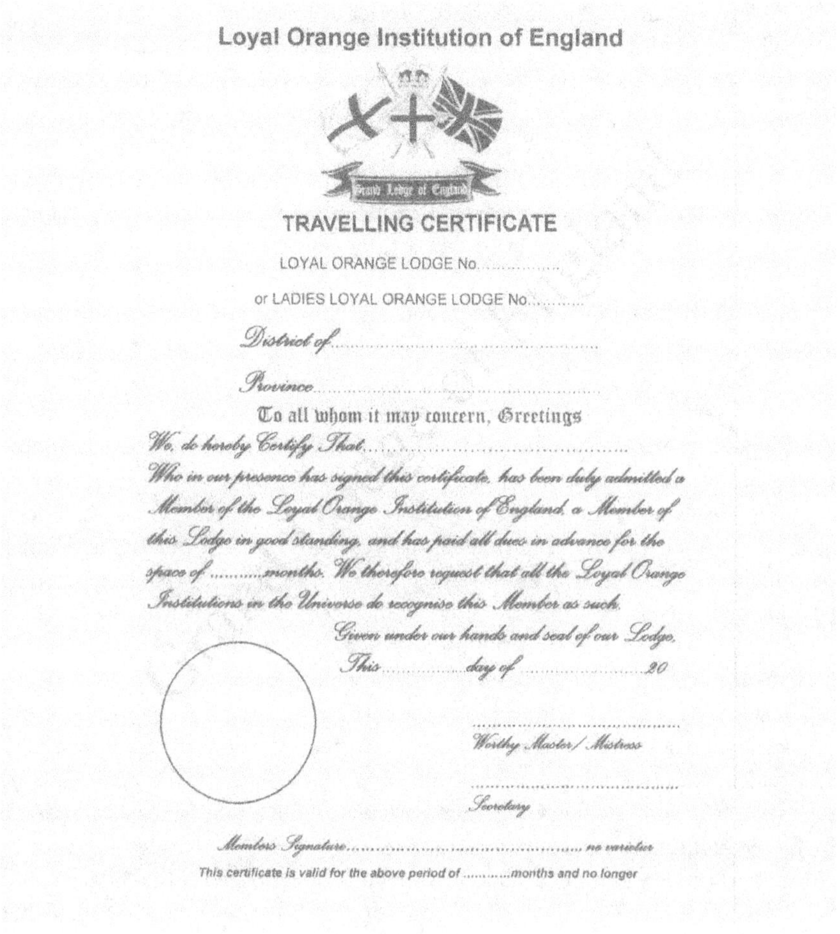

Loyal Orange Institution of England

Grand Lodge of England

TRAVELLING CERTIFICATE

LOYAL ORANGE LODGE No. ....

or LADIES LOYAL ORANGE LODGE No. ....

District of ....

Province ....

To all whom it may concern, Greetings

We, do hereby Certify That ....

Who in our presence has signed this certificate, has been duly admitted a Member of the Loyal Orange Institution of England, a Member of this Lodge in good standing, and has paid all dues in advance for the space of ....months. We therefore request that all the Loyal Orange Institutions in the Universe do recognise this Member as such.

Given under our hands and seal of our Lodge,

This .... day of 20

....

Worthy Master/ Mistress

....

Secretary

Members Signature .... no variation

This certificate is valid for the above period of ....months and no longer

Figure 4.4 Travelling certificate. Migrant members were assured access to the familiar ambience of Lodge ritual and sociability.
Source: Enclosed with Garston True Blues LOL 64 Minute Book 1921–23

of outside lodges, as in July 1910 when Sons of the Boyne LOL 28 agreed 'that we grant 5s. to the appeal from Lodge 597 towards the brother who has lost a leg'.[86] In June 1887 the secretary of No. 2 District attended a meeting of Everett LOL 108 'and applied for assistance on the grounds of his being long out of work, having three children and his wife being near her confinement'—a gift of four

[86] Sons of the Boyne LOL 28 Minute Book 9 July 1910 LRO 306.ORA/6/1/1

shillings was agreed.[87] Members forced to leave home by lack of employment were also assisted. In February 1887 Cromwell 94 agreed 4s. 'to relieve Brother Thomas McCurley LOL 100 Gateshead he being a Brother on the road in search of work'.[88] On 3 May 1892 they gave 5s. to 'two brothers from Belfast who was in distress circumstances & could not get back'[89] and in June a 'Visiting Brother from Scotland' received 2s.8d. from Everett LOL 108.[90] Members moving from one lodge to another were gladly accepted, provided they had no outstanding lodge dues, a transfer fee had been paid and a fully authenticated transfer certificate was presented.

But despite the bonds of brotherhood, there were limits. In November 1913 the Sons of the Boyne LOL 28 learned that a brother had fallen ill and sent him 10s. He died shortly afterwards and was honoured with a memorial service. By January 1914 relations with his widow had deteriorated to the point at which the lodge authorised the secretary to 'send a sharp letter to the ... widow telling her we have finished with her'.[91] In some cases, there was a reluctance to accept applications from outside the lodge. Though Cromwell LOL 94 had been generous to their Belfast visitor, later that year it was noted that some of their own members were in difficulties and it was proposed 'that we do not reliefe [sic] anyone outside of our own Lodge while there is members of our lodge in distress'.[92] In late 1904 Everett LOL 108 decided not to support anyone outside their own lodge 'until we were on a sound financial basis'.[93]

In some lodges the assistance took the form of waiving the charges for entry to socials or participation in 12 July events. In 1908 the Sons of the Boyne LOL 28 decided 'that this Lodge grant to out of work Brethren a free ticket and 1/- for the 12 July anniversary'.[94] Garston True Blues LOL 64 had another approach in the economically troubled times of the early 1920s. At a lodge meeting in November 1921 it was agreed that all work in connection with the lodge should be given to Orangemen if possible;[95] on another occasion it was decided that photographic work would only be given to a non-member 'failing any of the

---

[87] Everett LOL 108 Minute Book 16 June 1887 LRO 306.ORA/1/1/1
[88] Cromwell LOL 94 Minute Book 8 February 1887 LRO 306.ORA/2/1/1
[89] Cromwell LOL 94 Minute Book 3 May 1892 LRO 306.ORA/2/1/2
[90] Everett LOL 108 Minute Book 21 June 1899 LRO 306.ORA/1/1/2
[91] Sons of the Boyne LOL 28 Minute Book 3 January 1914 LRO 306.ORA/6/1/1
[92] Cromwell LOL 94 Minute Book 1 November 1892 LRO 306.ORA/2/1/2
[93] Everett LOL 108 Minute Book 21 December 1904 LRO 306.ORA/1/1/5
[94] Sons of the Boyne LOL 28 Minute Book 10 July 1908 LRO 306.ORA/6/1/1
[95] Garston True Blues LOL 64 Minute Book 1921–23: 28 November 1921; held at Heald Street Orange Hall, Garston

brethren knowing an Orangeman in the business'[96] and early in the new year it was agreed that some printing would go to a member of LOL 108 in Dingle.[97]

In the early 1920s unemployment in Garston was so serious that the lodges set up the Distress Fund mentioned in Chapter Three. Operating between November 1921 and 1923, it held fund-raising events to provide grants for needy members. Rose of England LLOL 95 was requested to 'report any case of distress among widowed sisters and case would be attended to',[98] though it also decided, given a quorum, that they would 'render assistance in cases whenever possible to Brethren who land in this town and in want no less than five being in attendance...'[99] Funds were administered and distributed with tactful care. Visitors were appointed to call on applicants and evaluate their claims. In March 1922 it was recorded:

> A discussion arose re the application by Bro. P... he was called in... Bro. Grace then explained to him that all the work done by this committee was secret and that he was not to say anything as regards what he had received and that, when he was making an application, he was to do it and say nothing to anyone else.

A grant of 15s. was given.[100]

In May 1922 it was decided to give food parcels as well as money and a scheme was devised related to the family status of applicants and their frequency of application.

Members with Dependents

Provisions valued	5s
Money	7s
Total	12s

Second and Subsequent Applications

Money or Provisions valued	7s

Members without Dependents

Money	5s

---

[96] Garston True Blues LOL 64 Minute Book 1921–23: 30 December 1921; held at Heald Street Orange Hall, Garston

[97] Garston True Blues LOL 64 Minute Book 1921–23: 23 January 1923; held at Heald Street Orange Hall, Garston

[98] Garston True Blues LOL 64 Distress Fund Committee Minutes 11 January 1922; held at Heald Street Orange Hall, Garston

[99] Garston True Blues LOL 64 Distress Fund Committee Minutes May 1922

[100] Garston True Blues LOL 64 Distress Fund Committee Minutes 9 March 1922

Second and Subsequent Applications
Money   5s

**In the event of Sickness or Unforeseen Circumstances not
specified in the above or where provisions would not be required:**

On first application   12s

Second and Subsequent Applications   7s

The scheme was operated by the President, Treasurer and Secretary and its workings reported to the Committee each month.[101]

In some lodges applications were so frequent that cash was set aside for charitable purposes, often in a box for voluntary contributions, and guidelines rather than mere rule of thumb devised. When Lady Stanley LLOL 97 received an application in January 1908 it was decided to give 2s.6d. to a 'widow & 7 children of the late Bro... to be taken out of the bereavement box'.[102] In March 1914 it is clear that Old Swan Arch Purple Heroes LOL 810 was following well-established practice when they agreed 'the usual sum to a brother in distress'.[103]

In fact lodges had organised mutual benefit societies from quite early on. Rule books for such Orange societies are quite rare,[104] and it is fortunate that three survive from the early 1840s in Liverpool. The 1835 Parliamentary report on the Order had observed that, whilst 'religion' was the main object of the Institution, '[i]n Lancashire and other places funds have been collected for the assistance of decayed brethren, and thereby given, in some degree, the character of benefit, or benevolent societies, to Orange lodges'. It was also noted that, though Grand Lodge had described such groups as 'excrescences', it neither acknowledged nor forbade them so long as no rules were broken.[105] By the economically challenging 1840s attitudes had clearly shifted. The *Laws and Ordnances of the Loyal Orange Institution of Great Britain* in 1842 included Rule 50 stating '[t]his Institution recommends the establishment of a Benefit Society in connection with each lodge or District; but in such a manner as not to interfere with any of its rules'.[106]

There were two great fears in working-class life. One was to become so

---

[101] Garston True Blues LOL 64 Distress Fund Committee Minutes 12 May 1922
[102] Lady Stanley LLOL 97 Minute Book 8 January 1908 LRO 306.ORA/5/1/1
[103] Old Swan Arch Purple Heroes LOL 810 Minute Book 14 March 1914 LRO 306. OTA/8/1/1
[104] MacRaild, *Faith, Fraternity and Fighting*, p. 220
[105] Report of Select Committee, p. x
[106] *Laws and Ordnances of the Loyal Orange Institution of Great Britain*. Liverpool. Printed by Order of the Grand Lodge. 1842. LRO Town Clerk's papers 352 CLE/460, p. 19

impoverished that the family could only afford a pauper's funeral at public expense, leaving a widow and children in poverty. The second was to become so indigent that it was necessary to seek shelter in the workhouse. The rule book of Lodge No. 14 opens with a statement of underlying philosophy:

> Societies of this kind, possess the philanthropy of all well-disposed men, inasmuch as they tend to make them sober, industrious, and benevolent: affording them the means of providing for each other and themselves, at that period when all the sympathies of our nature are absorbed in affliction, personal or relative... it then comes to our assistance like the Good Samaritan...[107]

The funeral society rule book for Liverpool District in 1843 opens with the statement '[t]hat this Institution shall consist of an unlimited number of members, being Orangemen, whose object is the interment of their dead'.[108] After outlining details of governing structure, standing orders for calling and conduct of meetings and fees to be paid, it declares that, provided they are up to date with dues, on death the sum of £10 would be paid for a member's funeral; details are given of regalia to be worn by members attending the event. The rule books of both Lodge 13 and Lodge 14 make specific mention of the threat of entry into the workhouse. For Lodge No. 13 Rule 24 states that:

> [s]hould any member be reduced to the necessity of going into a Parish Workhouse, he shall forfeit his claim to sick allowance during the continuance therein, and should such member die in the said workhouse... his heirs shall be entitled to his funeral money, and the Society shall take care that he is decently interred... and further should such member leave such workhouse... all his arrears whilst in such workhouse shall be forgiven.[109]

As for those forced to migrate in search of work, 'any member leaving town for want of employment or any other lawful cause, shall obtain his card, signed by the President and Secretary'.[110]

Appreciation of the work of such societies is demonstrated by their extraordinary growth in numbers. The annual Friendly Societies Act of 1855 was the

[107] *Rules and Regulations, Lodge No. 14*, p. 3. LRO Town Clerk's Box 145
[108] *Rules of the Funeral Fund Association of the Order of Loyal Orangemen, Liverpool District* (Liverpool: Shaw, 1843), p. 3, Rule 1. LRO Town Clerk's Box 145
[109] *Rules of the Benefit Society of Loyal Orange Association Lodge No. 13* (Liverpool. Braithwaite: c. 1842) LRO Town Clerk's Box 145
[110] *Rules of the Benefit Society of Lodge No. 13*, p. 3

first serious effort at regulation but this was made permanent by legislation in 1879 which set up a national register under the oversight of a specially appointed civil servant. This framework of stability and legality led to a notable growth of societies within the Order. The experience of Cromwell LOL 94 and their lengthy struggle to maintain a society illustrate its importance for members. At a lodge meeting in early 1884 there was lengthy discussion of 'the formation of a funeral fund' and it was agreed 'to call a meeting together of themselves to draw up a code of rules for the working of such Funeral Fund'.[111] By August 1884 the society was in place and it was decided to appoint a committee of ten members to consider rules revision.[112] At a special meeting on 5 January 1885, they agreed membership charges, scrutinised the rules on sick pay and strengthened the sanctions on those found to be under the influence of drink or involved in gambling whilst receiving assistance.[113] These measures underline the perpetual anxiety over the danger of fraud. Members receiving sick pay were restricted in their movements and to ensure they followed the rules Sick Visitors were appointed to call and ensure they were at home within the prescribed times. Cromwell LOL 94 discovered a recipient had breached the rules by being away from home from 6 pm onwards on two successive nights, visiting his ill son in Denbigh. A Benefit Committee meeting on 25 February 1886 'after a long and careful consideration of the facts lasting nearly two hours were unanimous... that he be fined... 12/- for the first offence... and 20/- for the second offence'.[114]

Recipients were not always grateful. In a meeting of the Benefit Society in January 1891 doubts were expressed about the membership of an Orangeman who had received assistance and it was decided to send a letter informing him 'that we will not pay him any more sick money until he produce a certificate of his baptism as they think he has entered this society under a false age and you will have to prove otherwise before you receive any more club money'.[115] A further meeting on 28 March agreed to inform him that

> [a]t a meeting of the [benefit society] held March 1891 your wife brought some money there and thrown it on the table and we left it there for we don't understand it—so if you want your money you had better apply to the Hall Keeper for it. Therefore if you think that you are not justly treated you must make a personal application as we will take no notice of anyone els [sic].[116]

[111] Cromwell LOL 94 Minute Book 15 January 1884 LRO 306.ORA/2/1/1
[112] Cromwell LOL 94 Minute Book 26 August 1884 LRO 306.ORA/2/1/1
[113] Cromwell LOL 94 Minute Book 5 January 1885 LRO 306.ORA/2/1/1
[114] Cromwell LOL 94 Minute Book 25 February 1896 LRO 306.ORA/2/1/1
[115] Cromwell LOL 94 Minute Book 13 January 1891 LRO 306.ORA/2/1/1
[116] Cromwell LOL 94 Minute Book 24 March 1891 LRO 306.ORA/2/1/1

By the early 1890s it is clear that the society was struggling and, after some agonised discussion,[117] the annual meeting in December 1893 unanimously adopted the resolution 'that on account of the low state in which our society was in seeing that the expenditure far exceeded the income and our meeting on this occasion is to consider what can be done under the present circumstances that we dissolve the society'.[118] Other lodges such as Ivy LOL 783 decided not to run their own branch but to affiliate to the District society.[119]

The difficulties facing lodges and indeed Districts and Provinces, that tried to run their own societies plus the increased demand for their services generated by wartime casualties may have prompted Grand Lodge to organise The Loyal Orange Orphan Society of England in 1920 and descriptions of its activities began to appear in the annual report from 1932 onwards, when the Organising Secretary noted that income had increased 'mainly due to the splendid support of the members of the Liverpool Province, who have worked whole-heartedly by means of the 12th July Celebration and subsequent flag day'.[120] Subsequent reports appealed for lodges to affiliate, noting in 1936 that only 22 per cent of private lodges were involved.[121] In 1956 Liverpool was specially commended for the fact that the number of lodges affiliated had risen from 34 in 1954 to 44 in 1955 and 65 in 1956, with special mention of the collection boxes successfully used by 'Liverpool Sisters'.[122] Here too, the application process was closely vetted. At a meeting of No. 6 District in May 1961 an application from Garston Rose of England LLOL 95 for the support of three orphan children was informed that '[m]arriage lines, death certificate and three birth certificates were examined by the Provincial Grand Master... who found same in order...' The application was granted.[123]

The death of a lodge member was marked not merely by verbal and material expressions of support, but by elaborate ceremonial. The lodge stood for a minute's silence, a letter of condolence went to the bereaved family and a wreath would be sent. Orange funerals followed a carefully devised pattern. When Sons of the Boyne LOL 28 met after the death of a member it is recorded '[i]t is with sincere regret that we in this Lodge LOL 28 have to record the passing away of the late Brother... interred at Anfield Cemetery on June 14th with all

[117] Cromwell LOL 94 Minute Book: meeting of the Cromwell Benefit Society 18 July 1893; some Society minutes are incorporated with those of the lodge. LRO 306. ORA/2/1/1

[118] Cromwell LOL 94 Minute Book 9 December 1893 LRO 306.ORA/2/1/1

[119] Ivy LOL 783, *100 Years of History*, July 1905, p. 3

[120] Loyal Orange Institution of England Report 1932, p. 15

[121] Loyal Orange Institution of England Report 1936, p. 18

[122] Loyal Orange Institution of England Report 1956, p. 20

[123] Duke of York No. 6 District Minute Book 17 May 1961 LRO 306.ORA/13/1/2

Orange rites... [District Master and Chaplain] officiating at the graveside.'[124] Lodge members were encouraged to attend such funerals and when absent were expected to apologise. Some families were not happy with an official funeral. When the Treasurer of Daughters of Victory LLOL 11 died the officers who had visited the family reported they did not wish an Orange funeral because 'they feared it would be too much to bear the ceremonies at the graveside'.[125] In some cases the family requested the lodge to provide pall bearers.[126]

These 'ceremonies', or 'Orange rites', were laid down by Grand Lodge.[127] They specify that each member should wear a white rose on the point of a collar and a white ribbon on any wands carried; when walking in procession the youngest members should lead; the Chaplain should carry a bible; and the W.M. come last. On the return the W.M. and officers were to lead. When it came to the graveside service members were to form a broken circle and then complete the circle, presumably to symbolise the absence of the dead member and eventual reunion on death. Following hymns, specified bible readings, the Lord's Prayer, an address by the Chaplain, sympathetic references to the family and a hymn, the service should close with a benediction. Any departure from the specified order of the procession drew adverse attention, as in October 1921 when it was noted that formation of the ranks at a recent funeral had not quite followed prescribed ritual.[128]

The arrangements for such a funeral were quite a challenge for a lodge anxious to be precisely correct and to pay due public homage to their fellow member. This is illustrated by the meeting to prepare for a funeral at Garston in September 1957. The deceased had taken a leading role in local Orange affairs, having served as W.M. of Rose of England LLOL 95 for 35 years. At a joint committee of LLOL 95 and LOL 64 an officer explained that he had met with the family, 'they informing us that the wish of Sister D. to be buried an Orangewoman and they were leaving of the details with us'. The cortege included two bands, the warrant was carried, the graveside ceremony was conducted by female lodge members and a memorial service at the Orange Hall was planned for the following Sunday.[129] The sense

---

[124] Sons of the Boyne LOL 28 Minute Book 20 June 1922 LRO 306.ORA/6/1/2

[125] Daughters of Victory LLOL 11 Minute Book 16 July 1931 LRO 306.ORA/9/1/2

[126] Garston True Blues LOL 64 Minute Book 1950–53: 9 November 1952; held at Heald Street Orange Hall, Garston

[127] Loyal Orange Institution of England Burial Service for Departed Members of the Orange Order. Undated, probably early twentieth century; enclosed with Everett LOL 108 Minute Book LRO 306.ORA/1/1/3 for November 1903–March 1908. Probably subsequently amended.

[128] Garston True Blues LOL 64 Minute Book 1921–23: 24 October 1921; held at Heald Street Orange Hall, Garston

[129] Garston True Blues LOL 64 and Rose of England LLOL 95 Joint Lodge Committee

of satisfaction gained from such an occasion was expressed in the record of a
Lady Stanley lodge meeting in September 1935:

> We laid the remains of our Treasurer... to rest after service by the Vicar
> of St Polycarp's Church. Our Worthy District Master... conducted the
> Orange Ceremonies in a most suitable manner. We had a goodly number
> of Orange Brethren & Sisters present... representing Lady Stanley LOL 97.[130]

Here there is a sense of pride at having done justice in the prescribed manner
to a prominent, long-serving member of the lodge and the Order.

Conclusion

Liverpool Orange lodges emerge as overwhelmingly working-class organisations
the great majority of whose members are locally born and deeply rooted in
the life of their localities. The membership is closely bonded, not merely by
the formality of regular lodge meetings, but by an intensely active, communal,
social life in which informal socialising, dining together, entertainment and
leisure outings feature heavily. There is a long history of mutual support taking
many forms from the verbal and informal to the material and institutional in
the form of mutual aid societies in which members banded together against
poverty, unemployment and the impact of illness and bereavement. The result
is yet another layer of the dense associational network within working-class
Liverpool in the nineteenth and twentieth centuries, in this case amounting to
a densely woven working-class sub-culture fortified by a form of ultra-Protestantism reminiscent of a folk religion.

Meeting Garston True Blues LOL 64 Minute Book 1956–61: 2 September 1957; held
at Heald Street Orange Hall, Garston
[130] Lady Stanley LLOL 97 Minute Book 4 September 1935 LRO 306.ORA/5/1/2

5

Royalism, Patriotism, Empire and Commemoration

Introduction

This chapter discusses how loyalty to the British connection, its royal family, a willingness to serve in Britain's wars and pride in empire were defining features of the Orange Order. British participation in war is never questioned. Indeed, the Order is notable for heavy recruitment into the British forces, pride in its members' service and the casualties sustained, as reflected in the readiness to commemorate their deaths in parades and memorials.

Royalism

The loyalty of the Order to the British Protestant monarchy is vividly expressed on banners. By far the most popular personality on display is King William III, though Queen Victoria also frequently appeared, not only in part because her long reign (1837–1901) witnessed much of the history of the Order, but also because she presided over the wars that saw massive extension of the British empire, a development in which the Order took much pride. Devotion to royalty is also expressed in the singing of the national anthem at lodge, District, Provincial and Grand Lodge meetings, public parades and private social gatherings. Portraits of the current monarch have always hung in Orange Halls and resolutions of loyalty are a standard feature of 12 July rallies. Minutes of lodge meetings often end with 'God Save the Queen/King', but in one case with the condition 'God save the King and Queen as long as they remain Protestant'.[1]

The qualification indicates the only basis on which lodges have been prepared to express unhappiness with British royalty, namely the slightest possibility of dilution of their Protestantism. When in 1906 it was announced that Princess Eugenie, daughter of Princess Beatrix, the fifth daughter and youngest child

---

[1] Everett LOL 108 Minute Book 20 December 1905 LRO 306.ORA/1/1/3

of Queen Victoria, would marry King Alfonso XIII of Spain, necessitating a conversion to Catholicism, both Liverpool No. 3 District and Everett LOL 108 sent letters of protest to the press and the king.[2] Royal visits to the Vatican have provoked dismay, as in the case of the visit of King George V in 1923 and the state visit of Queen Elizabeth and the Duke of Edinburgh in May 1961.[3] Occasionally unhappiness has been expressed at the personal behaviour of royals, as in August 1965 when a member of Stuart McCoy Memorial LOL 2 'spoke of the example set by the Royal Family in the way they spend Sabbath Day... [and] objected to the Prince of Wales being allowed to play polo on a Sunday while we were fighting to uphold the Protestant cause in England and proposed a letter be sent... asking for a protest to be made'.[4]

The death of a monarch has been marked by parades and services. In May 1910 Garston True Blues LOL 64 held a memorial service for King Edward VII to which Everett LOL 108 were invited,[5] and Stuart McCoy Memorial LOL 2 planned a memorial parade for King George VI in February 1952.[6] The coronation service traditionally includes a declaration in which the monarch undertakes to uphold the Protestant faith whilst abjuring aspects of Roman Catholic doctrine. In 1910 King George V expressed unease with the declaration as insulting to his Roman Catholic subjects and requested amendments. There was considerable dismay within the Order. In May 1910 Enniskillen No. 5 District decided to send 'letters re proposed alteration of the King's Coronation Oath... to the Prime Minister, the Leader of the Opposition, Grand and Provincial lodges'[7] and a few days later No. 3 District weighed in with a unanimous resolution 'that this District sends a very strong protest against any alteration to the King's Accession Oath and that a copy of same be sent to the Prime Minister & also our local MPs...'; but it also took care 'that letter of sympathy be sent to His Majesty King George [on death of] his father the beloved King Edward the Seventh'.[8] At the coronation a revised version was used in which the monarch simply declared his Protestant faith and pledged to preserve the Protestant succession.[9] On the accession of Queen Elizabeth II in 1952 Stuart McCoy Memorial LOL 2 again raised the question of the coronation service and sent a letter expressing their views to the

---

[2] No. 3 District Minute Book 20 February 1906 LRO 306.ORA/3/1/1; Everett LOL 108 Minute Book 21 February 1906 LRO 306.ORA/1/1/3
[3] 1923 visit: No. 3 District Minute Book 20 February 1923 LRO 306.ORA/3/1/1; 1961 visit: Ivy LOL 783, *100 Years of History*, p. 32
[4] Stuart McCoy Memorial LOL 2 Minute Book 9 August 1965 LRO 306.ORA/12/1
[5] Everett LOL 108 Minute Book 18 May 1910 LRO 306.ORA/1/1/5
[6] Stuart McCoy Memorial LOL 2 Minute Book 11 February 1952 LRO 306.ORA/12/1
[7] Enniskillen No. 5 District Minute Book 11 May 1910 LRO 306.ORA/7/1/1
[8] No. 3 District Minute Book 17 May 1910 LRO 306.ORA/3/1/1
[9] Harold Nicolson, *King George V* London: Constable, 1984, pp. 162–63

Figure 5.1 Enduring loyalty. The Grand Lodge Report of 1937 proclaims its unshaken royalism after the year of three kings.
Source: Private collection

LOYAL ORANGE INSTITUTION OF ENGLAND

GRAND ORANGE LODGE OF ENGLAND

(Established 16th February, 1807)

Report of Proceedings

OF THE

ANNUAL MEETING

IN THE

CORONATION YEAR

OF THEIR MAJESTIES

KING GEORGE VI. and QUEEN ELIZABETH.

HELD AT

THE ORANGE HALL, UNIVERSITY ROAD, BOOTLE,

WEDNESDAY & THURSDAY, ——7th & 8th JULY, 1937.——

PUBLISHED ON BEHALF OF GRAND LODGE.

Home Secretary.[10] In Orange lodge records, only those of Lady Stanley LLOL 97 cover the period of the abdication of King Edward VIII in 1936 but they make no mention of the crisis, though the Grand Lodge Report of 1937 was at pains to celebrate the coronation of King George VI and Queen Elizabeth.

Royal events are celebrated with enthusiasm. In May 1886 Cromwell LOL 94 took part in a procession 'in honour of our most Glorious Majesty Queen Victoria's visit to Liverpool'[11] and in May 1902 Everett LOL 108 organised a picnic to celebrate the coronation of King Edward VII.[12] In June 1977 Kirby Defenders

---

[10] Stuart McCoy Memorial LOL 2 Minute Book 9 June 1952 LRO 306.ORA/12/1
[11] Cromwell LOL 94 Minute Book 4 May 1886 LRO 306.ORA/2/1/1
[12] Everett LOL 108 Minute Book 21 May 1902 LRO 306.ORA/1/1/2

Figure 5.2   Coronation portrait of King George VI and Queen Elizabeth
Source: Private collection

LOL 300 organised a dinner to mark the jubilee of Queen Elizabeth II and in
July 1980 members agreed 'Lodge send HM Queen Elizabeth queen mother a
birthday card on the occasion of her 80th birthday'.[13] In July 1981 they decided
to mark the wedding of the Prince of Wales and Lady Diana Spencer with a
specially designed jewel to be presented to each member.[14]

Patriotism

Loyalty to the royal family and Protestantism ran in tandem with unquestioning
patriotism. This is seen in the ubiquitous display of the union flag in Orange
Halls, at parades and processions and the ceremony of saluting the flag noted
in discussion of the juvenile lodges in Chapter Two. The question who should
carry the flag on public parades has been subject to serious discussion. In June
1951 Trevor LOL 820 noted with satisfaction: 'Union flag to be carried... for the
first time in front of [12 July] parade then to be handed over to No. 7 District

---

[13] Kirby Defenders LOL 300 Minute Book 10 June 1977 and 11 July 1980 LRO 306.
ORA/16/1/2
[14] Kirby Defenders LOL 300 Minute Book 8 July 1981 LRO 306.ORA/16/1/2

for the following year'[15] and in May 1960 the Provincial Processions Committee discussed how to hand over flags to the District leading the 12 July procession and subsequently expressed concern at the manner in which flags had been brought to the rostrum.[16]

The most challenging demand a state can make upon its citizens is that they risk their lives in time of war. The Order has always been notable for the heavy recruitment of members into the services. In some respects this is not surprising, given that it drew the great majority of its membership from the working class and the fact that many of the earliest lodges in Great Britain had their roots amongst serving and retired servicemen. Nowhere in the available records is there the least reservation about British involvement in the various colonial conflicts of the nineteenth and twentieth centuries. The Boer War broke out on 11 October 1899 and at a meeting of Everett LOL 108 the following month the lodge passed a resolution to be sent to Colonial Secretary Joseph Chamberlain and Arthur Balfour, Leader of the House of Commons:

> we the members of the above lodge hereby approves of the action of Her Majesty's government in regard to the South African affairs and also express its unbounded confidence in their ability to bring the war to a speedy and successful termination and also Express its confidence in the Commanders of Her Majesty's forces Sir Redvers Buller & General Sir G. White both of whom have our confidence & support to bring this trouble to a successful Settlement.

The lodge also sent £2.12s.9d. to the District to be forwarded to a fund for Liverpool reservists.[17] Despite initial heavy defeats for British forces, when General Secretary Touchstone addressed a Liverpool rally at Buckley the following 12 July he proposed a resolution

> which recognises with much satisfaction the marked ability, prudence and energy put forward by Her Majesty's Government... recognised with national pride the great military genius displayed by our generals commanding the bravest troops—Imperial and colonial—that have ever encountered mortal foe, defeating under difficult conditions the murderous deep laid plans of a treacherous and unscrupulous enemy and turning

---

[15] Trevor LOL 820 Minute Book 28 June 1951 LRO 306.ORA/14/1/1
[16] Liverpool Province Processions Committee Minute Book 27 May and 22 July 1960 LRO 306.ORA/1/1
[17] Everett LOL 108 Minute Book 17 November 1899 LRO 306.ORA/1/1/2

the tide of war with awful retribution against its crafty and intriguing instigators.[18]

The two world wars were a stern test of the Order, costing it heavily in both casualties and funds and seriously disrupting the routine of life at all levels.[19] In both conflicts all processions and annual Grand Lodge meetings were cancelled, essential business being left in the hands of leading officers sitting as a Standing Committee.[20] From quite early in the 1914–18 conflict some in the Liverpool lodges realised the likely impact. In August 1914 the District Master visiting Sons of the Boyne LOL 28 'spoke a few words about the war and other matters relating to the Institution, saying that it might affect us in so many ways in so many of our members being absent'.[21] The Treasurer of No. 3 District, warning that their efforts to maintain widows and orphans funds could come under strain, 'asked all to help us in case we should be called to do our duty in the near future'.[22] Exhortations to courage and endurance constantly recur. In November 1914 a member of Lady Stanley LLOL 97 'spoke about the upset the country was in and urge[d] the Sisters at home to do their best for our Brethren at the Front'.[23] In May 1916, addressing the annual meeting of Enniskillen No. 5 District, the presiding officer 'urged upon the brethren the necessity of holding firm to the group during the present national crisis'.[24]

There is little data on numbers serving, but it is recorded that 20 members of the Ivy LOL 783 served during 1914–18 and 21 in 1939–45.[25] They were looked on with pride and respect, particularly if given medals. When Old Swan Arch Purple Heroes LOL 810 met for their annual meeting in April 1916 the Deputy District Master took the chair and 'congratulated the members of LOL 810 for having one of their number to win the DCM [Distinguished Conduct

---

[18] *Liverpool Courier*, 13 July 1900; both generals had to be replaced the following year: Thomas Pakenham, *The Boer War* London: Abacus, 1979

[19] Fitzpatrick, *Descendancy*, pp. 21–40 for the Irish lodges in the conflict; McRaild, *Faith, Fraternity and Fighting*, pp. 68–69 suggests a lesser impact in the north-east of England

[20] Loyal Orange Institution of England Report of the Standing Committee, 1940, p. 7

[21] Sons of the Boyne LOL 28 Minute Book August 1914 LRO 306.ORA/6/1/1

[22] No. 3 District Minute Book August 1914 LRO 306.ORA/3/1/1

[23] Lady Stanley LLOL 97 Minute Book 11 November 1914 LRO 306.ORA/5/1/2

[24] Enniskillen No. 5 District Minute Book 10 May 1916 LRO 306.ORA/7/1/1

[25] Ivy LOL 783, *100 Years of History*, Appendix 3, p. 64; Loyal Orange Institution of England Report 1942, pp. 2–3 lists not only those who are described as having been 'killed in action' or reported 'missing' during the previous twelve months, but those 'killed by enemy action', presumably in the bombing of Liverpool. If so, it is notable for the number of women listed, the only acknowledgement of female members killed during the conflict that I have come across

Medal]'[26] and in 1918 the Sons of the Boyne LOL 28 sent a letter to their District secretary 'congratulating him on his son's distinction during this serious war'.[27]

The greatest reverence was reserved for those killed on active service. In late 1916 there is a particularly poignant entry in which two members:

> extended their feelings of sincere sympathy to the W. Sec. and family through the lamented death of his eldest son who was killed in action Sep. 9th 1916 and the brethren joined in same. Bro. McMurray thanked the brethren on behalf of himself, wife and family for the many kind expressions of sympathy they had received.[28]

In May 1917 Lady Stanley LLOL 97 sent letters of sympathy to two members 'who are bereaved by the loss of loved ones through the turmoil that we are now passing through'.[29] In February 1918 No. 3 District sent a letter of sympathy to the widow of Thomas Taft, killed in action in France, describing him as 'one of our most noble and fearless officers of our Institution... a past Deputy District Master of this District'[30] and Old Swan Arch Purple Heroes LOL 810 draped their warrant in black to honour a dead member.[31] In April 1945 Belfast Patriotic LOL 3 noted that 'we had lost another Brother through enemy action...' and sent a letter to his widow.[32]

When members on leave from active service attended meetings they were greeted as returning heroes. In June 1917 Old Swan Arch Purple Heroes LOL 810 expressed its congratulations to a member 'upon his return from France & in the name of the lodge wishes him every success'[33] and in December 1918 the W.M. 'expressed the members of the lodge wishes to Bro. Houghton for his presence there that night and hoped that God would take care of him until he returned again for good. Bro. Houghton suitably replied.'[34] The pattern was repeated in the next conflict when in May 1944 the Belfast Patriotic LOL3 and Pride of West Derby LOL 5, who were meeting together, were informed that a member had returned to the forces but 'hoped to be home again for next meeting'.[35] Efforts

---

[26] Old Swan Arch Purple Heroes LOL 810 Minute Book April 1916 LRO 306.ORA/8/1/1
[27] Sons of the Boyne LOL 28 Minute Book March 1918 LRO 306.ORA/6/1/1
[28] No. 3 District Minute Book 21 November 1916 LRO 306.ORA/3/1/1; McMurray, as Secretary, was the author of this minute
[29] Lady Stanley LLOL 97 Minute Book 10 May 1917 LRO 306.ORA/5/1/2
[30] No. 3 District Minute Book 19 February 1918 LRO 306.ORA/3/1/1
[31] Old Swan Arch Purple Heroes LOL 810 Minute Book February 1918 LRO 306.ORA/8/1/1
[32] Belfast Patriotic LOL 3 Minute Book 7 April 1945 LRO 306.ORA/11/1
[33] Old Swan Arch Purple Heroes LOL 810 Minute Book 13 June 1917 LRO 306.ORA/3/1/1
[34] Old Swan Arch Purple Heroes LOL 810 Minute Book September 1917, December 1918 LRO 306.ORA/3/1/1
[35] Belfast Patriotic LOL 3, Pride of West Derby LOL 5 Minute Book 6 May 1944 (joint

were made to keep in touch with lodge members on active service. In November 1914 Old Swan Arch Purple Heroes LOL 810 agreed 'that all members at the front have their monthly magazine free of charge until they return…' and a year later a member 'read some communication from the brethren at the front who wished to be remembered to all at home'.[36] The pattern was repeated in the Second World War. On 14 December 1939 Pride of West Derby LOL 5 decided 'a Christmas card to be sent to each brother serving in the army' and the following March, when letters were read from two members serving in the forces, it was agreed that the Secretary should send best wishes in reply.[37] The practice was retained in peace time: in March 1954 when Garston True Blues LOL 64 received a letter from a serving member sending best wishes for the success of the lodge, a gift was sent in return.[38]

Membership dues were suspended for those who enlisted and gifts were sent. In April 1939, Pride of West Derby LOL 5, clearly anticipating what was to come, agreed that any member joining the forces 'should stand clear with this lodge until his return, also that a letter be sent him'.[39] Again, this was followed in peace time, as in 1947 when Belfast Patriotic LOL 3 was informed of a member 'not yet out of the forces and going away again for two years' and it was decided he should be 'free on the books until his return…' and wishes sent for 'good luck on his journey'.[40] Gifts could take practical form, as in September 1914 when Kirkdale's Glory LLOL 80 contributed £1 to a local fund to buy wool for making up into comforts for troops; and a collection for the Red Cross was taken in November 1916.[41] Again, some lodges continued their generosity after 1945—in November 1953 Belfast Patriotic LOL 3 agreed a 10s. Christmas gift for every lodge member in the forces;[42] and in July 1982, in the aftermath of the recapture of the Falkland Islands, Kirby Defenders LOL 300 agreed the purchase of tickets for a 'South Atlantic Social'.[43]

Perhaps the most ambitious and successful project for assisting Orangemen on active service in the First World War was the special ward for injured members

---

meeting) LRO 306.ORA/11/1

[36] Old Swan Arch Purple Heroes LOL 810 Minute Book 3 November 1914, November 1915 LRO 306.ORA/8/1/1

[37] Pride of West Derby LOL 5 Minute Book 14 December 1939, 17 March 1940 LRO 306.ORA/10/1/1

[38] Garston True Blues LOL 64, Minute Book 1953–55: meeting 10 May 1954; held at Heald Street Orange Hall, Garston

[39] Pride of West Derby LOL 5 Minute Book 18 April 1939 LRO 306.ORA/10/1/1

[40] Belfast Patriotic LOL 3 Minute Book 23 October 1947 LRO 306.ORA/11/1

[41] Kirkdale's Glory LLOL 80 Minute Book 14 September 1914 and 14 November 1916 LRO 306.ORA/4/1/2

[42] Belfast Patriotic LOL 3 Minute Book 24 November 1953 LRO 306.ORA/11/1

[43] Kirby Defenders LOL 300 Minute Book 8 July 1982 LRO 306.ORA/16/1/1

attached to the Trent Bridge Red Cross hospital at Nottingham. With the Ulster unionist leader Sir Edward Carson as patron, fund raising was launched in October 1916 and the first part of the ward was opened the following January. Appeals were sent out to all lodges, with female members particularly active in the project.[44] Analysis of the Liverpool lodge records reveal that Old Swan Arch Purple Heroes LOL 810 made a donation in November 1916,[45] but that same month Enniskillen No. 5 District decided that the matter should be dealt with by Province and Sons of the Boyne LOL 28 put the matter aside until funds were 'better'.[46]

These last two responses reveal the fact that many lodges struggled to cope. The absence of so many members plus the waiver on dues meant that, with a sharp decline in income and a rise in outgoings, finances at all levels of the Institution were under severe strain. Consequently, in late 1917 Old Swan Arch Purple Heroes LOL 810 'decided that all discharged soldiers of this Lodge commence payment after one month',[47] Sons of the Boyne LOL 28 declared that 'we cannot assist [G.S.] Bro. Ewart as regards Bibles for soldiers'[48] and in late 1921 No. 3 District decided that members who had not paid dues in wartime but had historic debts could only be readmitted if these were cleared, whilst noting there was a right of appeal to Province.[49] The problems were recognised quite early on when it was realised that the war was likely to create increased demands on the small-scale widow and orphan funds organised by lodges, District and Province. As early as November 1914 the Treasurer of No. 3 District warned of the difficulties likely to be 'occasioned by the call to arms of so many of our brethren in defence of King and Country'.[50] A proposal to increase payments into these schemes provoked strong reactions. A special meeting was called for 17 April 1915 and one speaker provided a glimpse of the struggle involved in coping with the demands of wartime civilian life in working-class communities when he 'quoted all the hardships that we were faced with the increase in the price of food met us everywhere and also the maintaining of home and family affairs'.[51] A compromise was eventually accepted, but as late as June 1916 there

---

[44] McPherson, *Women and the Orange Order*, pp. 68–71

[45] Old Swan Arch Purple Heroes LOL 810 Minute Book November 1916 LRO 306. ORA/8/1/1

[46] Enniskillen No. 5 District Minute Book 8 November 1916 LRO 306.ORA/7/1/1; Sons of the Boyne LOL 28 Minute Book November 1916 LRO 306.ORA/6/1/1

[47] Old Swan Arch Purple Heroes LOL 810 Minute Book 10 October 1917 LRO 306. ORA/8/1/1

[48] Sons of the Boyne LOL 28 Minute Book 17 August 1917 LRO 306.ORA/6/1/1

[49] No. 3 District Minute Book 15 November 1921 LRO 306.ORA/3/1/1

[50] No. 3 District Minute Book 17 November 1914 LRO 306.ORA/3/1/1

[51] No. 3 District Minute Book 17 April 1915 LRO 306.ORA/3/1/1

was still some discontent, with rumours of lodges seceding from the District.[52] In July 1920 the experience led to the organisation of the nation-wide Loyal Orange Orphan Society of England noted in Chapter Four.

Every aspect of lodge life was disrupted by the world wars, but the 1914–18 conflict proved particularly devastating. The signing-in book for Everett LOL 108 has survived for the period 1904–23. In 1913 attendees numbered 14, by 1917 there were 10 and in 1918 9. Numbers returned to pre-war levels in 1923.[53] Records for Lady Stanley LLOL 97 in the period from July 1914 to September 1919 reveal the impact on a female lodge.[54] The absence of large numbers of men meant that female members took on responsibility for all aspects of household life plus handling the household finances. Consequently, attendance at lodge meetings was much less of a priority and posts formerly occupied by men in many Liverpool female lodges fell vacant. The records show that there was a sharp decline in the frequency and regularity of lodge meetings. After November 1914 there were no meetings until the annual meeting of April 1915, when it was decided that 'present officers retain their seats for ensuing year',[55] a pattern followed in other lodges. Meetings are recorded for August 1915, 10 September 1916 and 10 May 1917. At that event 'the lack of numbers present to open lodge' was noted and the (male) Chaplain 'addressing the sisters earnestly appealed to them to be more determined than ever to shew [sic] their unity and loyalty to one another by sticking together and trying to keep the old flag flying through this terrible conflict until our brave lads return home once again'.[56] The next meeting recorded is 10 April 1919 when the minutes occasionally become a retrospective on the wartime experience and its lingering impact. It is explained that they were meeting

> for the purpose of reopening the meetings that had since May 1917 been temporarily suspended through the anxiety and trouble that members were passing through caused by the Great War and the many causes that would not permit the gathering together month by month of the few members left in this lodge... we now feel and trust that this is the beginning of a new lease of life in this lodge...

The District Master sent apologies for being 'detained by other business', the nature of which emerged when it was agreed

---

[52] No. 3 District Minute Book Special Meeting 8 June 1916 LRO 306.ORA/3/1/1
[53] Everett LOL 108 Signing-in book 20 January 1904–16 May 1923 LRO 306.ORA/1/2/1
[54] See Diane Urquhart, 'Unionism, Orangeism and war', *Women's History Review*, 27,3, 2018, pp. 468–84 for the impact of the First World War on the role of women in unionist politics
[55] Lady Stanley LLOL 97 Minute Book 14 April 1915 LRO 306.ORA/5/1/2
[56] Lady Stanley LLOL 97 Minute Book 10 May 1917 LRO 306.ORA/5/1/2

that we send letter of sympathy to Bro. & Sis. Weekes and their family in that recent bereavement by the calling home of their beloved and devoted son who had passed through the turmoil of this great war on several fronts only to come home for a few days and pass away.[57]

In June 'the lack of sisters attending for the lodge meeting caused it to be adjourned'.[58] Regular meetings resumed in September 1919.

Lodges had to find replacements for officers who had joined up, as in the case of Sons of the Boyne LOL 28 whose incumbent Treasurer was 'away serving with the colours as a Royal Engineer'.[59] Some relief was provided for Old Swan Arch Purple Heroes LOL 810 when informed by the D.M. chairing their annual meeting that 'any Officer could hold two offices in present circumstances'. Special meetings were held when necessary, as in April 1918 when a member of this lodge was raised to the Royal Arch Purple as he was about to be called up.[60]

At a meeting of Enniskillen No. 5 District on 14 November 1917 a member shared his distress at the situation in his lodge and, given the intense pride and loyalty members invested in their lodges, aired a radical suggestion:

> giving report on lodge meetings during the present times [he] suggested that all Lodges in Group work together for the time being, the numbers being unable to attend, their own lodges were unable to open. The W. Master, who expressed his sympathy... spoke of the meagre meetings of his Lodge, & it was suggested... that lodges should meet together with a view to making a united lodge during the war.

The meeting agreed. The District had already acknowledged wartime difficulties at its annual meeting earlier in the year when 'owing to the present national crisis calling so many of our members away the District officers elected *en bloc*'.[61] The suggestion for joint meetings was put into effect in early 1918 by Old Swan Arch Purple Heroes LOL 810 when they agreed 'that we extend a hearty note of thanks to the Brethren of LOL 782 for coming along to join us for the duration of the war... District Master then gave us an [account] of the way in which they desired to amalgamate'. Separate meetings were resumed in August 1919.[62]

[57] Lady Stanley LLOL 97 Minute Book 10 April 1919 LRO 306.ORA/5/1/2; possibly a victim of the 1918 influenza epidemic

[58] Lady Stanley LLOL 97 Minute Book 9 June 1919 LRO 306.ORA/5/1/2; four attended, one short of a quorum

[59] Sons of the Boyne LOL 28 Minute Book October 1915 LRO 306.ORA/6/1/1

[60] Old Swan Arch Purple Heroes LOL 810 April 1916, 27 April 1918 LRO 306.ORA/8/1/1

[61] Enniskillen No. 5 District Minute Book 9 May 1917 and 14 November 1917 LRO 306. ORA/7/1/1

[62] Old Swan Arch Purple Heroes LOL 810 Minute Book 13 March 1918 and 3 August

Similar measures were taken in the Second World War. Pride of West Derby LOL 5 decided in November 1939 to meet on the third Sunday of each month, possibly because of the wartime demands of the working week, and then at the annual meeting in 1940 decided to meet jointly with Belfast Patriotic LOL 3, an arrangement which lasted until May 1949.[63] Disruption of lodge life by military service was not confined to wartime. In 1958 Garston True Blues LOL 64 received an appeal from the band for new members to replace two who had been called up to national service and,[64] in August 1982, a member of Kirby Defenders LOL 300 gave his apologies for absence from the next meeting 'as he will be away with army'.[65] In view of the unprecedented disruption of the previous five years it is little wonder that, at a meeting of Old Swan Arch Purple Heroes LOL 810 in July 1919, a member 'referred to peace being signed in which all the brethren stood up & were asked to sing the first verse of the national anthem'.[66]

There was a determination to celebrate when serving members were demobilised. As early as May 1915 the Sons of the Boyne LOL 28 placed a box on the table at lodge meetings in support of a reception for 'our Bros. who are fighting for our country when the war is over...',[67] and by late 1918 a Soldiers and Sailors Reception Committee had been set up 'for the benefit of our brave heroes upon their return'.[68] At their meeting in September 1919 Lady Stanley LLOL 97 agreed to a proposal for a welcome home event for the returning servicemen of LOL 116, the lodge which traditionally appointed their Secretary. At their meeting in March 1920, they agreed to volunteer for 'the Catering & Waiting Tables etc. at the LOL 116 Male Lodge[']s welcome'.[69] Clearly the traditional relationship had been renewed. Their efforts were appreciated at a subsequent District No. 3 meeting.[70] The custom was followed in the next war when it was decided by Belfast Patriotic LOL 3 in late 1944 that, when members were demobilised, they would 'give them a real good time'.[71]

From quite early on the feeling emerged that in addition to letters of condolence and wreaths, permanent forms of commemoration would be needed. As early as November 1916 a proposal for a roll of honour was discussed at a meeting of Enniskillen No.5 District and the idea also surfaced at a meeting of

1919 LRO 306.ORA/8/1/1

[63] Pride of West Derby LOL 5 Minute Book April 1940 LRO 306.ORA/10/1/1

[64] Garston True Blues LOL 64 Minute Book 1956–61: 14 April 1958; held at Heald Street Orange Hall, Garston

[65] Kirby Defenders LOL 300 Minute Book 12 August 1982 LRO 306.ORA/16/1/1

[66] Old Swan Arch Purple Heroes LOL 810 Minute Book 9 July 1919 LRO 306.ORA/8/1/1

[67] Sons of the Boyne LOL 28 Minute Book May 1915 LRO 306.ORA/6/1/1

[68] No. 3 District Minute Book 19 November 1918 LRO 306.ORA/3/1/1

[69] Lady Stanley LLOL 97 Minute Book 10 September 1919, March 1920 LRO 306. ORA/5/1/2

[70] No. 3 District Minute Book 19 November 1920 LRO 306.ORA/3/1/1

[71] Belfast Patriotic LOL 3 Minute Book 4 November 1944 LRO 306.ORA/11/1

No. 3 District in May 1918.[72] There was also a proposal that the Order should strike a campaign medal for all serving members.[73] In late 1918 the Pride of the North LOL 841 was given permission to commemorate a member killed in the war by renaming themselves the Thomas Taft Memorial lodge.[74] It was also decided to designate a proposed District Orange Hall as a memorial.[75]

The most common form of permanent memorial that emerged was a tablet engraved with the names of the dead and placed in a prominent position in an Orange Hall. Garston True Blues LOL 64 formed a War Memorial Committee which by late 1921 was discussing arrangements for a formal unveiling. This was to take place on 5 November, three other lodges were invited, members would wear regalia, warrants would be draped and the flag flown at half-mast. Subsequently, it was decided to place a wreath at the foot of the plaque each Armistice Day and in 1922 a parade was held to mark the anniversary of the unveiling.[76] The dedication of the Cenotaph in London's Whitehall and the burial of the Unknown Warrior in Westminster Abbey in 1920, the invention of the tradition of the annual national commemoration service and parade in London on the Sunday closest to 11 November, and processions to local memorials resonated deeply with the history and ethos of the Order. Processions on Armistice/Remembrance Day with regalia, flags and banners, wreath-laying at memorials, a short religious service and two minutes' silence were effortlessly folded into the Order's ceremonial calendar, along with parades to mark significant battles.[77] Liverpool Province ruled that on 12 July, when lodges were on the way to nearby Lime Street station for trains to the rallying point, bands were to be silenced within 100 yards of the cenotaph on the nearby St George's plateau.[78]

Imperialism

Here I am a loyal Orangeman just come across the sea
For singin' and for dancin' I hope that I please thee

---

[72] Enniskillen No. 5 District Minute Book 8 November 1916 LRO 306.ORA/3/1/1; No. 3 District Minute Book 21 May 1918 LRO 306.ORA/3/1/1

[73] Enniskillen No. 5 District Minute Book 9 May 1917 LRO 306.ORA/7/1/1

[74] No. 3 District Minute Book 18 November 1918 LRO 306.ORA/3/1/1

[75] No. 3 District Minute Book 16 May 1922 LRO 306.ORA/3/1/1

[76] Garston True Blues LOL 64 Minute Book 1921–23: 29 September, 10 November 1921, 22 September 1922; held at Heald Street Orange Hall, Garston

[77] Protestant Martyrs LOL 35 Minute Book 15 October 1959 LRO 306.ORA/15/1/1

[78] Liverpool Province Processions Committee Minute Book 24 March, July, 25 August 1961 and 25 October 1969 LRO 306.ORA/1/1

> I can sing and dance like any man they did in times of yore
> And on the 'Twelfth', I'll always wear the Sash my Father Wore.[79]

The song dates from at least the mid-nineteenth century and resounds wherever Orange lodges parade. It underlines the fact that alongside, and interacting with, the patriotism so deeply embedded within Orangeism, there was always an awareness that the Order and the reach of the British state were not confined to Britain and Ireland. Indeed, the fact that the Order in Britain originated from Ireland was never lost on members, giving rise to a protean diasporic awareness. The earliest overseas lodges were founded in British military garrisons and, like those in Britain, subsequently attracted local civilians and Irish Protestant immigrants. One such lodge was formed in Halifax, Nova Scotia, in 1799, and the first 12 July parade in Canada, later a powerful Orange stronghold, was held in 1818. A military lodge opened in Australia in 1830, another in New Zealand in 1842 and by the early twentieth century there were lodges in west Africa and Egypt.[80] In 1867 an Imperial Orange Council was established with triennial meetings. When a special representative of the Grand Orange Lodge of British America spoke to the annual meeting of the Grand Lodge of England in 1928 he claimed that 'the first Deputy Grand Master of all the provinces of British North America, with the dependencies etc. belonging and adjacent thereto, had been appointed by the Grand Lodge of England... on April 19th 1832'.[81]

At local level members were constantly reminded of the overseas lodges thanks to the traffic in transfers. In March 1905 Everett LOL 108 learned that 'Bro. Baillie of LOL 1560 Vancouver BC then applied for admission & secretary was asked to see him but Bro. Baillie was not having this year's imperial pass it was decided not to admit him at present'; however, at the next meeting 'it was decided to admit him pending the receipt of his certificate'.[82] Six years later the Sons of the Boyne LOL 28 received an application 'from Geo. Hy Orme Royal Navy late of LOL 802 Hong Kong, China, to join this lodge was read by the W.S.... and he was enrolled in this Lodge unanimously'.[83] News from overseas lodges was carefully noted. In March 1924 'Bro. Glennon... gave a very able account of how orange lodges were doing over in New York where he is a frequent visitor and gets highly welcomed by all over there'.[84] In July 1948 the combined Belfast Patriotic LOL 3 and Pride of West Derby LOL 5 passed a 'hearty vote of thanks to Bro. Metcalfe of USA... [who] said he was very glad to be with us and gave

[79] Haddick-Flynn, *Orangeism*, p. 393; there are several variations on the wording
[80] Haddick-Flynn, *Orangeism*, pp. 393–94
[81] Loyal Orange Institution of England Report 1928, p. 17
[82] Everett LOL 108 Minute Book 15 and 21 March 1905 LRO 306.ORA/1/1/3
[83] Sons of the Boyne LOL 28 Minute Book 9 December 1911 LRO 306.ORA/6/1/1
[84] Sons of the Boyne LOL 28 Minute Book 8 March 1924 LRO 306.ORA/6/1/2

a very good talk which was much appreciated'.[85] But fraternity had its limits. The archives report several appeals for support from brethren in South Africa, Ontario and Hong Kong requesting financial help to build an Orange Hall, but Liverpool lodges found they were unable to help.

Throughout the period under discussion the archives reveal emigration of lodge members to territories of the British empire, particularly Canada, reinforcing the steadily growing sense of imperial awareness. In 1867 the Imperial Grand Orange Council was formed, held its first meeting in London and has since gathered every three years except in wartime. It was one manifestation of the steadily growing sense of popular imperial enthusiasm within British society as a whole, expressed and encouraged by the Royal Titles Act of 1877 which endowed the monarch with the title of Empress of India. In the 12 July procession of 1880 it was noted there was 'a representation showing "the cause of England's greatness" which illustrates the familiar story of the Queen presenting a bible to the chief of a savage race'.[86] These were reproductions of a portrait painted in 1862-3 in which the Queen presented a bible to a kneeling black chieftain shown receiving the gift with smiling gratitude. The scene and the sentiments, intertwining patriotism, popular imperial pride, Protestant providentialism and latent racial superiority, resonated deeply with the Order and was to be reproduced on banners for generations to come.

There were recurring imperial references in the Grand Lodge annual reports from the mid-nineteenth century onwards. In the 1865 report of the Grand Protestant Association there was an item from the Grand Secretary of the Western Province of Canada and Lodges of British North America.[87] In 1881 the Grand Secretary informed members that he was in touch not only with members in Britain and Ireland but also those in 'the colonies' and reminded all that 'London is the seat and heart of Government... and the heart as it were of the body politic, according to the beatings of whose pulse the affairs of the mightiest empire on earth are conducted'.[88] Recurring efforts were made to ensure uniformity of degree rituals and annual passwords throughout the empire. In 1904 it was reported to No. 3 District that the General Secretary was arguing an imperial pass should be given to all lodge officers for passing on to any member going abroad.[89] It was noted that at the 1905 meeting of the Imperial Grand

---

[85]   Belfast Patriotic LOL 3, Pride of West Derby LOL 5 Minute Book 22 July 1948 (joint meeting) LRO 306.ORA/11/1

[86]   *Liverpool Courier*, 13 July 1880. See L. Nead, 'The secret of England's greatness', *Victorian Culture* 19,1, 2014, pp. 161–82

[87]   Report of the Grand Protestant Association of Loyal Orangemen of England 1865, p. 12

[88]   Loyal Orange Institution of England Report 1881, p. 13

[89]   No. 3 District Minute Book 16 August 1904 LRO ORA/3/1/1

Figure 5.3 'The Secret of England's Greatness'. Based on the original by Thomas Jones Barker *c.* 1862–63 in the National Gallery, London, referencing the Order's emphasis on biblical Protestantism, royalty and empire. *Source: Courtesy LLOL 68*

Council that 'three and a half million Orangemen were represented'.[90] Four years later one of the toasts at the annual Grand Lodge dinner was 'the Orange Order all over the world' and the proposer noted that 'in every quarter of the globe they found "Orange Trees" whose branches were spreading far and wide'.[91] In July 1914 there was great satisfaction that '[o]ur foreign bodies in India, China, Straits Settlements and Arabia are doing splendidly'.[92] By the early 1920s lodges had also been recruited from local inhabitants in Nigeria, Togo and the Gold Coast (Ghana).

The conviction that pride in empire should be imbued in future generations is illustrated by Garston True Blues LOL 64. In 1921 they were so impressed by the manner in which a local Boy Scout had sounded the 'Last Post' at a

---

[90] Loyal Orange Institution of England Report 1905, p. 8
[91] Loyal Orange Institution of England Report 1909, p. 27
[92] Loyal Orange Institution of England Report 1914, p. 18; clearly military lodges

recent Armistice Day service that they sent him a letter of appreciation and a copy of the life of General Gordon, the devoutly Christian British general who had been killed in the Sudan in January 1885 when the armies of an Islamic revival movement stormed the city of Khartoum. Gordon's death had made him a popular imperial hero, who for several decades was held up to school-children as the model British Christian martyr courageously defending imperial power, civilisation and dignity in the face of fanatical savagery.[93] Empire Day, inaugurated in 1905 and renamed Commonwealth Day in 1966, was regularly celebrated with a parade of juvenile lodges.

Empire became a standard trope of 12 July gatherings. At the Liverpool 1899 event Grand Secretary Touchstone carefully defined the current war as a reaction to Boer invasions of imperial territories, paying tribute to 'troops both imperial and colonial... who fell courageously fighting, even in the cannon's mouth, for the preservation of the Empire'.[94] Other public issues were placed in an imperial context, most notably the successive Irish home rule bills, condemned in 1886 as an attempt 'to pluck a... gem from the imperial diadem',[95] in 1893 as 'the traitorous designs of Mr Gladstone to break up this mighty empire' and,[96] at the 1913 rally, as 'not only injurious to Ireland, but... against the best interests of the Empire' with an appeal to '[s]tand united for the glory of the Empire and a glorious triumph for Protestantism'.[97]

From the mid-nineteenth century the steady rise in emigration caused concern. The archives carry details of quite frequent occasions when members were about to depart. In 1887 Everett LOL 108 received a letter from a former local District Master who had emigrated to Canada 'giving an account of his settlement in Toronto and of his warm reception by the brethren there'.[98] In 1914 they received a final payment of dues from a member about to leave for Australia.[99] Grand Lodge was aware of the trend and at the 1910 meeting the Grand Secretary 'mentioned the fact that several Brethren had gone to Canada, Brethren having wished them God-speed before their departure'.[100]

Lodges were anxious to ensure that emigrant members made contact with local lodges on arrival. In 1921 the Grand Lodge reported that they had received a letter from the Grand Secretary of New South Wales 'to notify you that should any members of the Institution be coming to Sydney, they are requested to call at this office on arrival so that if we can help them with any information or

[93] Michael Asher, *Khartoum: The Ultimate Imperial Adventure* London: Penguin, 2006
[94] *Liverpool Courier*, 13 July 1900
[95] *Liverpool Courier*, 14 July 1886
[96] *Liverpool Daily Post*, 13 July 1893
[97] *Liverpool Courier*, 14 July 1913
[98] Everett LOL 108 Minute Book 16 June 1887 LRO 306.ORA/1/1/1
[99] Everett LOL 108 Minute Book May 1914 LRO 306.ORA/1/1/4
[100] Loyal Orange Institution of England Report 1910, p. 16

anything of that sort, we shall be glad to give them all the help we can in a fraternal spirit'.[101] In 1926 the Grand Secretary assured members that '[a] watchful eye has been kept on all cases of emigration which have come to my notice with a view to their welcome and retention in the Order'.[102] That year the annual gathering was addressed by the Grand Master of British America who made it clear that their concern went beyond personal welfare:

> The foundations of the Order are the basic foundations on which the British Empire had been built up… for future consideration, he would throw out the hint that the various Grand lodges of the world should consider… the question of Emigration work, and co-operate in the selection and placing of Emigrants, particularly those in their 'teens'. The Roman Church had been particularly active in the matter recently in placing such people of their Faith in the dominions. The great problem in Canada was keeping Canada British.[103]

Two years later Grand Lodge heard an address by the significantly titled Special Immigration Representative of the Grand Orange Lodge of British America who 'gave a lucid account of conditions in Canada, where the Orange Order had undoubtedly been a main factor in retaining a dominant British prestige and influence, and explaining the purpose of his sojourn in the British Isles—to encourage and assist emigration to Canada under the splendid scheme instituted by the Grand Lodge of British America'.[104] He was clearly energetic: in August 1929 the Daughters of Victory LLOL 11 received a letter from the Grand Secretary 'relating to help and information to anyone interested to emigrate to Canada[;] there was a representative of the Grand Lodge of Canada residing now in Belfast wishing to give advice and prospects of a good home in Canada to those strictly Protestant towards loyal Empire building'.[105]

At the 1931 Grand Lodge meeting the Secretary outlined the workings of the scheme. Administrators requested details of the migrant's name, lodge name and number, destination, boat name, date of sailing and promised

> [u]pon receipt of this information we will arrange to meet the Brother upon arrival in this City, and extend to him the right hand of fellowship, and furnish any such information and advise [sic] as he may require or do anything in our power to direct him to his final destination. We will

[101] Loyal Orange Institution of England Report 1921, p. 15
[102] Loyal Orange Institution of England Report 1926, p. 18
[103] Loyal Orange Institution of England Report 1926, p. 15
[104] Loyal Orange Institution of England Report 1928, p. 17
[105] Daughters of Victory LLOL 11 Minute Book 15 August 1929 LRO 306.ORA/9/1/1

further put the brother in touch with the Lodge nearest to his future home, so that he will find himself amongst friends upon his arrival.[106]

Emigration from the United Kingdom resumed in the mid-1940s, and from 1948 to 1975 inside the front cover of the annual report of the Order, under 'Special Notices', there was a reminder:

> Lodge Secretaries are earnestly requested to notify the Grand Secretary under seal through the Provincial Grand Secretary of their Province of any Brethren or Sisters Emigrating to any of the Dominions and to supply the following particulars: a) Name of Member; b) No. of Lodge; c) Date of Sailing; d) Name of Ship; e) Port of Destination; f) Address in Dominion to which proceeding.[107]

The difficulties and emotions surrounding the emigration process, for both migrating and remaining lodge members, are borne out by two examples. Early in 1954 a member of Lady Stanley LLOL 97 was on the verge of emigrating. At the February lodge meeting the lodge made:

> a presentation... to [the Sister] who is going to S. Africa to live wishing her and her family every success in this venture and hope that she will always remember that she would keep in touch with Lodge by writing to us. [She] replied that this would always remind her of Ladies Stanley lodge and many happy Lodge meetings she had attended.

At the April meeting it was noted the lodge had received a letter thanking them for their gift.[108]

The departure of a member of Stuart McCoy Memorial LOL 2 was a more protracted affair, illustrating the strength of lodge loyalty. In December 1953 he

> told the Lodge that he would be leaving us very soon as he was emigrating to Canada, but still wished to remain a member of our lodge. He promised to send his dues to the Worthy Master and hoped he would return home sometime and be able attend lodge. [A Brother] on behalf of the Lodge wished him every success in his new venture [and] also wished him Godspeed and said he would be sure of a warm welcome if he could visit

---

[106] Loyal Orange Institution of England Report 1931, p. 19
[107] Loyal Orange Institution of England Report 1948: inside front cover
[108] Lady Stanley LLOL 97 Minute Book February and April 1954 LRO 306.ORA/5/1/2

a lodge in Canada [Secretary] said he would find a Brother to write to in Canada and would let him know.[109]

At the March 1954 meeting the Secretary read a letter describing how the former member was faring and requesting a travelling pass; in April it was agreed that the secretary should write to the 'Grand secretary of British America, Toronto, thanking him on behalf of the Lodge for the assistance he has given…' and in September there was a letter from the migrant member 'telling of his experiences of Lodges in Canada'.[110] But by early January 1956 it was reported that he had returned, become lodge Treasurer and then in March 1957 'said that this would be his last meeting before he sailed for Canada… Deputy W.M.… on behalf of the Lodge wished both him and his wife Godspeed. In reply [he] thanked members and said he still wished to be a member of the Lodge and promised to let us know how he was going on.' At the meeting in March 1959, it was reported he wished to retain lodge membership and promised to pay all dues owed, but there is no trace of any further contact.[111]

Clearly the migration process was not always a simple one, but it reminded members that they belonged to an international order within an imperial framework. This thrilling sense of worldwide bonding was expressed in material form in the late 1940s. In the immediate post-war period there was quite strict food rationing in the United Kingdom. The empire rallied to support the home country. In 1947 the Grand Master reported he had received a letter from the secretary of a New Zealand female lodge announcing that food parcels would begin to be despatched in April that year.[112] In the 1948 report it was stated that five schemes would shortly be in operation, based in New Zealand, Canada and the USA, with some Canadian lodges sending food to English lodges which they had 'adopted'.[113] In 1949 the Grand Secretary noted that '[t]o date, 80 parcels have been despatched from WLOL New Zealand, of these 74 have been received and distributed. Canada—This scheme is in "full blast"; also parcels are being sent from New Brunswick. All are being received in good condition and are much appreciated.'[114] In Liverpool the W.M. of Belfast Patriotic LOL 3 reported 'the parcel he had received from Canada was a bit to [sic] large for one person…' and he asked for it to be distributed among needy female members.[115] In May 1950 a

---

[109] Stuart McCoy Memorial LOL 2 Minute Book 14 December 1953 LRO 306.ORA/12/1
[110] Stuart McCoy Memorial LOL 2 Minute Book 9 March, 12 April, 8 November 1954 LRO 306.ORA/12/1
[111] Stuart McCoy Memorial LOL 2 Minute Book 9 January 1956, 11 March 1957, 9 March 1959 LRO 306.ORA/12/1
[112] Loyal Orange Institution of England Report 1947, p. 17
[113] Loyal Orange Institution of England Report 1948, p. 13
[114] Loyal Orange Institution of England Report 1949, p. 14
[115] Belfast Patriotic LOL 3 Minute Book 22 July 1948 LRO 306.ORA/11/1

Figure 5.4
Scott Memorial
Orange Hall,
Winnipeg, Manitoba.
A migrant Ulster
Orangeman executed
by rebellious local
insurgents in March
1870, Scott's death
elevated him to
martyr status in
Canada's Orange
diaspora.
*Source: Author's
collection*

meeting of Duke of York No. 6 District agreed that a box of dripping received from Australia should be divided between three female lodges.[116]

The Order was acting as an international mutual aid society and migrant support network, an extended version of the welfare work discussed in Chapter Four, but within the framework of the empire and with the hope of helping maintain the Order's British and Protestant nature.[117]

---

[116] Duke of York No. 6 District Minute Book 15 May 1950 LRO 306.ORA/13/1/1
[117] Don MacRaild, '"Wherever Orange is worn": Orangeism and Irish migration in the nineteenth and early twentieth centuries', *Canadian Journal of Irish Studies*, 28,2/29,1 2002/03, pp. 98–117; 'The associationalism of the Orange diaspora' in D.A. Wilson (ed.), *The Orange Order in Canada* (Dublin: Four Courts Press, 2007), chp. 1, pp. 25–41

Conclusion

Aside from occasional reservations over personal behaviour and diplomatic visits to the Vatican, the Orange Order remained firmly loyal to the British Protestant monarchy throughout the period. Unquestioning patriotism was expressed through military service in both world wars, sustaining heavy losses not only in casualties but in the expenditure of financial resources in support of both those serving in the field and their families, widows and orphans. Normal lodge life was devastated with so many on active service, leading to meetings being thinly attended or cancelled and some lodges temporarily combining to maintain a quorum. At the conclusion of the First World War the newly invented commemoration traditions were immediately adopted by the Order since they resonated strongly with the historic military roots of the movement and provided yet another occasion for the parades with regalia that were such a defining feature of the Order.

As the nineteenth century unfolded, popular patriotism developed an imperial dimension which the Order enthusiastically embraced and this was reinforced by the steady growth of emigration to the white dominions, encouraged by the Grand Lodges, especially those in Canada, anxious to maintain the British Protestant majority of the dominion. Throughout the period the espousal of Protestantism at home and abroad and faith in the superior civic virtues it imbued remained unquestioned, though it was gradually coming under pressures which reflected deep-seated socio-economic and cultural shifts within British society.

6

Defending Protestantism

Introduction

This chapter will discuss the continuing centrality of Protestantism to the Order, the monitoring of applicants and members and the tensions generated by the unease of some of the more devout with aspects of traditional working-class life. It will demonstrate that whatever the differences of emphasis amongst members, they united in the face of the growing Anglo-Catholic movement within the Church of England, which was contested through tactics from the verbal and written to public protest and direct action, occasionally leading to bitter sectarian conflict and exasperation with the established church.

Monitoring members

Applicants for membership were interviewed and on occasion birth and baptismal certificates and marriage lines requested. Once accepted, members were expected to avoid contact with Roman Catholicism and were admonished if they erred. In 1907 it was noted that a lodge member had helped out at a Catholic event and a letter was sent from District 'disapproving of her assisting at Roman Catholic concerts'.[1] Protestant Martyrs LLOL 91 reminded members that '[a]ny Sister who goes to a Roman Catholic church for any service or other function [is] to be reprimanded by members of their lodge and can be severely dealt with...'[2] and the male lodge declared that 'RC clubs and churches are out of bounds to all members'.[3]

Regular social contact with Catholics was condemned. In 1922 a member of Garston True Blues LOL 64 was accused of 'keeping company with a young

---

[1] No. 3 District Minute Book 21 May 1907, LRO 306.ORA/3/1/1
[2] Protestant Martyrs LLOL 91 Minute Book November 1967 LRO 306.ORA/15/1/3
[3] Protestant Martyrs LOL 35 Minute Book 9 March 1973 LRO 306.ORA/5/1/2

woman who is an RC and also supporting an RC ball him at the same time being an R.A.P. member'.[4] Another explained 'that the girl he keeps company with was brought up a Protestant but she was confirmed in an RC chapel'. The Secretary explained 'that if he married her he would cease to be a member of this Lodge'.[5] Expulsion for life was the ultimate sanction and lodge Secretaries recorded such decisions with great care, aware there could be appeals to District, Province and Grand Lodge. At the October 1931 meeting of Lady Stanley LLOL 97, the Secretary noted the decision that a member 'be expelled for marrying a R. Catholic', underlining the words in red ink.[6] One suspect member had to prove his bona fides with documentation confirming baptism, confirmation and first communion in the Church of England.[7] Another accused of being present when the Pope appeared in St Peter's Square in Rome explained he had been on a trip and was merely passing through.[8] Other appeals were deemed less convincing, as when an applicant explained that 'after marriage he found out his wife to be a Roman Catholic'. He was refused membership and told he 'should have been more discreet before marrying'.[9] Such measures policed the boundaries and confirmed the exclusively Protestant and anti-Catholic nature of the Order, but there were internal fissures, often centred around boisterous features of traditional working-class life.

The Puritan tradition

Observers have noted a puritan streak within the Order that sits uneasily with its overwhelmingly proletarian membership.[10] Most of the clergy within the Order were conservative evangelicals stressing regular church attendance, bible reading, prayer, traditional family life and a serious-minded, sober lifestyle. Along with some of the more devout lodge members they were dismayed by the low level of church attendance amongst their brethren. Gatherings such as church parades were an opportunity to scold these brothers for neglect of duty. The preacher addressing a church parade at Garston parish church in 1892 was notably direct:

[4] Garston True Blues LOL 64 Minute Book 1921–23: Special Meeting 7 April 1922; held at Heald Street Orange Hall, Garston
[5] Garston True Blues LOL 64 Minute Book 1921–23: 26 June 1922; held at Heald Street Orange Hall, Garston
[6] Lady Stanley LLOL 97 Minute Book 14 October 1931 LRO 306.ORA/5/1/2
[7] Everett LOL 108 Minute Book 14 March 1899 LRO 306.ORA/1/1/2
[8] Garston True Blues LOL 64 Minute Book 1956–61: 3 June 1957; held at Heald Street Orange Hall, Garston
[9] No. 3 District Minute Book 17 February and 18 May 1920 LRO 306.ORA/3/1/1
[10] Gray, *The Orange Order*, pp. 9–10

Did they think it right that so many of them should be standing on the street corners unwashed during divine service on the Lord's Day? Was this pleasing to God, or in accordance with the principles that they were sworn to defend? The reverend gentleman urged them... to remember that shouting for these principles would not commend them to the world unless they lived them in their everyday life.[11]

But the problem persisted. At a meeting of Ivy LOL 783 in December 1964 the Chaplain, minister of the Protestant Reformers' Church, asked how many members attended church and expressed disappointment on seeing 'very few hands raised'.[12]

In the second half of the nineteenth century vigorous campaigns were mounted by temperance reformers in working-class districts and some lodge members were active in the cause. In July 1898 a dinner and presentation were held in honour of the W.M. of LOL 337 and his work 'in the formation and furtherance of Juvenile and Temperance Orange Lodges in the Province'. The recipient referred to the 300 youths under the W.M.'s leadership and declared '[h]is object was... to make them teetotal Orangemen and keep them out of the public houses...' Only tea was served.[13] In 1960 LOL 63, closely associated with the Protestant Reformers' Church, voted to insert the word "Temperance" into their title, with 17 in favour and 4 against.[14]

But temperance collided with the fact that from its foundation the Orange Order had a strong social dimension to all its gatherings, with food and drink figuring large. The 12 July celebrations, with lengthy processions, speeches, games and the sometimes enervating heat, undoubtedly generated a thirst. Even sympathetic reporters sometimes noted returning members had celebrated too well. In July 1872 '[t]he proceedings on the march out were of a very orderly character... but the return march was not performed in a manner so creditable to the Order, several of the members being perceptibly under the influence of drink...'[15] Lodge archives record severe penalties. Everett LOL 108 met on 24 July 1907 to consider a case of 'insubordination and drunkenness on the July demonstration'. A motion that the member 'be expelled from this Lodge & the Institution at large was carried without any further consideration'.[16]

Some clergy were concerned about events following the return from the main July celebrations. In 1870 a group left the procession, gathered at Mr Johnson's

---

[11] *Garston & Woolton Reporter*, 16 July 1892
[12] Ivy LOL 783, *100 Years of History*, December 1964, p. 34
[13] *Protestant Standard*, 23 July 1898
[14] Recorded in Protestant Martyrs LOL 35 Minute Book 11 January and 7 February 1960 LRO 306.ORA/15/1/2
[15] *Liverpool Courier*, 13 July 1872
[16] Everett LOL 108 Minute Book 24 July 1907 LRO 306.ORA/1/1/3

Cattle Market Inn for a meal and '[a]fter the prandial business, the festive party—the gentler sex predominating—launched into the gayer recreation of dancing, with songs, recitals, and the like diversions and... "danced all night till the broad daylight".' But at a 'grand Orange demonstration' the same evening the Ulster-born Reverend Gustavus Carson condemned:

> the numerous other gatherings and attractions held by other of the brethren. He remarked that the anniversary they were celebrating was one that specially called up the religious feelings of Orangemen... He thought there was a tendency to gather into their dancing assemblies those whose moral character was not such as it ought to be, and he said it without fear of rebuke, that the association of Orangemen with persons of that description throw mud and mire on the glorious Order to which they belonged.[17]

Church parades often created problems. In May 1923 a member of No. 3 District 'spoke of the disgraceful scenes outside a church at a recent parade by concertina bands playing tunes to the amusement of girls which we all deeply deplored and ask for better behaviour in the future'.[18] As time passed there was increasing official unhappiness with the music played on such occasions. One band was asked 'not to play tunes usually played on the 12th July on an ordinary church parade',[19] and there was a complaint about 'the singing of party tunes' with a warning 'the practice must cease'.[20] Garston True Blues LOL 64 devised a compromise in 1921—they would play marches *en route* to a Watch Night Service but 'sacred music' on the return.[21]

Any suspicion of drunkenness on such occasions was taken very seriously. In February 1899 a lodge conducted 'a very exhaustive inquiry' into a charge that a member had 'been the worse of drink in Church Parade', but concluded the report was unfounded.[22] A recurring practice that drew constant censure was the tendency for some members to parade but not enter the church. In 1908 Sons of the Boyne LOL 28 held a lengthy discussion following a recent church parade and decreed that in future 'any member not attending church be fined 1/-'.[23] In early 1954 one local cleric had clearly lost patience. He informed Ivy LOL 783 that the parades would no longer be welcome in his church for two reasons, namely

[17] *Liverpool Courier*, 13 July 1870
[18] No. 3 District Minute Book 15 May 1923 LRO 306.ORA/3/1/1
[19] Pride of West Derby LOL 5 Minute Book 25 June 1956 LRO 306.ORA/10/1/2
[20] Duke of York No. 6 District Minute Book 18 June 1957 LRO 306.ORA/13/1/2
[21] Garston True Blues LOL 64 Minute Book 1921-23: 23 December 1921; held at Heald Street Orange Hall, Garston
[22] Everett LOL 108 Minute Book 24 February 1899 LRO 306.ORA/1/1/2
[23] Sons of the Boyne LOL 28 Minute Book 12 December 1908 LRO 306.ORA/6/1/1

it was noted that many members of the order had been seen walking away from the church rather than attending the services... it has been further reported to him that members of the order had been urinating at the rear of the church which, quite rightly, offended the congregation who had to clear after we'd gone.[24]

There was also unhappiness within the Order over the various forms of gambling popular in working-class communities, particularly football pools, raffles and draws, all easily incorporated into lodge fund-raising events. Some lodges were unsure how to proceed. In November 1952 Stuart McCoy Memorial LOL 2 queried the legality of a football draw, provoking 'a general discussion between the members about football pools and the Orange Institution...' There was no definite decision but six years later it is recorded 'we the members of LOL 2 protest strongly against the Orange Hall Committee letting rooms for the purpose of running football pools...'[25] Financial pressures gradually forced a rethink. In October 1958 the Protestant Martyrs LOL 35 realised a fund-raising raffle 'though excellent in character' would encounter clerical opposition.[26] In 1970 Kirby Defenders LOL 300 agreed to participate in a 'Spot the Ball' competition and to make a monthly donation from the proceeds towards work amongst juvenile lodges.[27]

This was symptomatic of growing realisation that without additional sources of revenue the future of the Order was in question. As early as November 1922 the Hall Committee of Garston True Blues LOL 64 recommended that the lower rooms of the hall be opened as a licensed social club. Lodge meetings left the idea on the table until April 1923 when 'after a debate, which lasted several hours, it was decided that it would be impossible to run a Social Club, with intoxicating liquors, owing to the fact that this procedure would be detrimental to juvenile lodges'.[28] The proposal met the same fate 30 years later at a joint meeting with the Entertainments Committee.[29] However, economic pressures were such that, by April 1952, a weekly 'Tote' was in operation. This helped pay for refurbishment of the Orange Hall, but the lack of a drinks licence was increasingly felt to be a problem. A committee was formed to investigate the possibility of a social

---

[24] Ivy LOL 783, *100 Years of History*, February 1954, pp. 42–43

[25] Stuart McCoy Memorial LOL 2 Minute Book 11 November 1952, 13 October 1958 LRO 306.ORA/12/1

[26] Protestant Martyrs LOL 35 Minute Book 16 October 1958 LRO 306.ORA/15/1/1. Harry Dixon Longbottom (see Chapter Seven) was minister of the church at this time

[27] Kirby Defenders LOL 300 Minute Book 19 August 1970 LRO 306.ORA/16/1/1

[28] *A Glimpse into 125 Years*, pp. 12, 17.

[29] Garston True Blues LOL 64 Hall Committee Minute Book 3 September 1951; held at Heald Street Orange Hall, Garston.

club on separate premises and this was formally launched in February 1954, apparently the first social club to be owned by a private lodge.[30] However, there was lingering unease at erosion of the temperance tradition.

Whilst there could be some disagreement over alcohol at social events, sexual immorality was unreservedly condemned. In June 1911 a member of Sons of the Boyne LOL 28 was accused of having sex with the daughter of an R.A.P. member. The case wound its way through the Order and the law courts for seven years, resulting in an expulsion from the Order in early 1918.[31] In 1923 Lady Stanley LLOL 97, faced with a confession of adultery by a member, quickly agreed her expulsion 'for conduct not becoming an Orangewoman'.[32] By 1953 attitudes had moderated and, after discussion, Garston True Blues LOL 64 eventually agreed to readmit an errant member.[33] But in 1978 Kirby Defenders LOL 300 were clearly faced with a puzzle when they decided to send a letter to District, Province and Grand Lodge 'regarding a ruling and guidance on a common law wife'.[34]

Lodge and church

For the great majority of Orangemen and -women lodge and church were quite compatible. For clergy the situation could be rather more problematic. Those in the evangelical tradition were sympathetic towards the Order's emphasis on the historic significance of the Reformation and opposition to both Anglo- and Roman Catholic beliefs and practices. The Reverend Richard Hobson personified the ambivalence of some. His patronising rationalisation for not actually joining was his puritan abhorrence of dancing, playing cards, the theatre, opera and music hall, though he was totally silent on the sectarian strand within the Order.[35] It is this combination of carefully distanced support with the occasional scolding for lax behaviour that could provoke resentment amongst the rank and file, fuelling what at least one observer has suggested is a strand of anti-clericalism within the Order.[36]

Some clerics did not hesitate to join. One, who applied for a transfer into Belfast Patriotic LOL 3, promised 'he would do his best to work for the good of

[30] *A Glimpse into 125 Years*, p. 17
[31] Sons of the Boyne LOL 28 Minute Book 10 June, 9 September, 14 October, 11 November 1911, December 1917 LRO 306.ORA/6/1/1
[32] Lady Stanley LLOL 97 Minute Book 7 May 1923 LRO 306.ORA/5/1/2
[33] Garston True Blues LOL 64 Minute Book 1950–53: 12 May, 3 June, 14 July, 11 August, 8 September, 13 October 1952, 13 July 1953; held at Heald Street Orange Hall, Garston
[34] Kirby Defenders LOL 300 Minute Book 14 April 1978 LRO 306.ORA/16/1/1
[35] Croft, 'Richard Hobson and the Anglican church', , pp. 57–67; Hobson, *What God Hath Wrought*, p. 44
[36] Kennaway, *The Orange Order*, p. 15

the cause'. He was warmly welcomed.[37] Some served as Chaplains, conducting the devotions that feature in all gatherings and occasionally giving talks at lodge meetings. Their outlook was well expressed by the Reverend Theodore Howard, vicar of St Matthew's Church, Toxteth, who, welcomed as a new member by Everett LOL 108 in February 1902, clearly saw the Order as an opportunity for evangelism, declaring that 'his great work in this life should be the uplifting of the brethren and to instruct them how to use their great and mighty power to advantage so that the Church we all loved so dearly might benefit by it...'[38] Reverend Anthony of the Protestant Martyrs church served as lodge and District Chaplain, seeing the R.A.P. as 'a degree only for a Christian man'.[39]

The close link between some lodges and local churches is seen in use of church premises and schools for lodge meetings. Of the 138 lodges in the city of Liverpool that submitted details of venues to the annual report of 1910 45 (32.6 per cent), together with two Districts, met on church premises.[40] News of local church events was regularly circulated amongst lodges together with appeals for attendance and financial support. In April 1901 the vicar of St Cleopas sent a letter to Everett LOL 108 'inviting the members... to attend Divine Worship... on Sunday 28th to assist the clear off of the church expenses which were exceptionally heavy...' It was agreed 'to march in a body to church... [and] grant the sum of £1.10s. to the Vicar in aid of the church expenses'.[41]

A particularly close relationship developed between the Order and the Protestant Reformers' Church founded in 1903 by the redoubtable George Wise, of whom more shortly. In some ways this was the most notable example of the development of independent conservative evangelical churches as a reaction to what was deemed the inadequate response of Church of England authorities to the growth of Anglo-Catholicism. Hardly surprisingly, notable numbers of Orange Order members were attracted to these churches. The records display the closeness of the relationship that developed, especially with Protestant Martyrs LOL 35 which drew heavily on church membership. The church was in regular contact with the lodge, inviting them to special Gift Days,[42] asking for help in the purchase of Christmas cards towards church funds,[43] requesting items for a Christmas Fair[44] and publicising the harvest festival.[45] The assumption that lodges and church were closely interwoven was well expressed by one hall committee

[37] Belfast Patriotic LOL 3 Minute Book 23 October 1947 LRO 306.ORA/11/1
[38] Everett LOL 108 Minute Book 19 February 1902 LRO 306.ORA/1/1/2
[39] Protestant Martyrs LOL 35 Minute Book 16 December 1959 LRO 306.ORA/15/1/2
[40] Loyal Orange Institution of England Report 1910, pp. 25–42
[41] Everett LOL 108 Minute Book 17 April 1901 LRO 306.ORA/1/1/2
[42] Protestant Martyrs LOL 35 Minute Book 7 February 1960 LRO 306.ORA/15/1/2
[43] Protestant Martyrs LOL 35 Minute Book 6 September 1960 LRO 306.ORA/15/1/2
[44] Protestant Martyrs LLOL 91 Minute Book November 1967 LRO 306.ORA/15/1/3
[45] Protestant Martyrs LLOL 91 Minute Book March 1975 LRO 306.ORA/15/1/3

member who pledged 'he would always do his best for all members of Church and Hall'.[46] One lodge member was clearly dismayed to discover that 'there is members on church council that is not in the Institution'.[47]

Since so many members of the Order took it for granted that the state church was a bulwark of what they regarded as traditional Protestantism there was widespread dismay at the growing influence of the Anglo-Catholic movement within the Church of England in the second half of the nineteenth century.

The enemy within

What is variously known as the Oxford, Tractarian, Anglo-Catholic or high church movement was simply 'Ritualism' to opponents. It originated in the 1830s amongst a group of Church of England clergy who sought to restore to the church some aspects of historic belief, liturgy and ritual rejected at the Reformation which they believed were quite compatible with standard church teaching.[48] The movement originally centred around a gifted group of young Oxford clergy who set out their ideas in a series of publications, the most controversial being Tract 90 by John Henry Newman, which strove to argue that the Church of England's foundational Thirty-Nine Articles of belief were perfectly compatible with a Catholic outlook. In the ensuing controversy several of the most prominent were received into the Roman Catholic church, including Newman in 1845. Those who remained, often referred to as 'high church', emphasised the need for restoration of a numinous sense of worship in services. They regretted what they saw as the great losses incurred at the Reformation in terms of liturgy, ritual and internal church embellishments. They sought to restore elaborate church buildings and interiors with statues, lighted candles, incense, colourful clergy vestments, auricular confession and celebration of mass rather than communion. The first bishop of this outlook was appointed in 1854. By the end of the nineteenth century Anglo-Catholics were an integral part of the Church of England, with their own advocacy group, the English Church Union, founded in 1860. It has been argued that by then one-third of parochial clergy were of this outlook, with particular strongholds in the London region and adjoining home counties.[49]

For those of a traditional ultra-Protestant outlook this was an appalling development which they viewed as an existential threat attempting to overturn

---

[46] No. 6 District Hall Management Committee Minute Book 15 August 1960 LRO 306. ORA/13/2/1

[47] No. 6 District Hall Management Committee Minute Book 21 September 1964 LRO 306.ORA/13/2/2

[48] J. Munson, 'The Oxford Movement by the end of the nineteenth century: the Anglo-Catholic clergy', *Church History: Studies in Christianity and Culture*, 44,3, September 1975, pp. 382–95

[49] Munson, 'The Oxford Movement', pp. 393, 385

the sixteenth-century Reformation, subvert the state church and the Protestant constitution and return Britain to Roman Catholicism. From the mid-1860s there are traces of growing anxiety within Orangeism. At its Bradford gathering in 1864 the Grand Protestant Association noted a local cleric had been arguing for the return of monasticism and resolved 'this Meeting entirely reprobates and condemns all such conduct'.[50] It was an opening shot in an agitation that climaxed in the early twentieth century and has been termed the last of a long tradition of popular campaigns on the issue.[51] In Liverpool the Orange Order was notably vocal. In July 1898 one commentator on that year's events suggested: '[o]f late years such demonstrations have shown a tendency to diminish... in the numbers participating in them, but recent events in the shape of vigorous protests against Ritualism have infused fresh vitality into the Order itself, and brought its principles into greater prominence with the public'.[52] In November 1900 a recruit to Everett LOL 108 explained his motivation: 'he thought it time to join the Orange Order for there was so much Papacy in the church and was much pleased with the Order'.[53]

The anxieties underlying the agitation are revealed in the terminology deployed. One constantly recurring theme was the alleged conspiratorial nature, deceit and dishonesty of the clergy involved. In July 1864 they were described as 'sappers and miners secretly and stealthily undermining Protestantism',[54] and four years later a speaker at the 12 July celebrations warned that 'the National Church is exposed to peril, as well from secret and treasonable foes within as from open and avowed enemies without...'[55] The result: 'clergymen who had crept into our church of England and were preaching Romish doctrines'.[56] The allegation was not merely treason to the doctrines of the Church of England but betrayal of the Protestant constitution. High church clerics were described as embracing 'doctrines and practices... and formulations which proves their disloyalty to the Throne as well as their rebellion against the church...',[57] since the eventual intention was 'to undo the work of the Reformation, and many of its supporters hope to hand the Church of England over bodily to Rome'.[58] They

---

[50] *Report of Proceedings*, The Grand Protestant Association of Loyal Orangemen of England, 1864, Appendix 1, p. 14
[51] G.I.T. Machin, 'The last Victorian anti-ritual campaign', *Victorian Studies* 25,3, 1982, pp. 277–302
[52] *Liverpool Courier*, 13 July 1898
[53] Everett LOL 108 Minute Book 21 November 1900 LRO 306.ORA/1/1/1
[54] *Liverpool Daily Post*, 13 July 1864, Supplement
[55] *Liverpool Courier*, 14 July 1868
[56] *Liverpool Courier*, 15 July 1902
[57] *Liverpool Courier*, 15 July 1902
[58] *Liverpool Daily Post*, 10 July 1933

were frequently described as 'the traitors in their church...', successful because 'so insidious',[59] their behaviour 'unconstitutional, un-English...'[60]

Observers noticed that the Liverpool campaign attracted a notable working-class element. Speaking to a meeting of LOL 62 in July 1873 the District Master of Duke of York District No. 6 referred to 'our society, being composed of men chiefly of the working class who have many a time had to fight their own battles...' and was applauded when he called on them 'to do their utmost to expel Ritualism or semi-Popery from the National Church'.[61] In 1885 the Reverend Carson, now Provincial Grand Chaplain, also implied a class divide when he described the ritual party as an effete elite comprising 'a strong, well organised conspiracy, in which were involved men of undoubted talent and ability...'[62] In August 1898 the District Master addressed lodges LOL 119 and 719, condemning 'ritualism' which he alleged 'has no doubt been encouraged by the upper class who desire something showy in in their services... so great had this evil become that at last the working man has taken up the question ...' and went on to draw attention to the person he regarded as the most effective Protestant champion: 'Mr George Wise is doing noble work and has the sympathy and support of every intelligent working man...'[63]

Wise was to become the dominant figure in the Liverpool anti-ritual campaign and a warm favourite of the Orange lodges. Born in the Bermondsey district of London in 1855, he converted to Christianity in 1872, joined the Christian Evidence Society and began to give open-air lectures, leaving secular employment in 1886. He first visited Liverpool that year, giving lectures on Christian doctrine and classes to Sunday school teachers, and debating with high churchmen and Roman Catholic clergy. In 1887 he returned and was increasingly drawn into the anti-ritual campaign. When he organised a protest outside a local Anglo-Catholic church the Christian Evidence Society withdrew their support, but T.H. Bromley-Moore, a wealthy local merchant, financed the purchase of rooms over a shop, where Wise began to hold services and founded the anti-ritual British Protestant Union.

In personal terms Wise was unimpressive: short, stocky, be-whiskered and short-sighted. But he was energetic, a good organiser and administrator, a fluent public speaker, a shrewd political tactician and a perceptive opportunist with an intimate understanding of his constituency. For many in the Orange lodges he was McNeile come again (see Chapter Two). He took care to flatter the working-class element amongst his followers as representing the true spirit

[59] *Protestant Standard*, 2 July 1898
[60] *Protestant Standard*, 6 August 1898
[61] *Liverpool Daily Post*, 15 July 1873
[62] *Liverpool Courier*, 13 July 1885
[63] *Protestant Standard*, 8 August and 17 September 1898

Figure 6.1 George Wise. Self-educated polemicist, skilled organiser with an astute understanding of his constituency, founder of the Protestant Reformers' Church and the Protestant Party.
Source: LRO

THE LATE PASTOR WISE.

and values of their country. At an open-air meeting in July 1898 he praised 'the bona fide workingmen of England...'[64] for their opposition to ritualism. At another such event he made it clear that 'they wanted the press and the public to see that the people he was leading were nor "cornermen" but true, genuine, Protestant workmen, who were the mainstay, let it be noted, of their Protestant constitution'. One speaker warned it was possible some people might try to disrupt future plans by violence, in which case 'they looked to the Protestant workingmen to avenge their cause. (Loud cheers.)'[65] The faithful were warned they faced a vast conspiracy of ritualists working quietly in the dark and already far more extensive and influential than they realised. At a meeting of the evangelical Church Association in 1900 Archdeacon Taylor concluded melodramatically that in many churches '[t]hey had the mass, the confessional, and in fact essential Romanism'.[66]

---

[64] *Protestant Standard*, 2 July 1898
[65] *Protestant Standard*, 6 August 1898
[66] *Liverpool Courier*, 20 February 1900

By the early years of the twentieth century the controversy had generated a network of around 50 short-lived ultra-Protestant pressure groups.[67] They published a vast amount of literature in which they claimed to trace the secretive machinations of the Anglo-Catholic movement. The Liverpool version was The League of Latimer and Ridley, which appeared in 1902 and within a short time was producing a programme of regular meetings and the monthly *Protestant Searchlight*. In May, June and July 1902 it claimed to have outed '[l]ocal Clergy helping the Romeward movement in the National Church', listing names and churches and detailing links with ritualist fraternities.[68] They named 69 clergy, most certainly an exaggeration in a region noted for the relative weakness of the movement.[69] Particularly concerned at the spiritual threat to the royal family, in 1904 the League warned that a viscountess who had been a friend of Queen Victoria was a keen supporter of the Church Union.[70]

The anti-ritual movement also traded on traditional sexual innuendoes about Catholic clerical behaviour, particularly focused on the restoration of auricular confession.[71] Grand Lodge took up the issue as early as 1877, condemning 'a practice sinful and demoralizing...' and encouraging members who discovered clergy conducting it to 'report them to diocesan officials'.[72] That year a speaker at the Liverpool 12 July celebrations asked '[w]ould they submit to their daughters, their modest daughters, coming to him or any other person... to tell the secrets of their hearts (No, and cheers)... Would they allow their sons to go to confession?'[73] Some called on the government to 'suppress the anarchy and safeguard the moral character of our wives and children from the power of a servile priesthood',[74] convinced, like George Wise, that 'the men who would go to hell were the men who corrupted boys and women in the confessional box'.[75]

There were hints of darker practices. A favourite tactic was to hold meetings at which the main speaker was claimed to be a former Roman Catholic cleric. At a Liverpool gathering in March 1899 one such speaker suggested some high church clerics were secret Jesuits: 'of all people in the church of Rome the most cunning and diabolical...' and claimed there was a training college at which

---

[67] Machin, 'The last Victorian anti-ritualist campaign', p. 282

[68] *Protestant Searchlight*, 1 May: 7 names, 1 June: 15 names and 1 July, 1902

[69] Peter Toon and Michael Smout, *John Charles Ryle: Evangelical Archbishop* Cambridge: James Clark and Company, 1976

[70] *Protestant Searchlight*, 1 March 1904

[71] This is the confession of wrongdoing by an individual in private to a priest, requiring penitence, punishment and absolution

[72] Loyal Orange Institution of England Report 1877, p. 30

[73] *Liverpool Courier*, 13 July 1877

[74] *Protestant Standard*, 4 March 1899

[75] *Protestant Standard*, 2 February 1902

one Jesuit Father [is] so astute as to spy that he would go round the boys dormitories and hearing a boy speaking in sleep would softly join in the conversation and thus worm secrets out. If the sleeper was disturbed, the priest would pretend to cover him and say: 'Yes, my son, I thought you were getting cold.' (Laughter). This... is an art very much practised by Jesuits in their colleges.[76]

The reappearance of convents attracted particular ire. In 1869 Edward Harper, G.M. of the Loyal Orange Institution, visited Liverpool to lecture on Fenianism but took the opportunity to condemn ritualism and, to loud applause, urged 'throwing open of the Bastil[l]es where women called nuns, or spouses of Christ, were unlawfully confined to carry out the behests of the Romish priests'.[77] Another speaker was unable to resist some titillation when he

> produced certain items which he said were used for the chastisement and mortification of the nuns, one of which was a prickly chain... He then proceeded to read from a book in reference to the mortification of the nuns... and he produced the articles alluded to, including cats of nine... tails... having a significance which he could not name in the presence of a respectable meeting... The nuns not only whipped themselves but were whipped.[78]

Demands for legislation authorising inspection of convents became staple fare. In 1876 a former G.M., speaking at the Liverpool July demonstration, noted that a bill to this end had recently failed to pass Parliament, declaring to cheers: '[t]hese institutions were altogether illegal and therefore... pull them down...' and noting with approval that one MP had referred to them as 'nothing but brothels'.[79] Grand Lodge was regretting the lack of legislation as late as 1910.[80]

Some campaigners hinted that the entire Anglo-Catholic movement was in fact a cover for homosexuality. The allusions, tapping into the visceral homophobia so long a feature of British popular culture, were easily decoded by listeners. Legislation strengthening the law against male homosexuality was passed in 1885, Oscar Wilde was successfully prosecuted in a series of sensational trials in 1895 and the overall social climate had become decidedly more hostile.[81] The theme of 'perversion' constantly recurred in discussion of ritualism, as in 1905

---

[76] *Protestant Standard*, 4 March, 1899
[77] *Liverpool Courier*, 7 February 1869
[78] *Liverpool Courier*, 7 February 1869
[79] *Liverpool Courier*, 13 July 1876
[80] Loyal Orange Institution of England Report 1910, p. 15
[81] D. Hilliard, 'Unenglish and unmanly: Anglo-Catholicism and homosexuality', *Victorian Studies* 25,2, 1982, pp. 181–210

when Grand Lodge described supporters of ritualism as 'dangerous perverters of God's Truth...'[82] The use of elaborate clergy vestments came in for almost obsessive attention. At a public meeting on ritualism in Hope Hall, Liverpool in 1898, John Kensit senior, a militant anti-Catholic agitator, took up the theme when describing what he had witnessed during a service in a local church:

> [t]he officiating clergyman had on a lot of petticoats—(laughter). He knew the Roman Catholic name for them but as an Englishman he objected to use those names (cheers). Also, as a married man he objected to see men in petticoats. They wanted manly men as ministers of the gospel.[83]

The contrast was with the 'Protestant workingmen' of the city. Here, true masculinity, Protestantism and patriotism were conflated.

Tactics

As the Anglo-Catholic movement gradually found acceptance within the state church, attention increasingly turned to the possibilities of legal action. Prime Minister Disraeli, though proud of his Jewish cultural heritage, was nominally a member of the Church of England and happy to take communion at the local parish church when at Hughenden, his country home. Though caring nothing for theology or doctrine,[84] he was convinced that religion was a priceless social bond in support of the public good and valued the tolerant inclusiveness of the state church.[85] However, when the recently retired Gladstone came storming back in 1874, as terrible as ever on the rebound, and thunderously condemned a private bill to check ritualism,[86] Disraeli discerned a splendid opportunity to wrong-foot his opponent. Having modified the bill he championed its passage through the Commons, condemning high church communion as 'the mass in masquerade'.[87] The measure established a court in which action could be taken against a cleric employing unauthorised liturgy or ritual or implements in the conduct of services. The bishop retained the right to veto such proceedings.

The Act elevated Disraeli to hero status amongst ultra-Protestants and the Orange Order, not least in Liverpool, but as a check on 'ritualism' it was totally counter-productive. It was difficult to prove a case and even when successful

[82] Loyal Orange Institution of England Report 1905, p. 19
[83] *Protestant Standard*, 6 August 1898
[84] David Cesarani, *Disraeli: The Novel Politician* New Haven, CT: Yale University Press, 2016, pp. 162–79
[85] Douglas Hurd and Edward Young, *Disraeli, or Two Lives* London: Vintage, 2016, pp. 35–36
[86] Roy Jenkins, *Gladstone* London: Macmillan, 1996, pp. 383–84
[87] Robert Blake, *Disraeli* London: Eyre & Spottiswoode, 1967, pp. 506–07

punishment of guilty clergy attracted public sympathy. Liverpool was the scene of a famous, long-running case. In 1880 the city, previously part of Chester diocese, became a separate see. Disraeli, about to be replaced by Gladstone, hurried to appoint John Charles Ryle, deemed politically ideal in both secular and church terms, as first bishop. By the mid-1880s it has been estimated that there were nine Anglo-Catholic churches in the city. James Bell-Cox, curate and then vicar of St Margaret's, Toxteth, from 1869 to 1923, was the best known and liked, thanks to his tireless work in a notably deprived area. But in January 1885 a member of the congregation launched legal action. This triggered a 17-year legal saga that resulted in Bell-Cox serving 16 days in gaol, from which he emerged a hero to those who shared his outlook and viewed with sympathy by a general public quite unable to understand why a clergyman should be sent to prison for conducting a certain style of service. Ryle later regretted allowing the action to proceed.

Church authorities were repeatedly forced to return to the issue. Each year from 1899 there were unsuccessful Parliamentary efforts in bring in more effective bills. Conservative members for Liverpool were so regular in their support that these became known as the 'Liverpool church discipline bills'.[88] In 1906 the report of a Royal Commission on Ecclesiastical Discipline was equally ineffective, simply recommending a more tolerant and flexible interpretation of canon law, leaving most questions in a state of ambiguity and suggesting such matters should be reserved to ecclesiastical courts. But the Parliamentary route was still strongly supported in the Orange lodges. As late as 1908 Sons of the Boyne LOL 28 called on all local MPs 'to be in their places on July 14th to support Mr Charles McArthur MP [Liverpool Kirkdale] in his Church Disorders Bill'[89] and Ivy LOL 783 made a similar appeal,[90] but the bill was yet another failure.

In the ranks of the Liverpool Orange Lodges this strengthened a growing conviction that authorities in both church and state were dragging their feet over 'the errors and false doctrines which were been [sic] introduced...',[91] leading to a growing sense of 'the present crisis in our church...'[92] There was increasingly direct criticism of episcopal authority. In March 1899 Wise held a public meeting a short walk from Ryle's official residence, and alleged that the priest in charge of nearby St Catherine's Church in Abercromby Square was planning 'two distinctly Popish services practised within 20 yards of your own Palace, and yet it seems absolutely impossible to get you to act'.[93]

---

[88] Machin, 'The last Victorian anti-ritualist campaign', pp. 298–99
[89] Sons of the Boyne LOL 28 Minute Book 28 February 1908 LRO 306.ORA/6/1/1
[90] Ivy LOL 783, *100 Years of History*, February 1908, p. 7
[91] Everett LOL 108 Minute Book 18 May 1898 LRO 306.ORA/1/1/1
[92] Everett LOL 108 Minute Book 17 May 1899 LRO 306.ORA/1/1/2
[93] *Protestant Standard*, 4 March 1899

Exasperation now led to increasing militancy. The first visit of Wise to a ritualistic church seems to have been to St Thomas's, Warwick Street in mid-July 1898, when he sat quietly through the proceedings but at a subsequent open-air meeting condemned what he had seen.[94] He returned the following Sunday 'accompanied by a considerable number of Protestant workingmen...' Towards the end of the service he brandished a written protest; an effort was made to remove him but he was quickly surrounded by supporters:

> The uproar was terrific. Hats, sticks and umbrellas were waved about, people stood on the seats and chairs, and... for some minutes a perfect pandemonium prevailed... The floor was strewn with hymn-books and prayer-books, many chairs were overturned and in some cases broken... Nobody, however, was seriously hurt.

Wise and a colleague then addressed a crowd outside the church.[95] This established a pattern of direct action that drew increasingly large crowds and generated considerable publicity, confirming Wise as the most active champion of the anti-ritualist movement in the city.

It was becoming clear to the organisers of the campaign that ritualistic practices were slipping down the official agenda of the Church of England. At the local level it was also noticeable that, whilst the evangelical tradition was firmly established as the dominant form of churchmanship within the diocese, there was now a tendency for most clergy to distance themselves from Wise, his language and his methods. A prominent evangelical layman decried his open-air speeches as offensive 'to all who value the cause of true religion' and the future Archdeacon Madden condemned the violence associated with Wise's activities as mere 'brickbats and rowdyism... bastard Protestantism'.[96]

It was against this background that Wise took the decision to separate from the Church of England. A former Welsh Methodist church in Netherfield Road North was bought and reopened as the Protestant Reformers' Church on Christmas Day 1903 with Wise as pastor.[97] Within a short time it was the best attended place of worship in the city, 'making rapid strides and producing a powerful influence in the North-end...' Wise built up an intense pattern of activity. In addition to Sunday services there were weekday activities, both religious and secular. The best-known organisation was probably the Men's Bible

[94] *Protestant Standard*, 16 July 1898
[95] *Protestant Standard*, 23 July 1898
[96] John Bohstedt, 'More than one working class: Protestant and Catholic riots in Edwardian Liverpool', in Belchem, *Popular Politics, Riots and Labour*, chp. 8, pp. 204–05
[97] R.F. Henderson, *George Wise of Liverpool: Protestant Stalwart Twice Imprisoned for the Gospel's Sake* Privately published 1967

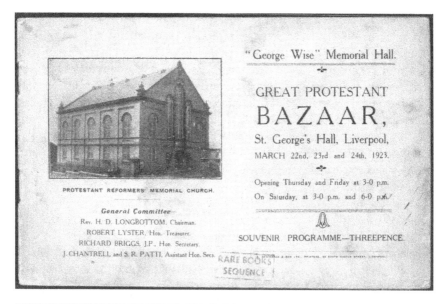

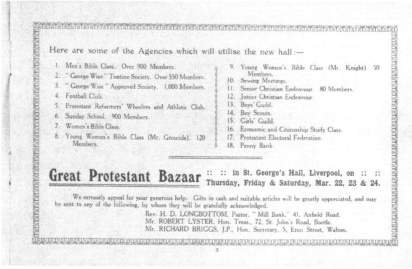

Figure 6.2   Protestant Reformers' Church bazaar 1923. The list of groups
underlines the intensity of activity centred on the church. Briggs was prominent
in the Royal Black Institution.
Source: *LRO*

Class, which had been founded in 1898. This paraded to and from the church and by 1909 was estimated to muster around 1,600 'almost entirely working men...'[98] and was claimed to be 'perhaps the largest Sunday afternoon gathering of men in Lancashire'.[99] There were bible classes, sewing groups for young girls, organised bands and what was claimed to be the largest cycling club in Liverpool.[100] Demonstrating an awareness of the problems within his largely working-class congregation, Wise founded a Boys Anti-Smoking League, a tontine society[101] and the Kirkdale Social Institute to support those who had problems with alcohol and gambling. For those who were actively involved the total effect was to bind the members into a close and intense pattern of fellowship and belonging deeply embedded in the locality.

Another response to what was regarded as the indifference of church authorities to 'ritualism' was to revert to all the ancient tropes, language and tactics of traditional, atavistic, anti-Catholicism, which in fact had never been far beneath the surface.[102] Public meetings became increasingly rowdy and violent fist fights began to break out as local Irish Catholics took offence. When Wise appeared before magistrates in May 1901, he was ordered to alter the venue of a planned meeting and at another hearing he was fined for conduct likely to lead to a breach of the peace. This served his purpose, as he took on the role of a martyr, championing not only Liverpool Protestantism but traditional British rights to freedom of speech and assembly.

In early 1902 the picture was complicated with the announcement that Kensit senior was planning a series of meetings in the city. Born in London into a working-class family in 1853, Kensit was utterly convinced that the ritualist movement was an existential threat aiming at the return of Roman Catholic hegemony. In 1889 he founded the Protestant Truth Society, which focused on the dissemination of literature, and subsequently the Wycliffe Preachers who held anti-ritual lectures, meetings and demonstrations. Adopting increasingly militant tactics, in January 1897 he interrupted the service to consecrate the new Bishop of London but his career as a publicist took off from April 1898 when his disruption of a service at an Anglo-Catholic church was followed by considerable disorder. In early 1900, with his family and the Wycliffe Preachers, he began a series of tours where they deployed similar tactics.

Kensit senior had visited the city and delivered lectures in 1898, when he and Wise had held a joint public meeting, but there is no indication that

[98] Neal, *Sectarian Violence*, p. 224
[99] *Protestant Searchlight*, 1 April 1904
[100] Neal, *Sectarian Violence*, p. 225
[101] Henderson, *George Wise*, p. 27
[102] Neal, *Sectarian Violence*, pp. 198, 202

Wise had invited or indeed welcomed him.[103] The new series of meetings was launched on 1 August 1902, the leading role being taken by John Kensit junior. Though nominally protests against Anglican ritualism they usually elided into anti-Catholic demonstrations and by early September counter-demonstrations and disruption by inflamed Irish Catholics were common. On 7 September fighting broke out and the following day Kensit junior appeared in court and, refusing a pledge to keep the peace and not hold any further meetings for twelve months, was sentenced to three months' prison.

It was a successful bid for martyr status. Wise probably realised his 1901 decision to modify his campaign made him seem faint-hearted and he set about orchestrating a series of increasingly noisy rallies and processions in Kensit's support, with the Orange lodges a notable presence.[104] Kensit senior came to Liverpool to conduct the final meeting of their campaign in Birkenhead on 25 September. This passed off peacefully, but when he and colleagues were about to board the ferry to Liverpool a heavy metal file was thrown, which struck Kensit on the head; he was rushed to hospital and died on 8 October. His son was immediately released by the Home Secretary. For Kensit's supporters he had been 'Faithful Unto Death… The First Protestant Martyr of the Twentieth Century'.[105] At the Liverpool memorial service a eulogist praised his campaigns against 'those reactionary principles which brought about degeneracy leading to apostasy and also to Mariolatry and idolatry'.[106] The Kensit organisation, now led by his son, continued to campaign in the south end of Liverpool, where it displaced Wise and his followers as the chief banner carriers of ultra-Protestantism.[107]

But for the rest of the city Wise was now the unchallenged champion of anti-ritualism, and what had long been implicit now came to the forefront, namely the fact that the anti-ritual campaign was simply tapping into historic, visceral, anti-Catholicism. On the day that Kensit died, Wise appeared in court and agreed to be bound over to good behaviour for six months. In the new year he announced plans to hold a series of public meetings at Everton's St Domingo Pit, a recreation ground that had become a traditional spot for Protestant open-air gatherings. At a court hearing on 20 March he was asked to give sureties and pledges of good behaviour for twelve months. He announced that in the interests of defending Protestantism and free speech he would go to prison, which he did on 8 April, proceeding to Walton gaol through thousands of cheering supporters. In the following weeks there was a series of sometimes rowdy public meetings and demonstrations, letters and petitions for his release

[103] Neal, *Sectarian Violence*, p. 207
[104] Neal, *Sectarian Violence*, pp. 209–11
[105] *Protestant Searchlight*, 1 November 1902
[106] *Protestant Searchlight*, 1 November 1902
[107] Neal, *Sectarian Violence*, pp. 225–26

were circulated and when he emerged on 5 June he was again greeted by large crowds. With martyr status now well established and much energy diverted into the Protestant Martyrs church and political matters discussed later, he was less active in the next few years. Outbreaks of conflict were fewer and more limited in scale, often little more than drunken fist fights.

But in 1908 it became clear that the fire still smouldered. The Roman Catholic hierarchy announced that later in the year there would be an International Eucharistic Congress in London and that it was planned to hold a ceremonial procession on 13 September with the consecrated host and robed clergy. Traditional Protestants angrily cited the 1829 Catholic Emancipation Act, which restricted such processions to the immediate grounds of Catholic churches. Wise and Louis Ewart, local leader of the Wycliffe Preachers and later Grand Lodge Secretary, held a large protest demonstration in Liverpool on 5 September and there were similar gatherings elsewhere. Following hurried consultations the procession did take place but the host was not carried,[108] though in subsequent months it was carried at Eucharistic processions in Manchester and Reading. When in early 1909 it was announced that the Liverpool Catholic parish of Holy Cross would hold a procession on 9 May to celebrate their 60th anniversary, rumours circulated that the host would be carried. Wise and local Orange leaders were quick to demand the procession be banned. A trouble-free procession was eventually held without the host and was a colourful event, with street decorations and shrines, clergy and lay orders in regalia, banners and statues carried and bands playing,[109] demonstrating the growing public confidence of the local Catholic community.[110]

But for traditional Protestants this was an example of the burgeoning threat from Rome, and a watchful edginess was further sharpened by the news that on the same day the host had been carried in a London procession. Consequently, the announcement that there would be another Catholic parish parade in the north end of the city roused Protestant ire. The Orange Order planned counter-demonstrations, and the police suggested to the clergy that images should not be carried and care be taken not to break the law. Some 600 police were put on standby, large crowds turned out from both communities, riots broke out, police charged the crowds and made arrests and the procession was drastically modified into a modest local affair. It was the opening phase of a summer of intense sectarian conflict. Churches and shops were attacked, fist fights were common, some 50

---

[108] Roy Jenkins, *Asquith* London: Fontana Collins, 1967, pp. 210–14; C. Devlin, 'The Eucharistic Procession of 1908: the dilemma of the Liberal government', *Church History: Studies in Christianity and Culture* 63,3, 1994, pp. 407–25

[109] Bohstedt, J., 'More than one working class', pp. 181–82

[110] T. Horwood, 'Public opinion and the 1910 Eucharistic Congress', *British Catholic History*, 25,1, 2000, pp. 120–32

schools in the north end were closed, people were attacked on the way to and from work and Protestants and Catholics who were a minority in their local district abandoned their homes, seeking refuge in areas of their own persuasion, sharpening the pattern of residential segregation.[111]

Though avoiding counter-demonstrations, Wise held meetings and parades at which he and his followers assailed both the Catholic church, its doctrines and followers and the local police, accusing the latter of ill treatment of Protestants and favouritism towards Catholics in the recent riots. So strongly did the Order feel about alleged mistreatment that the Province decreed a 1s. per head levy towards the legal expenses of members facing prosecution and 'suffering through the police brutality on Sunday 29th...'[112] It was decided to exclude juvenile members from the 12 July processions 'owing to the present disturbed state of the town'.[113] When Wise announced yet another parade over a sensitive route, he was arrested and ordered to keep the peace but refused, and was imprisoned for four months on 23 October. Again a vast crowd accompanied him to the prison gates. Once again there were demonstrations, petitions and localised outbreaks of sectarian violence. There were also demands for an inquiry into recent police behaviour and in November, in response to a request from the city council, the Police (Liverpool Inquiry) Act was passed. Wise was released on condition he would use his influence to calm community feelings and not organise open-air meetings. He agreed, though sailed close to the wind by holding church-based gatherings.[114] The Inquiry set up by the Act reported in March 1910. It cleared the police of charges of excessive force and showing partiality towards Roman Catholics and laid a good deal of blame on the activities of Wise and Orange Order processions and bands parading at historically sensitive times and places. Realising that the recurring riots had given the city an appalling reputation, there were tentative council discussions on legislative regulation of public gatherings.[115]

The final spur for reform was provided in 1911 when there was such a prolonged outbreak of violent industrial unrest that there were fears of anarchy and total social breakdown. Casual employment of a great part of the labour force meant that trade union organisation had progressed fitfully and was marked by locally organised 'unofficial' strikes and, given the long-lived popular tradition of rowdy parading and conflict, outbreaks of violence.[116] In 1911 industrial disputes originating with firemen and seamen escalated until the entire seaborne and

[111] Neal, *Sectarian Violence*, pp. 231–34

[112] Lady Stanley LLOL 97 Minute Book 7 July 1909 LRO 306.ORA/5/1/1

[113] No. 3 District Minute Book 26 June 1909 LRO 306.ORA/3/1/1

[114] Bohstedt, 'More than one working class', pp. 186–88; Neal, *Sectarian Violence*, pp. 235–38

[115] Neal, *Sectarian Violence*, p. 239

[116] Eric Taplin, 'False dawn of new unionism? Labour unrest in Liverpool, 1871–73', in Belchem, *Popular Politics, Riot and Labour*, chp. 6, pp. 135–59

land-based transport system in the city came to a halt.[117] Troops were deployed to move food supplies and the cruiser HMS *Antrim* was anchored in the Mersey. Mass rallies were held, the largest on 'Bloody' or 'Red Sunday' 13 August when 90,000 were present. Police and troops charged the crowds, over 200 people were injured, 1 constable died and 200 people were arrested. Sporadic rioting continued for two days. Though there were some signs of class solidarity at the funerals of two people shot when prison vans were attacked on 15 August, there was also sporadic sectarian fighting, opportunistic looting and local score-settling.[118]

The city was in a deeply disturbed, nervous state, vividly reflected in a meeting of No. 3 District who had received a letter from LOL 235

> to ask the District to call the attention of the Watch Committee to the fact that it had been unsafe for Protestant workmen to go through several streets off Scotland Road to or from their work and ask for more police protection in that district… after several of the brethren had voiced their feelings upon this subject it was thought that at this time it would be unwise to send the resolution as to the disturbed state of the city caused by the railway strike and general unrest.[119]

On 24 August there was a general return to work under a settlement that tended to favour the strikers.[120] Fears of revolutionary disorder finally moved local elites to address the long-running question of the use of the city's public spaces. Under government pressure local MPs T.P. O'Connor (Irish Nationalist, Scotland Road) and George Kyffin-Taylor (Conservative, Kirkdale), together with a Home Office advisor, were appointed to the Strike Conciliation Commission, the brief for which gradually widened to consider means of avoiding damaging civic conflicts. Lord Derby joined the group, adding his prestige and authority to its work; he served as Lord Mayor for 1911–12 and steered discussion towards closer regulation of public events. The result was the Liverpool Corporation Act of 1912 permitting the Council to endow the Watch Committee with the oversight of public meeting places, processions, carrying of emblems and weapons and the playing of music. It was the framework for all future public demonstrations in the city, including those of the Orange Order.

Wise was now the popular hero of Liverpool Orangeism. With an eye to

[117] Eric Taplin, *Near to Revolution: The Liverpool General Transport Strike of 1911* Liverpool: Liverpool University Press, 1994; P.J. Waller, *Democracy and Sectarianism: A Political and Social History of Liverpool 1868–1939* Liverpool: Liverpool University Press, 1981, pp. 252–58; Bohstedt, 'More than one working class', p. 212

[118] Neal, *Sectarian Violence*, p. 242

[119] No. 3 District Minute Book August 1911 LRO 306.ORA/3/1/1

[120] H.R. Hikins, 'The Liverpool transport strike, 1911', *Transactions of the Historic Society of Lancashire and Cheshire*, 113, 1961, pp. 169–95

School Board elections he had joined the Order in 1900. At the 12 July celebrations that year 'Bro. Geo. Wise, who wore his regalia, having been recently elected...' seconded a resolution and made a speech condemning government inaction over ritualism in the church.[121] In September he gave a lecture to Everett LOL 108, who were clearly impressed, and the following month members were encouraged to vote for him.[122] He subsequently served as a District Grand Master and Chaplain and was a regular speaker at the July rallies, most often supporting resolutions on ritualism. At Knowsley in July 1902 he expressed his growing dismay at both government and church policy on the issue and went on: 'taken as a whole he maintained that the bishops were not doing their duty...'[123] When observers condemned the procession for rowdy behaviour and anti-Catholic slogans, he wrote condemning '[t]he Shameful Attack on Orangemen', praised the work of total abstinence lodges and pointed out that his bible class was 'composed of many who are good, honourable and sober members of the various lodges of the district'.[124] His Protestant Reformers' Church regularly hosted lodge church parades. In 1904 it was noted with some smug satisfaction that '[t]he Orange Parade (Bootle District) to Pastor Wise's Church, on Sunday, Feb. 14th, was dignified and Christian, not a single Orangeman remained outside the building'.[125]

Lodges fully endorsed his outlook and tactics. In September 1908 Everett LOL 108 expressed thanks 'for the noble stance he took re the Eucharistic congress'.[126] Early the following year Ivy LOL 783 were clearly convinced that the procession planned by Holy Cross church would go through Protestant districts, their records stating that they had been asked 'to turn out in force to stop this procession. They and others (including a boatload from Belfast) did, and the procession was kept in its own area.'[127] Sons of the Boyne LOL 28 were equally convinced that the host would be carried and authorised a letter of protest to the Watch Committee.[128] When Wise was imprisoned the Secretary of Enniskillen No. 5 District sent him a letter of sympathy:

> In the Orange Order you have won golden opinions on account of your high administrative abilities... the brethren earnestly hope that you may be immediately restored to the sphere of your wonted activities to the great benefit of the whole of our Protestant friends.

[121] *Liverpool Courier*, 13 July 1900
[122] Everett LOL 108 Minute Book 19 September, 17 October 1900 LRO 306.ORA/1/1/2
[123] *Liverpool Courier*, 12 July 1902
[124] *Protestant Searchlight*, 1 August 1902
[125] *Protestant Searchlight*, 1 March 1904
[126] Everett LOL 108 Minute Book September 1908 LRO 306.ORA/1/1/5
[127] Ivy LOL 783, *100 Years of History*, p. 8
[128] Sons of the Boyne LOL 28 Minute Book 15 May 1909 LRO 306.ORA/6/1/1

The District also passed a resolution of support and sent a copy to the local press:

> we... place on record our unabated sympathy with Bro. Pastor G. Wise
> D.G.M.P.G.C. who through continued enforced imprisonment is prevented
> from attending our meetings, which is keenly felt by the Brethren and is
> it earnestly hoped that the Home Secretary will... sanction his immediate
> release and restore him to the sphere of his wonted activities to the great
> benefit of the Institution in general and the Church of which he is the
> beloved Pastor.[129]

No. 3 District was of the same mind, sending a letter in August when he was
first prosecuted and pledging to rally in sympathy outside Walton gaol.[130]

Wise died after a long illness in November 1917, probably through exhaustion
from his work in church and the political party he founded. It was noted that

> [t]he funeral procession to the cemetery was headed by representatives of
> Orange lodges, wearing their regalia... [who] wore their badges of office...
> there was a huge concourse of mourners, and crowds gathered at every
> point along the route. In the neighbourhood of Netherfield-road numerous
> places of business and shops were closed., and the blinds of private houses
> were drawn as a mark of respect to the dead pastor.[131]

Grand Secretary Ewart was amongst the mourners.

Conclusion

The significance of Protestantism as the defining feature of the Orange Order
is never in question and measures are taken to police and protect members
from meaningful contact with Roman Catholics and their beliefs and practices,
with expulsion as the ultimate sanction. But there have been stresses within
the Order, most vividly seen in the collision between the puritan tradition
and various aspects of traditional working lifestyle and behaviour. For some
members the rhythms of church activity and lodge life are mutually reinforcing,
but there have been traces of an ambiguous attitude towards clergy, some
acquiring heroic status, though the strong temperance principles of others were
resented. However, the Order was as one in opposition to the Anglo-Catholic
movement within the Church of England. Various tactics were employed, from

---

[129] Enniskillen No. 5 District Minute Book 10 November 1909 LRO 306.ORA/7/1/1
[130] No. 3 District Minute Book 15 August and 16 November 1909 LRO 306.ORA/3/1/1
[131] *Liverpool Courier*, 5 December 1917

legislation to direct action, sometimes sparking violent public disorder when the latent anti-Catholicism underlying the anti-ritual movement came to the fore. By the early twentieth century there was something of a distancing between established churches and Orange concerns, exemplified by the establishment of an independent church by the most notable local Protestant champion. However, when wider political concerns emerged, central to the origins and principles of the Order, solidarity was restored with the local Conservative party renewing its traditional alliance of convenience.

7

Politics: Local and Irish

Introduction

This chapter discusses the extent and nature of Orange Order involvement in the politics of Liverpool and Ireland from the 1860s onwards. Previous literature is discussed and lodge records, local newspapers and the publications of various ultra-Protestant publications examined to establish where the Order stood in relation to the pattern of party politics in the city and its enduring interest in Irish affairs.

Local politics

The exceptional nature of Liverpool has long been recognised, being described by one analyst as a 'devils' cocktail'.[1] The relative Liberal weakness in nineteenth-century Liverpool has attracted analysis and much effort has focused on the inability of the Labour Party to win the majority of the city's Parliamentary seats until 1945 and control of the city council until 1955. But the remarkable ability of the Conservative Party to attract a large section of the working-class vote well into the twentieth century and the role of the Orange Order have received relatively little scrutiny until recently.[2]

Comparison has been made with Glasgow, which also had a large Irish immigrant element and potential for sectarian polarisation, but where there was

---

[1] Paz, *Popular Anti-Catholicism*, p. 199; see also MacRaild, *Faith, Fraternity and Fighting*, p. 46; Joan Smith, 'Class, skill and sectarianism in Glasgow and Liverpool', in R.J. Morris (ed.), *Class, Power and Social Structure in British Nineteenth-Century Towns* Leicester: Leicester University Press, 1986, pp. 158–215

[2] Neal, *Sectarian Violence* and Waller, *Democracy and Sectarianism*, recognised the significance of the Order but lacked access to lodge records

a notable Liberal and later Labour hegemony.[3] It is argued that the two cities had contrasting histories of class relations and civic cultures.[4] Glasgow is seen as having a deep-seated culture of class antagonism dating from landlord–tenant relationships following land consolidation, enclosure and clearance. It is argued this fed neatly into classic Liberalism and later the socialism of the notably energetic Independent Labour Party, and was strong enough to hold embryonic sectarianism in check, though without eliminating it entirely.[5]

It is suggested Liverpool had two alternative traditions of 'commonsense' diverting the political loyalties of significant sections of the population into channels besides the Labour Party. One was Irish nationalism rooted in the long-established, Irish Catholic, dockside neighbourhoods dominated by the intense, parish-based, associational culture discussed in Chapter Two.[6] From the 1870s to the 1920s these elected 48 Irish Nationalist councillors and the MP T.P. O'Connor and, whilst living and working conditions were very relevant issues, a large portion of the Irish Catholic working class was diverted from the burgeoning Labour movement until Irish independence in 1921.[7] A second stream of 'commonsense' was provided by a local Conservative Party which constantly reinvented itself into one of the most successful urban electoral machines in British political history. The foundations had been laid in the 1830s and 1840s by Hugh McNeile, his associates and successors. Their fusion of patriotic royalism, ultra-Protestantism and apocalyptic anti-Catholicism created an ideology ideal for mobilisation of working-class Protestants, leading one observer to declare McNeile 'the real creator of the modern Conservative party'.[8]

Ideology was reinforced by institutional heritage, leadership style, organisational effectiveness and sheer pragmatism. The various anti-Catholic campaigns from the 1820s onwards generated ultra-Protestant protest groups, some ephemeral, others more enduring. Many, with 'Operative' or 'Workingmen' in their titles, specifically aimed to attract working-class men into Conservative

[3] Joan Smith, 'Labour tradition in Glasgow and Liverpool', *History Workshop Journal*, 17, 1984, pp. 2–53
[4] Smith, 'Labour tradition', p. 33
[5] Tom Gallagher, *Glasgow: The Uneasy Peace* Manchester: Manchester University Press, 1987; McFarland, *Protestants First*
[6] Belchem, J., 'The immigrant alternative: ethnic solidarity and sectarian mutuality among the Liverpool Irish during the nineteenth century' in O. Ashton, R. Fyson and S. Roberts (eds), *The Duty of Discontent: Essays for Dorothy Thompson* London: Mansell, 1995, chp. 11, pp. 231–50; R. Dye, 'Catholic protectionism or Irish nationalism? Religion and politics in Liverpool, 1829–1845', *Journal of British Studies*, 40,3, 2001, pp. 357–90
[7] Brady, *O'Connor and the Liverpool Irish.*
[8] Barbara Whittingham-Jones, *The Pedigree of Liverpool Politics: White, Orange and Green* (Liverpool: privately published, 1936), p. 34

ranks and always had a considerable Orange element in the membership.[9] The Liverpool Workingmen's' Protestant Reformation Society, formed in 1853, was still active in 1878. It was one element in the dense network of clubs and associations, often linked to local Conservative branches and deeply embedded in the Protestant working-class neighbourhoods of the city.

The Conservatives were also notable for a remarkable series of leaders who adopted an outlook combining Protestantism, flexibility, paternalism and inclusiveness. Samuel Holme founded the Liverpool Tradesmen's Conservative Association in the mid-1830s, recruiting amongst shopkeepers, merchants and tradesmen. Following adverse general election results in 1848, this morphed into the Constitutional Association, stressing encouragement of manufacturing and transport facilities and voter registration.[10] In 1868 the Workingmen's Conservative Association (WMCA) was formed and became the enduring workhorse of Liverpool Conservativism. It pitched its appeal to working-class Protestant men, stressing its aim 'to unite in maintaining Protestantism...'[11] alongside a lively social calendar. By 1914 it had 24 branches, approximately 8,000 members and had spawned a Junior Conservative Club.[12] In all its shapeshifting forms the Liverpool Conservative Party demonstrated a pragmatic ability to adjust to alterations in the franchise, constituency boundaries and social structure.

There was a conscious effort to generate an inclusive party ethos of convivial, earthy heartiness in an organisation where the working man was valued alongside the landed aristocrat and the wealthy businessman. In 1837 Viscount Sandon, the local Conservative MP, agreed to speak to the Lyceum, an organisation of merchants and engineers set up by Holme.[13] Almost 50 years later Sandon's son, also serving as the local MP, adopted the appropriate style at the 12 July procession of 1881. He welcomed the occasion: 'when good friends like ourselves meet together as we do to-day...', expressed thanks for Orange Order support and continued in flattering terms:

> You are a very important body of men. I know what you are by having met you in many a work yard, and in many a manufactory where busy men congregate. I know many of you are men in workshops, many of you are

---

[9] Wardle, 'Life and times', p. 110
[10] John Belchem, '"The church, the throne and the people: ships, colonies and commerce": popular Toryism in early Victorian Liverpool', *Transactions of the Historic Society of Lancashire and Cheshire*, 143, 1993, pp. 35–55
[11] Samuel Salvidge, *Salvidge of Liverpool: Behind the Political Scene 1890–1928* London: Hodder and Stoughton, 1934; the author is Sir Archibald's son
[12] Waller, *Sectarianism and Democracy*, pp. 17–18, 350; Bohstedt, 'More than one working class', p. 204
[13] Belchem, 'The church, the throne and the people', p. 42

headmen in manufactories. I know you are men who think for yourselves, weigh matters for yourselves, are watching for yourselves the course of events, and are accustomed to judge for yourselves.[14]

But it was recognised that it was also necessary for the MP to address the material living and working conditions of the population, especially as the franchise extended and the Labour Party appeared on the scene. This approach was championed by Archibald Salvidge, who became chair of the WMCA in 1892 and of the Constitutional Association from 1919, developing a leadership style unique in British cities, provoking comparisons with the 'boss' politics of Chicago and Boston, USA. Tough minded, autocratic, a skilled electioneer, he was well aware of the combined political appeal of patriotism, Protestantism and municipal works. Consequently, 'knowing the feeling of the workingmen of the city', he insisted on a fair wage clause in all corporation contracts,[15] thereby rendering Liverpool Conservatism a unique brand.[16] His successor Sir Thomas White, a member of the Orange Order, shared the management style but lacked Salvidge's political skills. The Liverpool Conservative Party was strong enough in popular appeal, organisational structure and leadership to weather internal stresses and maintain electoral success until the 1950s. In this respect it was much better placed than its competitors.

The Orange Order and local politics

Observers were convinced that Liverpool Conservative hegemony was down to the all-pervading influence of the Orange Order. When, in September 1907, the Conservatives won a by-election in staunchly working-class Kirkdale the rising Labour star Ramsay MacDonald remarked to Salvidge '[i]t is astonishing how in Liverpool, whatever the issue appears at the start, you always manage to mobilize the full force of Orangeism', to which Salvidge replied that he would prefer the term 'constitutionalism'.[17] The Order was the organisational expression of the deep-seated convictions of a considerable portion of the Liverpool Protestant working class, regularly performed in the colourful public

[14] *Liverpool Courier*, 13 July 1881
[15] Salvidge, *Salvidge of Liverpool*, pp. 45 and 35
[16] D. J. Dutton, 'Lancashire and the new unionism: the Unionist Party and the growth of popular politics 1906–14', *Transactions of the Historic Society of Lancashire and Cheshire*, 130, 1980, pp. 131–48; S. O'Leary, 'Re-thinking popular Conservativism in Liverpool: democracy and reform in the later nineteenth century', in M.J. Turner (ed.), *Reform and Reformers in Nineteenth Century Britain* Sunderland: Sunderland University Press, 2004, chp. 9, pp. 158–74; Smith, 'Class, skill and sectarianism', pp. 176–78
[17] Salvidge, *Salvidge of Liverpool*, p. 80.

demonstrations discussed in Chapters One and Three and carried into the political life of the city. However, it should be borne in mind that examination of the archive shows that municipal politics only occasionally surfaced at lodge meetings, which were generally taken up with the quite mundane business discussed in Chapters Three and Four. In the life of some lodges political matters seem never to have arisen. This is true for Cromwell LOL 94 between 1894 and 1905,[18] and for Kirkdale's Glory LLOL 80 from 1904 to 1923.[19] In the examples where political matters do surface this may reflect the interests of individual officers or lodge tradition.

For the Conservative Party the lodges were a handy pool of electoral resources. The frequent use of Orange Halls as election committee rooms and venues for fund-raising events has been noted. Candidates took care to visit lodges, reassure members of their Protestant credentials and request support. In October 1899 two local council candidates attended the lodge meeting of Everett LOL 108:

> Bro. Roberts... gave a very eloquent speech giving a very good account of his stewardship while representing the Dingle ward... and a large number of the brethren volunteered their services as workers for him in the forthcoming election. Bro. Killip... spoke in a very touching manner about his candidature for Brunswick ward... Provincial Grand Master Bro. Wilson... dwelt on the forthcoming Election pointing out... why we as protestents [sic] should rally round & give our help... as nothing but the return of Staunch Conservative protestents & Orangemen would ever gain our cause.

Roberts subsequently 'thanked the members of the lodge for the manner in which they worked for him at November election and said he knew full that his splendid majority was due to the Protestants for Toxteth & 108 members in particular'.[20] For the 1908 Board of Guardian elections one member 'offered the use of his Waggon for the speakers and a light conveyance to follow the procession'. The following year a member volunteered to go out with a band and deliver hand bills for the candidates and at the April meeting a member thanked lodge members 'most heartily for the splendid services they had rendered... in returning him at the head of the poll'.[21] Once elected, representatives were expected to champion Protestant concerns. At the meeting of Everett LOL 108 in March 1907 the W.M. urged members to support a fellow Orangeman, who replied 'giving us an idea

---

[18] Cromwell LOL 94 Minute Books 1894 to 1905 LRO 306.ORA/1/1/1/ and 1/1/2
[19] Kirkdale's Glory LLOL 80 Minute Books 1904 to 1923 LRO 306.ORA/4/1/1 and 4/1/2
[20] Everett LOL 108 Minute Book October and November 1899 LRO 306.ORA/1/1/2
[21] Everett LOL 108 Minute Book 19 March and 16 April 1902 LRO 306.ORA/1/1/2

of what occurs with the Guardians & exposing the Roman Catholics in their duties...'[22] Astonishment was expressed at a meeting of Duke of York No. 6 District in February 1956 when 'Bro. Wilkes pointed out the gravity of an R.A.P. brother voting Councillor O. Hare to become an Alderman... stating that as soon as the full facts were to hand, he would take suitable action'.[23]

The link between Conservativism and Orangeism persisted despite the ban on the Order in 1836. In July 1841 when lodges gathered for their now traditional dinners, speeches and toasts '[t]hey were joined by numbers of staunch and upright Conservatives who have never belonged to the Order',[24] but the relationship was not always harmonious. At a lodge dinner in a local Conservative hall in July 1845, reservations were expressed at Prime Minister Peel's 'expediency policy' on Maynooth College.[25] This was to be a recurring pattern. For the Order the relationship was conditional upon the Conservatives following what they regarded as a Protestant stance, meaning opposition to any policies that seemed to threaten erosion of the Protestant nature of the British constitution and established church. The result was the alternation of periods of close alliance whenever Liberals were in power, interspersed with exasperation when Conservative governments were deemed insufficiently Protestant. The strains are illustrated by the gathering in July 1862 when G.M. Harper, though describing himself as a Conservative, declared that when it came to defence of Protestant interests 'in the leaders of the Conservative party he regretted to find no... faithfulness'.[26]

With the election of Gladstone's Liberal government in 1868 the relationship was restored. In July 1869 Gladstone's proposal to disestablish the Irish Church was condemned at an evening rally and at the dinner of LOL 10 toasts included '[t]he Conservatives Peers and the Commons' and '[t]he Workingmen's Conservative Association'.[27] The Irish Land Act of August 1870 and abolition of religious tests at Oxford and Cambridge in 1871 confirmed the relationship. At a July 1873 rally the return of the sitting Conservative MP was urged and at the LOL 14 dinner the same evening Forwood, the Conservative leader, took the chair and a speaker urged support for the bible in education and opposition to ritualism in the Anglican church, declaring 'I don't anticipate any difficulty in obtaining the support of the Conservative party'.[28]

The relationship was cemented by Disraeli's Conservative government of 1874–80, when successive speeches and resolutions at the July rallies expressed delight with the Church Discipline Act discussed in Chapter Six. In 1875 the

[22] Everett LOL 108 Minute Book 20 March 1907 LRO 306.ORA/1/1/3
[23] Duke of York No. 6 District Minute Book 15 February 1956 LRO 306.ORA/13/1/2
[24] *Liverpool Courier*, 16 July 1841
[25] *Liverpool Courier*, 16 July 1845
[26] *Liverpool Courier*, 16 July 1862
[27] *Liverpool Courier*, 13 July 1869
[28] *Liverpool Daily Post*, 15 July 1873

G.M. noted that 'the Protestant succession to the Throne, as well as the social and moral well-being of the people is safer in the hands of the Conservative government...'[29] But the return of the Conservative government under Lord Salisbury in 1886 proved disappointing. At dinner with LOL 103 in July 1888 the District Secretary suggested that at election times members 'should not particularly consider the political opinions of candidates, but support the man who would pledge himself to uphold the traditions of the Orange Institution...'[30] Two years later a speaker urging support for the government found it necessary to remind listeners that Salisbury 'on a public platform had declared that he would support nothing but the true and right principles of Protestantism. (Cheers)... Such a statement removed any doubt there might have been about Lord Salisbury.'[31]

Aware of the disquiet, at the 1897 rally Salvidge reassured his hearers that:

> the association of which he had the honour to be chairman was in the closest possible affinity with the order to which they belonged. (applause)... the fundamental principles of the association were not only to be loyal to the Constitution and to their Queen, but also to protect their Established Protestant Church (applause)... it would be a very bad day for the Conservative Party when those who had those strong Protestant instincts were forced [to] become lukewarm to that party. (Applause).[32]

The following year the Liverpool Provincial Grand Master expressed unhappiness at the appointment of Anglo-Catholic bishops and argued '[t]hey must show the world that they were Protestants first and Conservatives afterwards'.[33] At a mass meeting against ritualism that evening Salvidge again reassured hearers that '[i]nterested as he was in one side of politics, he would not in the future move hand or foot for any candidate who would not pledge himself to maintain the Protestant character of the Church of England... the Roman Catholics must leave the Church of England (tumultuous cheers).'[34] But this was not enough to stem the rising undercurrent of discontent. A few months later, one ultra-Protestant outlet stated that '[m]odern Conservatism... has lost both the confidence and respect of the honourable, truth loving and loyal section of the Protestant community'.[35] In July 1899 '[s]everal of the speakers animadverted to the absence

---

[29] *Liverpool Courier*, 13 July 1875
[30] *Liverpool Courier*, 13 July 1888
[31] *Liverpool Courier*, 14 July 1890
[32] *Liverpool Daily Post*, 13 July 1897
[33] *Liverpool Echo*, 13 July 1898
[34] *Liverpool Daily Post*, 13 July 1898
[35] *Protestant Standard*, 10 September 1898

of members of Parliament and town councillors who used on former occasions to attend these demonstrations'.[36]

An independent Protestant political challenge was in the making. Having joined the Order, George Wise addressed the July 1900 rally, condemned Conservative Irish policy and ritualism, queried the religious views of Lord Salisbury and declared that sometimes an anti-Catholic Liberal MP would be preferable to a Conservative.[37] He was clearing the ground for his candidature in the School Board elections. Following his visit to Everett LOL 108 in September 1900 it was agreed the following month that £1 be donated to his campaign and a member 'hoped we would do all we could as he had been canvassing for a month and had got over 100 pledges for him'.[38] Wise, standing simply as 'Protestant', was swept to the head of the poll, with 107,063 votes, 'much greater than has ever before been registered for a candidate for the School Board ...'[39] He had successfully short-circuited the political system and demonstrated his vote-pulling power amongst the Protestant working class.[40] The extent of the growing dissatisfaction with the Conservatives surfaced at the annual meeting of Everett LOL 108 in April 1901 when a member even queried the position of the venerable Grand Secretary Touchstone. The Provincial Grand Master replied that 'he was only employed at election times by the Conservatives and payed [sic] by them for the work done...'[41]

Wise was the main speaker at the 1901 July demonstration, declaring '[h]e was not a Conservative first but an Orangeman—(applause)—Speaking of members of Parliament, he said that if they did not vote straight for the church and for the coronation oath they would throw them over'. Loud applause greeted another speaker who asserted 'the Conservative government had forfeited the confidence of the Orangemen'.[42] The language was increasingly colourful and personal. When in 1902 Victoria Total Abstinence LOL 724 celebrated the unfurling of a banner on which Wise was depicted the District G.M. commented on 'the Romish actions of the Cecil family... When the next general election took place he believed that Orangemen would know how to deal with such gentlemen...'[43]

The agitation over ritualism, Kensit senior's death in October 1902, the dispute over the use of public spaces for open-air meetings and the imprisonment of Wise in April fused the growing plethora of ultra-Protestant organisations. On 23 May 1903 at a meeting in Liverpool the National Protestant Electoral Federation

[36] *Liverpool Daily Post*, 13 July 1899
[37] *Liverpool Courier*, 13 July 1900
[38] Everett LOL 108 Minute Book 19 September and 17 October 1900 LRO 306.ORA/1/1/2
[39] *Liverpool Courier*, 17 November 1900
[40] *Liverpool Courier*, 16 November 1900
[41] Everett LOL 108 Minute Book 17 April 1901 LRO 306.ORA/1/1/2
[42] *Liverpool Courier*, 15 July 1901
[43] *Liverpool Courier*, 14 July 1902. 'Cecil' was the Salisbury family name

was founded with local Orangeman Thomas Massey as chairman. Presented as 'a crystillization [sic] from the great Protestant agitation in this city...',[44] the aim was to focus Protestant electoral support on candidates they regarded as 'sound' regardless of party political labels, vowing 'in view of common danger to cast their politics to the winds'.[45] The following month Conservative Charles Rutherford, whose brother was Lord Mayor, MP and future Grand Master of the Order, was defeated by a Liberal in a local government by-election, the Federation claiming this was because they had withheld their support.[46] A speaker at the July rally drove the point home, expressing dismay that 'the present so-called Conservative government, which they did so much to help into power, has grossly betrayed them... the ballot-box would tell what the Protestants of Lancashire really meant (Hear, hear)...'[47]

The November 1903 local elections displayed the electoral strength of militant Protestantism. Three of the four Protestant candidates were elected and the fourth defeated by a single vote. The Conservatives had lost two seats to Protestant insurgents and the Liberals one. Outside the town hall counting centre

> a crowd of nearly ten thousand persons gathered... several Protestant bands arrived and played lively airs... It was apparent from the cheers which were raised that there was a solid body of Protestants gathered... The success of Mr George Wise was received with tremendous cheers... in a few minutes after [his] result was known the bands marched away, taking a great proportion of the crowd with them...

Commentators heralded the new element on the Liverpool political landscape: '[u]ndoubtedly the great feature of the of the contests was the success which attended the efforts of Mr George Wise and his supporters'.[48] The Protestant insurgents made every effort to maintain the initiative. At the 12 July rally in 1904 a speaker proposed a resolution urging all members to vote 'on behalf of true Protestant candidates only...'[49] In November they gained another two seats, one commentator noting that '[t]he Protestant element... was a matter to be considered and in not a few cases they rather upset the calculations of the political parties, who have been accustomed to fight on purely party lines'.[50]

But by November 1905 there were signs of loss of momentum, with the Protestants losing one seat and drawing widespread condemnation for

44 *Protestant Searchlight*, 1 June 1903
45 *Protestant Searchlight*, 1 November 1903
46 *Protestant Searchlight*, I June 1903
47 *Liverpool Courier*, 14 July 1903
48 *Liverpool Courier*, 3 November 1903
49 *Liverpool Courier*, 16 July 1904
50 *Liverpool Courier*, 2 November 1904

the anti-semitism deployed against a Conservative candidate.[51] Conservative confidence was restored by a triumph in the 1906 local elections, Salvidge declaring '[h]e was proud that those he represented that night, the Conservative workingmen of Liverpool, had done their part'.[52] In subsequent local elections up to 1913 the Protestant Party narrowed their territorial focus, simply defending what they held. Electors were puzzled by their tactics as they switched support between candidates from election to election regardless of party, depending upon whether the candidate was deemed 'sound' on Protestant issues. The withdrawal of Wise from the City council, possibly to focus more on church affairs and the street campaign against ritualism, may also have weakened their impact. Salvidge rode out the Protestant insurgency by stressing his personal Protestant and anti-ritual credentials and those of the WMCA, and warning against disunity, though some local branches had to be purged of pro-Wise sympathisers.[53] The infighting was reflected within some lodges. Wise took care to cultivate his links with the Order. In September 1904 he offered to revisit Everett LOL 108 and 'give a lecture for the benefit of the lodge', though members were clearly conflicted. In May 1907 they agreed to support the Federation, but at the June meeting there was a move to rescind the minute of that decision, though this was defeated by 21 votes to 6. At the same meeting Wise 'received a hearty welcome [and] delivered a stirring address on Home rule, Education Bill & convent Inspection...'[54] LOL 108 continued to allow the WMCA to hire their hall but, as shown in Chapter 6, also sent their support to Wise when he was imprisoned in 1909.

Signs of reconciliation emerged when the Conservatives chose not to oppose a sitting Protestant councillor in 1907 and Wise endorsed the successful, ultra-Protestant, Conservative candidate for the Kirkdale Parliamentary by-election of 1910. The process is personified by the political trajectory of Robert Griffith, founder of The League of Latimer and Ridley and the *Protestant Searchlight*, which he also edited. An early supporter of the Electoral Federation and a Protestant Party member, he gave them generous publicity and twice stood unsuccessfully as a local election candidate. A keen Orangeman, he addressed the 1909 July demonstration.[55] At his funeral in February 1914 it was noted he was Chaplain of LOL 76, that 11 officers of the Order were present and that he was 'a prominent member of the Conservative Association'.[56] By then the Irish home rule crisis of 1910–14 was proving a potent unifying force in Liverpool Protestant ranks.

[51] *Liverpool Courier*, 2 November 1905; Waller, *Democracy and Sectarianism*, p. 213
[52] *Liverpool Courier*, 2 November 1906
[53] Waller, *Democracy and Sectarianism*, pp. 203–13; Salvidge, *Salvidge of Liverpool*, pp. 46–47
[54] Everett LOL 108 Minute Book 21 September 1904, 15 May 1907 LRO 306.ORA/1/1/3
[55] *Liverpool Courier*, 13 July 1909
[56] *Protestant Searchlight*, 1 December 1903; *Liverpool Courier*, 3 February 1914

In an effort to explain the extraordinary hold of Wise, his church and the Protestant Party on a significant section of the Liverpool Protestant working class it has been argued that he appealed on the basis of an ideology comprising defence of freedom of speech and conscience, social reform and temperance, populist insurgency and self-presentation as a martyr. However, this is a collection of causes rather than a coherent, analytical, ideological world view. Essentially he succeeded through a shrewd populist exploitation of traditional prejudices and anxieties, leavened by ad hoc efforts to address the everyday material concerns of his congregations and voters.[57] This was equally true of Harry Dixon Longbottom, who succeeded him as both church minister and party leader in August 1919. Fiery, energetic and combative, Longbottom was as anti-Catholic and ultra-Protestant as his predecessor, because, as he explained at the 12 July celebrations in 1925, he believed '[t]hey in Liverpool... were closer up against the Roman Catholic menace then they were in any other part of the country'.[58] He maintained the existing pattern of evangelistic services, bible classes, leisure-time activities and social improvement societies and was an active member of the Orange Order. The notable overlap in membership between the Orange lodges and church membership was personified by Richard Briggs who was both secretary of the Protestant Reformers' Church and a leading officer of the English chapter of the Black Institution.

But it is clear that novel political creeds were beginning to impinge on the awareness of lodge members. The inter-war period saw, on the left the rise of the Labour movement in the form of both the Labour Party and communism, and on the right the advent of fascism. Liverpool Labour Party had long battled against the appeal of Conservative ultra-Protestantism and Irish nationalism for significant elements of the working class, but by 1919 the party was able to win ten council seats and in March 1923 it gained its first Parliamentary seat in a by-election in Edge Hill constituency. Superficially, the disarray in nationalist ranks following the setting-up of the independent Irish Free State in 1922 benefited Labour as former Nationalist voters sought a new political home. Archbishop Keating sought to retain a distinctive Catholic voice by encouraging a Catholic Representation Association and some nationalists regrouped in a Catholic, later Centre, Party, but from August 1928 Keating's successor Richard Downey set a different course. Following discussion with party leaders he encouraged Catholics to take an active part in civic affairs but not in a confessional party, refused the use of 'Catholic' in a party label, forbade clergy to stand as candidates and banned the use of church property for party purposes.[59] In late

---

[57] Bohstedt, 'More than one working class', especially pp. 195–202
[58] *Liverpool Daily Post*, 14 July 1925
[59] Doyle, *Mitres and Missions*, pp. 208–12

1929 Labour took 5 Parliamentary seats, gained 13 council seats and recruited 5 former Centre Party councillors and aldermen.[60]

But the recruits brought with them their Catholic views on some public concerns.[61] They now formed the largest block within the Labour Party and held the safest seats. When the electoral tide flowed away from Labour they dominated the council party group, giving it a decidedly Catholic tinge. Moreover, given the presence of a notable left-wing element dominated by Jack and Bessie Braddock, there was bitter infighting. Two issues inflamed sectarian feeling and inflicted heavy electoral damage. The first arose when the Poor Law Guardians were abolished and the nine-acre site of the old workhouse on Brownlow Hill came on the market in March 1930. The council voted to accept a bid from Downey who saw it as an ideal site for a long-planned Catholic cathedral. This immediately drew heavy fire from ultra-Protestant elements, Longbottom declaring he would prefer a germ factory on the site. The council Labour group divided 37 to 21 against the sale, some members defecting to contest local elections as Independent Democratic Labour, resulting in heavy electoral losses, the deposing of the group leader at one point and, despite restoration of surface unity, faction fighting which simmered throughout the 1930s.

It resurfaced with sectarian overtones in the late 1930s over education, a traditional Catholic concern. The 1936 Education Act raised the school leaving age to 15 and authorised local authorities to provide grants of 50–75 per cent of the extra costs for the additional places. Most council and churches accepted the settlement but in Liverpool sectarian sentiments were reignited. The Conservatives opposed grants, doubtless with an eye to the Protestant Party's noisy campaign against 'Rome on the Rates'. Despite national party antipathy to faith schools the local Labour Party supported a 75 per cent grant. Downey set aside his normal reticence and in October 1937 wrote to one of his clergy:

> I appeal to the Catholics of this city, on this occasion, because of the peculiar peril in which we are placed... at the November elections to register their votes without fail against any candidate who supports the official policy of the Conservative Party of this city. I shall be grateful if you will kindly have this letter read from the pulpit at all Masses on the Sundays preceding the elections.[62]

[60] A. Shallice, 'Liverpool Labourism and Irish nationalism in the 1920s and 1930s', *Bulletin of the North West Labour History Society*, 8, 1981, pp. 19–28; Sam Davies, *Liverpool Labour* Keele: Keele University Press, 1990, pp. 114–15

[61] Belchem, *Irish, Catholic and Scouse*, pp. 295–96

[62] Metropolitan Cathedral Archives Series 2: Elections and Voter Representation: Municipal Elections, 15.10.1937.S21C; John Davies, '"Rome on the Rates", Archbishop Downey and the Catholic schools question 1929–39', *North West Catholic History*, 18, 1991, pp. 16–32

Figure 7.1 Liverpool
Province responding
to Archbishop
Downey's call for
Catholics to withhold
their vote from the
Conservatives in the
1937 local elections.
The result was a record
Conservative majority.
Source: LRO

ORANGE LODGES and R.C. GRANTS

The following resolution was passed by the executive committee of the Liverpool Province of the Loyal Orange Institution of England, at Orange Hall, Everton-road, Liverpool, on Tuesday, October 26th, 1937.

"This meeting having considered the challenge thrown down by Archbishop Downey on the question of a 75 per cent. grant to assist in the building and equipping of Roman Catholic senior schools in Liverpool, and his declaration to all Roman Catholics to vote against those who are pledged to give no grant for such a purpose, hereby **calls upon all members of the Orange Lodges in Liverpool to cast their votes on November 1st only for those Protestant and Conservative candidates who have definitely pledged themselves to a policy of ' No Grant.' "**

ORANGE MEN AND WOMEN! TAKE THE ADVICE OF YOUR LEADERS AND

Vote Only for Protestant & Conservative Candidates

ON MONDAY, NOVEMBER 1st.

Protestants reacted by rallying to the Conservatives, who gained a record council majority. This created an *impasse* with the national government which withheld funds because of council policy. Following legal opinion in May 1939 a scheme was accepted under which the local authority constructed 15 new schools which were to be leased to the Catholic church. While the council appointed staff the church had a veto on the appointment of heads and teachers of religious education.[63]

Despite internal troubles the political left was presenting a new challenge to traditional, Liverpool Protestant, working-class loyalties. This was recognised with the attempt to organise a Protestant alternative in the form of the Loyal

[63] John Davies, 'Sensible economy? Sectarian bigotry? The Liverpool Catholic schools question 1938–9', *Transactions of the Historic Society of Lancashire and Cheshire*, 155, 2006, pp. 85–120

British Patriotic Labour Party, which sent a speaker to address Kirkdale's Glory LLOL 80 in early 1920,[64] and a letter to Garston True Blues LOL 64 in 1922 appealing for recruits to help form 'a strong Protestant and Orange Party in Liverpool...' The lodge 'left to Brethren own discretion whether to join or not'.[65] In June 1920 a mass meeting was held in Sheil Park, partly in response to a recent May Day rally. Several Orange lodges in regalia attended the event, which was presided over by Richard Briggs, who declared their purpose was to demonstrate the patriotism and loyalty of Liverpool working men and proceeded to conflate Sinn Fein, Bolshevism, Irish nationalism and the Labour movement. The sense of unease was reflected in February 1922 when a member of Garston True Blues LOL 64 alleged that two Sinn Fein candidates were standing for election to the Board of Guardians and 'appealed to the brethren to bring every possible voter to the poll and keep the Sinn Fein out'.[66]

In 1925 the (male) Treasurer of Daughters of Victory LLOL 11 proposed a letter be sent to their local MP congratulating him 'on his notable stand against Bolshevism... and his ultimate victory against those who[se] aim and object is to destroy the freedom of our dear old country'.[67] These anxieties led to a resolution of Grand Lodge in 1924 which declared that 'any Member of the Loyal Orange Institution of England who shall knowingly vote or work for the return of any Roman Catholic or Communist Candidate at any Parliamentary, Municipal or other Public Election shall be deemed guilty of conduct unbecoming an Orangeman or Orangewoman'. Reminders were sent to all adult lodges.[68] A copy of a draft new Candidate's Proposal Form was considered and approved by Enniskillen No. 5 District at their meeting of 16 February 1928. It included the question '[a]re you a Socialist, Communist, or member of the Independent Labour Party?'[69] There was anxiety that schools were a target, leading to support for the idea that teachers be requested to state that they were not socialist or communist.[70] A visiting speaker at Garston True Blues LOL 64 in late October 1929 'gave [an] outline of the coming municipal elections & the peril of the

---

[64] Kirkdale's Glory LLOL 80 Minute Book 9 March 1920 LRO 306.ORA/4/1/2

[65] Garston True Blues LOL 64 Minute Book 1921–23, 22 May 1922; held at Heald Street Orange Hall, Garston

[66] Garston True Blues LOL 64 Minute Book 1921–23: 27 February 1922; held at Heald Street Orange Hall, Garston

[67] Daughters of Victory LLOL 11 Minute Book 17 September 1925 LRO 306.ORA/9/1/1

[68] Daughters of Victory LLOL 11 Minute Book 20 November 1924 LRO 306.ORA/9/1/1; a copy is taped into the Minute Book

[69] Enniskillen No. 5 District Minute Book 16 February 1928 LRO 306.ORA/7/1/1; copy of Proposal From enclosed

[70] Garston True Blues LOL 64 Minute Book 1927–29: 15 August 1927; held at Heald Street Orange Hall, Garston

Figure 7.2 The Reverend Harry Dixon Longbottom. Eventual successor to George Wise in church and party, energetic, combative, Lord Mayor 1950–51, Grand Master of England 1945–56, died 1962.
Source: Author's collection

The Most Worshipful Bro.
ALDERMAN THE REV. H. D. LONGBOTTOM
Grand Master

Labour party getting the town hall & appealed to the brethren to defeat the object in view'.[71]

Longbottom took pains to publicise the work of both the Electoral Federation and the Protestant Party via his church magazine. In the February 1922 issue there was a reminder of the forthcoming Board of Guardian elections, in March there was a discussion of 'Rome on the Board of Guardians' and in November items on the municipal elections.[72] At the July 1924 rally Longbottom took the opportunity to castigate political enemies old and new: 'I feel that not only in Ireland, but in England, sinister efforts are being made to capture civic control... the attempt had been made by the Irish Nationalists to control and use the Labour party

---

[71] Garston True Blues LOL 64, Minute Book 1927–29: 14 October 1929; held at Heald Street Orange Hall, Garston

[72] *Protestant Reformers Memorial Church Magazine 1920–22*, February 1922, March 1922, November 1922

for their own ends'.[73] Though he briefly held a council seat the Protestant Party made little further progress in the 1920s, largely confining itself to Netherfield and St Domingo wards where it was in contention with the Conservatives and occasionally Labour. In the 1930s party fortunes revived thanks to the controversies over the Catholic cathedral and the education question, and a rising tide of antipathy against Irish immigration. Longbottom gained a council seat in 1930, followed by his wife in 1932, and there were further gains in 1934, 1935 and 1936, reflecting an unofficial understanding that the Conservatives would not contest St Domingo or Netherfield. It also led Longbottom to test his strength at the Parliamentary level, standing for Kirkdale constituency at the elections of 1931, 1935 and 1945.[74]

The rise of European fascism provided an additional challenge. In Britain the Union Movement under the leadership of Sir Oswald Mosley adopted much of the provocative iconography, parading, anti-semitism and noisy violence of the continental movements and staged events in London and other cities, including Liverpool, leading to violent clashes with opponents and the police. In 1935 Grand Lodge reported '[t]he Council having heard a report from the Grand Secretary, agreed that no member of the Sir Oswald Mosley party of Blackshirts may be admitted as a member of the Loyal Orange Institution of England' and the Grand Secretary shared his concern that members were not fully equipped to contend with 'Roman and Anglo-Catholicism, Communism and various other isms as well as the various parties of the "Coloured Shirts"'.[75] When Lady Stanley LLOL 97 met in August 1935 the District Master 'informed the sisters that Grand Lodge had decided that no Sister who is a member of the Black Shirts can remain a member of the Institution'.[76] Following a fracas in Liverpool when a Blackshirt rally had been opposed by local Labour and communist supporters, Longbottom fell back on traditional tropes to argue that both communism and fascism arose from Catholic teaching and only a return to Protestantism could secure democracy and worldwide brotherhood, and argued the League of Nations was ineffective because it had 'long since passed into the hands of Jesuits who owe their powerful position in mischief-making to the colossal ignorance of British statesmen on the Roman question...'[77]

The fascist preoccupation with what they defined as 'race' helped to reignite a historic concern, namely the level of Irish immigration. As early as February 1916 Enniskillen No. 5 District had expressed fears over 'the importation of

---

[73] *Liverpool Courier*, 15 July 1924; Waller, *Democracy and Sectarianism*, p. 295
[74] Coming third on each occasion
[75] Loyal Orange Institution of England Report 1935, pp. 13 and 17
[76] Lady Stanley LLOL 97 Minute Book 16 August 1935 LRO 306.ORA/5/1/2
[77] *Protestant Times*, 18 October 1937: LCLAD 331.TRA 17/3

Irish farm labour into England'[78] and in the early 1930s a growing number of voices took up the issue.[79] Longbottom was early in the field, appealing in October 1937 for 'Protestant employers to employ Protestant men. Employing Irish increases YOUR rates. Willing Protestant men are waiting for jobs...' He dwelt at length on recent events in Chorley where at a Trades Council meeting it was alleged that drunken Irishmen working at the local munition works deserved imprisonment and deportation. He also claimed that 'women and girls in the town were afraid to go out at night...' and argued 'a warning should be given to the girls of the town... There recently has been an increase in the disease figures, and this could only be attributed to the number of men who had been imported to the district.'[80]

Public animosity was fuelled by an IRA campaign in British cities launched in January 1939.[81] Explosive devices were set off in public buildings, cinemas, hotels, railway stations and letter boxes. Following passage of the Prevention of Violence Act in July the police conducted sweeps through Irish neighbourhoods leading to a series of trials, imprisonments and deportations. In Liverpool there were explosions in February, March and July, caches of explosives were discovered, arrests made and the first deportations occurred in August.[82] Anti-Irish sentiment reached new heights in the city at a public meeting on 18 January. Prominent Conservatives took a leading role, despite claims to be 'non-sectarian and non-political...' Speakers argued Irish immigrants were given preference in allocation of employment and municipal housing and were exploiting the welfare system. One speaker deplored their 'low cultural development which did no good to the city' and was applauded when she expressed the hope 'that if the bombing outrages continued Liverpool would rise in a body and clear the Irish out'.[83]

Perhaps dismayed that the campaign was trespassing on his territory, Longbottom beat the sectarian drum the following Sunday when he argued

> [y]ou cannot handle this question unless you face up to Rome behind it... If you had wanted support for our statements that the menace is not only a civil one but a national one, we have had it in the bomb outrages of the last few days... If there was an appeal made to the loyal, patriotic unemployed,

[78] Enniskillen No. 5 District Minute Book 9 February 1916 LRO 306.ORA/7/1/1
[79] John Davies, 'Irish narratives: Labour in the 1930s', *Transactions of the Historic Society of Lancashire and Cheshire*, 148, 1999, pp. 31–62
[80] *Protestant Times*, 16 October 1937
[81] Dermot Keogh, *Twentieth-Century Ireland: Nation and State* Dublin: Gill and Macmillan, 1995, chp. 2: 'De Valera and Fianna Fail in power, 1932–39'
[82] *Liverpool Daily Post*, 4 August 1939
[83] *Liverpool Daily Post*, 19 January 1939

I think the old sectarian riots in Liverpool would be surpassed... [carefully adding] I, for one, would not readily be a party to it.[84]

The following month the organisers of the meeting launched the 'Irish Immigration Investigation Bureau', whose report in August unsurprisingly restated their original arguments. The authors could not resist using the IRA campaign as an argument for careful counting and close surveillance of the Irish in Britain and control of immigration by a passport system.[85] The IRA campaign finally petered out in early 1940, but by then public discussion of Irish affairs was overwhelmed by a world war which set a very different public agenda for the city.

By mid-century, though Longbottom was still trading in his ultra-views, he had become something of a 'grand old man' in some circles and this may have led to his election as Lord Mayor in 1950, and his service as Orange Grand Master of England from 1946 to 1956; but the relationship soured, he fell out with the Order and he was formally expelled in 1961, though the Order was well represented by members in full regalia at his funeral in March 1962. He was succeeded at the Protestant Reformers' Church by pastor George Mason, who became a member of Ivy LOL 783. Protestant Party leadership passed to Ronald Henderson, a keen evangelical and member of Ivy LOL, who had been elected a St Domingo ward councillor in 1961. By then the chronic tensions between dwindling finances and the historic puritan tradition were resurfacing and dividing the party from the Order. At the March 1967 meeting of Stuart McCoy Memorial LOL 2 it was reported that Province had 'lodged an application for a licence in the Provincial Hall and had applied for a brewery to come and view'. The lodge agreed to send 'a strong protest to the Province through the District against this'.[86] In Ivy LOL 783 'there was a fair bit of resistance...'[87] In December the application for a licence was refused, members who had opposed it at the court hearing were disciplined, with the expulsion of councillor Ronald Henderson and the resignation of his five fellow Protestant Party councillors in sympathy. In December 1967 the Province publicly distanced themselves from the Protestant Party. The Province did gain a licence, but the unhappiness lingered and at one point Stuart McCoy Memorial LOL 2 declared that 'they could not attend any meeting in the Provincial Orange Hall while there was a bar in it. All the members felt very strongly on the matter' and arrangements were made to meet in 'alternative premises'.[88]

The longevity of the Protestant Party in the north end of the city was

[84] *Liverpool Daily Post*, 23 January 1939
[85] Belchem, *Irish, Catholic and Scouse*, pp. 302–15
[86] Stuart McCoy Memorial LOL 2 Minute Book 13 March 1967 LRO 306.ORA//12/1
[87] Ivy LOL 783, *100 Years of History*, March, July, October 1967
[88] Stuart McCoy Memorial LOL 2 Minute Book 11 December 1967, 12 February 1968 LRO 306.ORA/12/1; letter from Liverpool Province to lodge 30 March 1968

attributable to its appeal to traditional fears and anxieties, reinforced in some cases by genuine religious conviction, but also by the intense social life based around the Protestant Reformers' Church and the local Orange lodges; plus the electoral truce with local Conservatives. It was certainly not derived from an analytical political world view, since Longbottom if anything had even less of a coherent ideology than Wise. His concerns were immediate, local and personal. He was well aware of the impact of alcohol and gambling on his overwhelmingly working-class congregation, his church magazine urging abstention because '[d]rink undermines the very foundation of life'.[89] But his response to such personal problems and to the wider ideological challenges of Irish republicanism, industrialisation, fascism and the burgeoning labour movement was to fall back on simplistic anti-Catholic tropes. Concern for 'our unemployed brethren' typified his narrow definition of the deserving. In late 1921 he set up

> a committee of loyalists... in order that the prospects of our men are not jeopardised by the action of revolutionary leaders in Liverpool... and also to raise a fund for the immediate relief of the more necessitous cases... we are proud to think that we have the confidence not only of our church members, but also of all patriotic citizens, and, not least, of the genuine unemployed.[90]

Fascist anti-semitism disturbed him. In the mid-1920s he was concerned that '[t]here are unhappy signs that an attempt is being made locally to create a strong anti-Jewish feeling'. Reminding his readers that Christ was a Jew, he recalled that Cromwell and William III had shown favour to the community and the Jews had supported the allies in the recent war. He conflated communism with Irish republicanism, arguing that 'Sinn Fein and Bolshevism joins hand in hand... What concord has Marxian Materialism with Romish priestcraft? This only, that in the main both are opposed to Britain and all that has made this country great.'[91] Underlying all such movements he discerned the old enemy:

> [t]here is, we admit, a sinister figure intriguing behind thrones and senates. A figure seeking the overthrow of the British Empire and stopping at nothing to attain that end. Using the assassin's dagger and the revolutionary bomb, but more often still, using the delicate weapon of diplomacy, and

---

[89] *Protestant Reformers Church Magazine*, 'Christianity and the menace of drink', September 1921 and 'The churches and gambling', May 1922
[90] *Protestant Reformers Church Magazine*, 'Our unemployed brethren', October 1921
[91] *Protestant Reformers Church Magazine*, 'Protestants and Liverpool extremists', June 1922

that figure is the black robed Jesuit. Before his devilry the atrocities of Bolshevist or Jew are but child's play.[92]

He argued that the divine transformation of the individual was the path to radical remaking of society, rather than violent revolution. He endorsed writings that condemned the materialism, alienation and class conflict flowing from industrial capitalism, but argued that change must be peaceful and for that to happen 'there must be a change of heart in all classes, a subordination of rival interests to the common good, a submission of industry, as of all other human activities, to the Kingdom of God as God's purpose of grace to all mankind'.[93]

By the mid-twentieth century a world view based on such arcane religious animosities had diminishing explanatory appeal for a public increasingly taken up with pressing material concerns. But there was an issue that could exert an atavistic pull on the Orange elements of the Protestant working class well into the second half of the twentieth century, namely Ireland.

The Liverpool Orange Order and Ireland

Given its origins it is hardly surprising that the Liverpool Orange Order has always had a special relationship with Ireland. This was constantly renewed by the many members who served there in the military, the ministrations of the Irish-born clergy discussed in Chapter Two and the transfer of Irish migrant members into the lodges. At a superficial level the link is reflected in titles such as 'Belfast Patriotic LOL 3' and 'Purple Daughters of Derry LOL 73'. In 1869 the significantly named 'County Down True Britons' LOL 847 carried a banner depicting William Johnston, independent Belfast MP and ardent Orangeman imprisoned for leading illegal 12 July processions.[94]

That special relationship was reinforced by the conviction that Ireland was the first line of defence for Protestant Britain and any weakening of the Irish Protestant position would be a precursor of events in Britain. This was the belief expounded in Liverpool by McNeile and colleagues appointed to Liverpool livings and perpetuated by the ethos they established. Daniel O'Connell's campaigns for Catholic emancipation in the 1820s and for repeal of the act of Union in the early 1840s, and the later home rule bills, fuelled this narrative. Consequently, when in 1868 the Gladstone government moved to disestablish the Church of Ireland, this was seen as another concession to Catholicism. At the Liverpool 12

[92] *Protestant Reformers Church Magazine*, 'Antisemitism', June 1925
[93] *Protestant Reformers Church Magazine*, 'Christianity and modern industrialisation', October 1923
[94] *Liverpool Courier*, 14 July 1868

July demonstration that year one banner carried the inscription '[t]he National Church of England and Ireland we will maintain and No Surrender'.[95] At Birkenhead the following year G.M. Harper deplored '[a] recreant government [who] have aimed a deadly blow at the national religion' and 'urged upon the Orangemen of Liverpool the importance of preparing for action...'[96]

Election of the Conservative government under Disraeli in 1874 and the church discipline bills discussed in Chapter Six brought great satisfaction, but by the early 1880s developments in Ireland again began to cause concern. The Irish nationalist movement was finding increasing confidence and organisational coherence under the leadership of Charles Stewart Parnell, who became chairman of the Home Rule Confederation of Great Britain in 1877, president of the Irish National Land League in October 1879 and chair of the Irish Parliamentary party in May 1880. Having already reached an understanding with the leaders of the Irish American community for a 'New Departure' involving a more disciplined Parliamentary party campaigning in militant fashion on the land question and home rule the result was an unprecedented concentration of Irish nationalist sentiment and Parliamentary power.[97]

The Land League embarked on a vigorous campaign for peasant ownership of land with mass meetings urging tenants to withhold rents and crops should landlords refuse to negotiate. If tenants were evicted from their holdings then the landlords, their agents and anyone who helped to harvest crops or occupied vacant holdings were to be socially ostracised. Running parallel with this was a clandestine nocturnal campaign of threats, cattle maiming, assault and arson. The most notable victims were Lord Erne on his Lough Mask estate in County Mayo and his agent Captain Charles Boycott, who had to rely on a contingent of Ulster Orangemen to take in the harvest under military protection, and bequeathed a new term to the English language.[98] The Order in England urged members 'to give practical proof of their sympathy with suffering Irish brethren...', and urged collection of money to be forwarded to Ireland. It was enormously proud of its role in the face of 'the most formidable scheme that has been adopted in modern times for driving Protestants out of Ireland... and as a consequence for separating Ireland from Great Britain'. There was particular satisfaction with the Liverpool reaction:

> Orange Relief Expedition—A notice having been given by the Orange leaders in Liverpool, that, owing to the difficulty experienced in some parts of Ireland in saving the crops, the aid was requested of Orangemen

---

[95] *Liverpool Courier*, 14 July 1868
[96] *Liverpool Courier*, 13 July 1869
[97] F.S.L. Lyons, *Charles Stewart Parnell* London: Fontana, 1977, pp. 79–83
[98] Bartlett, *Ireland: A History*, pp. 320–25

in Liverpool who might be willing to go on this mission of mercy... to help men... against whom a nefarious conspiracy existed. The original request was for only fifty men, but eight times that number at once responded, and sixty of these were at once dispatched... this undertaking... brought into bold relief the patriotic character of the Order, and shewed how in an emergency Orangemen could be relied on...[99]

At the July 1881 rally Lord Sandon MP applauded their response: '[a] more honourable course of action for the Orange body I cannot imagine than that which you have taken'.[100]

By July 1886 the Gladstone government had lost its home rule bill and suffered defeat in a general election, to the delight of those who gathered for the 12 July processions. Military language was to the fore; one speaker 'appealed to the Orangemen of Liverpool... to come forward manfully and do their duty in a noble manner' and Irish-born Grand Secretary Touchstone was certain that '[i]n the forefront of the fighting ranks would always be found the Orange brotherhood (Cheers). Let them close up their ranks... and if ever the emergency came let them stand by the old colours.'[101] In reaction to the recently defeated bill Irish unionists crystallised into a distinctive group in the House of Commons, led by the Orangeman Edward Saunderson. This moved Cromwell LOL 94 to adopt a resolution in April 1887 'that we the officers and members of this Lodge place every confidence in Colonel Saunderson M.P. for the noble manner in which he is speaking out for the loyalist cause in Ireland and against the severance of Ireland from the British empire...' The following year they donated £1 to 'the Johnston Ballykilbeg Redemption fund' for the notoriously impecunious member for South Belfast.[102]

The issue resurfaced with the election of another Gladstone government and the tabling of the second Home Rule Bill in February 1893. In April the Secretary of Everett LOL 108 'read a copy of a resolution from the G(rand) L(odge) condemning the Home rule bill & pledging ourselves to stand by our brethren in Ireland'.[103] The main speaker at the 12 July rally was Thomas Waring, G.M. of England and MP for North Down. Speaking to a resolution on the welfare of Irish loyalists he expressed some existential fears:

The grand question of the Home Rule scheme was the religious one... they believed that through Ireland England might be attacked successfully.

[99] Loyal Orange Institution of England Report 1881, pp. 14, 114
[100] *Liverpool Courier*, 13 July 1881
[101] *Liverpool Courier*, 13 July 1886; Alvin Jackson, *Colonel Edward Saunderson: Land and Loyalty in Victorian Ireland* Oxford: Clarendon Press, 1995
[102] Cromwell LOL 94 Minute Book 19 April 1887 and 18 September 1888 LRO 306. ORA/2/1/1
[103] Everett LOL 108 Minute Book 20 April 1893 LRO 306.ORA/1/1/1

Home Rule was desired by the Roman Catholic priesthood in order to make Ireland the place from which to attack the Protestantism of England... they might believe him that whatever was done in Ireland would come across the channel... with greater force.

Another speaker declared 'we solemnly pledge ourselves to render active assistance to our fellow Protestants and the Loyalists of the Sister Isle'.[104] With the defeat of the bill in the Lords in September and the election of successive Conservative governments from 1895 onwards the issue did not resurface until the advent of a Liberal administration in 1906. Their manifesto had vaguely committed merely to some form of eventual Irish self-government, but that was enough for some Orangemen. In August 1906 No. 3 District agreed to send a letter to the press supporting the opposition of the Irish Order to home rule,[105] and at a meeting of Everett LOL 108 in May 1907 a resolution was passed 'that we as a loyal body should give our brethren support in Ulster & that we send a resolution to the MP of this city'. When George Wise visited the following month, he included home rule in his 'stirring address'.[106]

Following the inconclusive general elections of 1910, the Liberals depended on Irish Nationalist and Labour support in the House of Commons and in April 1911 used this to replace the Lords' right of veto with delaying power. In April 1912 an Irish home rule bill was introduced in return for this Nationalist support. As it proceeded through Parliament it became one of the great issues of early-twentieth-century British politics and of increasing concern to the Liverpool Orange Order. At the July 1912 demonstration Touchstone, in his retiring address, moved a resolution expressing the Order's

determination by all legitimate means to oppose the passing of the Home Rule Bill and assuring its fellow Protestants of Ireland of its determination to stand by them in any action they might take and through any danger they might have to face... [declaring] he was not going to place their loyal, God-fearing, Empire-sustaining brethren in the North of Ireland under the thumb of the Roman Catholic church.[107]

The Ulster unionist leaders decided that there was a need for a peaceful, disciplined expression of popular feeling against home rule. This took the form of a 'Solemn League and Covenant' to be signed at a ceremony on 'Ulster Day', 28 September 1912, the unionist leader Sir Edward being the first to sign. Signatures

---

[104] *Liverpool Courier*, 13 July 1893
[105] No. 3 District Minute Book 20 November 1906 LRO 306.ORA/3/1/1
[106] Everett LOL 108 Minute Book 15 May and June 1907 LRO 306.ORA/1/1/3
[107] *Liverpool Courier*, 16 July 1912

Figure 7.3   Framed poster in Liverpool Province headquarters detailing Belfast
rally against Irish home rule in 1912.
Source: Courtesy Liverpool Province

were also collected in several cities in Great Britain, including Liverpool, where
copies of a British Covenant were available at premises in the city centre. Carson's
original intention was to leave Belfast the next day, passing through Liverpool
en route to London, but Salvidge perceived an opportunity and organised one of
the most spectacular political demonstrations in British history. Orange lodges
with banners and regalia, fireworks, music and patriotic songs generated a heady

atmosphere and local MP F.E. Smith became somewhat over-excited, promising that in the event of armed conflict between Ulster nationalists and unionists 'we will undertake to give you three ships that will take over 10,000 young men of Liverpool'.[108] The leaders subsequently reviewed a march-past in the city centre with Orange bands well to the fore,[109] and Ivy LOL 783 and Everett LOL 108 represented.[110]

Political tensions rose further with the foundation of the paramilitary Ulster Volunteer Force (UVF) in January 1913 and at the July events in Liverpool there was a decidedly militant edge to the speeches. The dominance of the home rule issue was underlined by '500 brethren of the City of Dublin... given the place of honour at the head of the procession...' A resolution pledged resistance to home rule and assured Irish Protestants of determination 'to stand loyally by them in any action they may take to take and through any danger they may have to face'. When Watson Rutherford suggested they might have to refight historic bloody battles he was greeted with 'cries of "And we will"'. The Irish Grand Master reassured them: 'It was not treason to refuse to forfeit their rights as subjects of the king and their privileges as members of the British Empire'.[111]

In February 1914 Liverpool District No. 3 endorsed a letter from a lodge urging 'Grand Lodge to move in way of helping our brethren in Ireland financially and otherwise in their efforts to resist the Home Rule Bill...'[112] In late April unionists smuggled 25,000 rifles and 3 million rounds of ammunition into Ulster and distributed them to UVF units amidst rumours that an Ulster provisional government would shortly be announced. By the July rally there was a widespread sense that the crisis was moving to a climax. A local MP informed the crowd that they would send a telegram assuring Carson that 'the men of Liverpool would stand by him and Ulster through thick and thin'. The rally resolved that if the home rule bill passed 'we shall hold ourselves justified in taking or supporting any action that may be effective to prevent it being put into operation...'[113] However, the First World War meant the rhetoric was not

---

[108] Montgomery Hyde, *Carson: The Life of Sir Edward Carson, Lord Carson of Duncairn* London, Constable, 1987, p. 323

[109] Daniel Jackson, '"Friends of the Union": Liverpool, Ulster and home rule 1910–1914', *Transactions of the Historic Society of Lancashire and Cheshire*, 152, 2003, pp. 101–32; Daniel Jackson and Don MacRaild, '"The conserving crowd": mass Unionist demonstrations in Liverpool and Tyneside, 1912–1913' in D.G. Boyce and A. O'Day (eds), *The Ulster Crisis, 1885–1921* Basingstoke: Palgrave, 2005, chp. 12, pp. 229–46

[110] Ivy LOL 783, *100 Years of History*, July 1912, p. 11; Everett LOL 108 Minute Book 18 September 1912 LRO 306.ORA/1/1/5

[111] *Liverpool Courier*, 14 July 1913

[112] No. 3 District Minute Book 17 February 1914 LRO 306.ORA/3/1/1

[113] *Liverpool Courier*, 14 July 1914

put to the test—the Home Rule Act was passed in September but suspended for the duration of the conflict.

With the general election of December 1918 and the advent of Sinn Fein as the main vehicle of a much more militant Irish nationalist movement the issue of Irish self-government returned to the agenda. Between January 1919 and July 1922 the IRA waged a guerrilla war in Ireland and in the cities of Britain. Liverpool was designated their No. 1 Area in Britain. Their Liverpool campaign opened in November 1920 with an arson campaign and £500,000 worth of damage to 34 warehouses, followed by attacks on road and rail links, outlying farms and ex-servicemen who had served in Ireland.[114] A truce was agreed in July 1921 and negotiations on a settlement began in London in October, though an element within the Conservative Party was deeply unhappy and the party conference in Liverpool in November 1921 was approached with some trepidation. However, Salvidge steered through a resolution supporting official policy and was believed to have saved the government from a damaging defeat.[115] The Anglo-Irish Treaty granting dominion status to the 26 counties of the Irish Free State was signed on 6 December 1921, but unhappiness lingered in some lodges. At a meeting in Dingle Orange Hall Longbottom claimed that 'we have roused the city...' and criticised Salvidge for his role.[116] A further meeting chaired by Provincial Grand Secretary Richard Briggs passed a resolution condemning 'the government's surrender to murderers and assassins, and further pledged itself to stand with Ulster, in whatever course she decided to take...'[117]

Once the government of Northern Ireland was established under the new Unionist Party leader and stalwart Orangeman Sir James Craig, the Liverpool lodges retained a keen interest in the affairs of the province. In October 1921 Garston True Blues LOL 64 agreed 'that a letter be sent to Bro. Craig... for the stand he is making in defence of our principles wishing him every success...'[118] In early February 1922 Briggs reported to Lady Stanley LLOL 97 on a recent visit to Belfast and 'spoke of our Orange Brethren in Ulster asking us to stand by them in their time of trouble & urged every member to give them every support possible'.[119] That same evening Old Swan Arch Purple Heroes LOL 810 and Ivy LOL 783 sent pro-Unionist resolutions to Downing Street.[120] Earlier that month

---

[114] Gerard Noonan, *The IRA in Britain, 1919–1923* Liverpool: Liverpool University Press, 2014, chp. 3, especially pp. 166–74

[115] *Liverpool Courier*, 8 December 1921; Salvidge, *Salvidge of Liverpool*, pp. 195–215

[116] *Protestant Reformers Memorial Church Magazine*, December 1921

[117] *Liverpool Courier*, 9 December 1921

[118] Garston True Blues LOL 64 Minute Book 1921–23: 24 October 1921; held at Heald Street Orange Hall, Garston

[119] Lady Stanley LLOL 97 Minute Book 8 February 1922 LRO 306.ORA/5/1/2

[120] Old Swan Arch Purple Heroes LOL 810 Minute Book 8 February 1922 LRO 306. ORA/8/1/1; Ivy LOL 783, *100 Years of History*, p. 15

the IRA had kidnapped 40 loyalists, including the County Grand Master of Tyrone. Garston True Blues LOL 64 Hall Committee had met to discuss catering arrangements but their chair 'proposed... that we write to Sir James Craig that this Committee... trust that he will use every means in his powers to obtain release of our brethren & loyalists who have been kidnapped & wish every success in your endeavours in the future'.[121] The victims were returned safely.

On 22 June 1922 the IRA assassinated Field Marshal Sir Henry Wilson, Unionist MP for North Down and former Chief of the Imperial General Staff. There was an angry public reaction, not least within the Orange Order. At a meeting of Liverpool District No. 3 the District Master

> spoke strongly against the action of our opponents the Sinn Fiens [sic] and the murder policy then engulfed in... it was resolved to send a telegram of sympathy to Lady Wilson and letters of protest to Speaker of the House of Commons, Sir J.S. Harmood Banner M.P. and the local press. The meeting then closed with Prayer.[122]

Garston True Blues LOL 64 also sent condolences, a member recalling army service under Wilson.[123]

The incident provoked angry reactions at a July demonstration at Knowsley Hall. Longbottom alleged that 'behind the Sinn Fein gunmen you have the mis-called spiritual power of an alien church...' while future Liverpool Conservative leader Thomas White described Wilson as 'one of the finest types of the British race we have ever possessed', declaring that the government now 'had got a sense of their responsibility towards Ulster, [due] to the solid stand which the Orange Order had taken'. A resolution pledging support for Craig declared that 'upon the preservation of the Order depends the future welfare of our homeland and the great Empire of which it forms a part'.[124] The following year the rally returned to Knowsley and 'a number of Loyalist refugees from southern Ireland were present on the platform' and a resolution proposed by White and Longbottom congratulated Craig and expressed particular sympathy with loyalists living in areas close to the Irish border.[125]

In early 1924 the part of the 1921 treaty that had left precise alignment of the Irish border to a Boundary Commission was activated. By mid-1924 three commissioners were collecting evidence on which to base their recommendations.

---

[121] Jonathan Bardon, *A History of Ulster* Belfast: Blackstaff Press, 1992, pp. 486–87

[122] No. 3 District Minute Book 23 June 1922 LRO 306.ORA/3/1/1; Banner was MP for Everton from 1905 to 1924

[123] Garston True Blues LOL 64 Minute Book 1921–23: 26 June 1922; held at Heald Street Orange Hall, Garston

[124] *Liverpool Courier*, 13 July 1922

[125] *Liverpool Courier*, 15 July 1924

Unease at the possible implications for the territorial integrity of Northern Ireland was simmering in the Liverpool lodges and a protest meeting was organised by Liverpool Province for 17 September. A meeting of No. 3 District was under way on the 16th when

> the members were greatly surprised by the entry of Bro. Charnock P.G.S. along with Bros J.F. Gordon and Wm. Grant MPs for Northern Ireland and they were given a rousing reception, and then we were treated to an excellent opportunity of having from our two brethren across the water some details of the experience that they were going through... at the hands of the Gunmen... and what they expected from the brethren of Liverpool to help them when the time came for deeds and not words... refreshments were handed round and a most successful meeting brought to a close.[126]

The visitors were the main speakers the following evening with Thomas White, Richard Briggs and Harry Dixon Longbottom present. White declared '[w]hether it was money or territory which the Free State desired from Ulster, they would never get a penny or an inch...' Gordon was equally adamant that, faced with drastic loss of territory to Northern Ireland, 'from this meeting we shall light a torch and carry it to the outposts of the Empire... We open our campaign in loyal Liverpool... I ask you to strike with the battleaxe of Liverpool such a blow as shall resound throughout the empire.'[127] He later claimed he had raised three battalions of the UVF in the city to oppose the commission.[128]

At the July procession the following year a resolution recorded 'determination on behalf of the Orangemen of England, never to allow any of Ulster's territory to be taken from her...'[129] By early November there was a first draft of the Commission report but on 7 November the Conservative *Morning Post* published leaked details together with a map of the changes to be recommended. They were quite minor, leaving Unionists well satisfied but bitterly disappointing nationalist hopes of an emasculated Northern Ireland being forced to join the Free State. The British and Irish governments agreed that the Commission report should be suppressed and the border left untouched in return for financial changes to the 1921 treaty in favour of the Free State.[130]

---

[126] No. 3 District Minute Book 16 September 1924 LRO 306.ORA/3/1/1. Gordon and Grant were both Orangemen, trade unionists and members of the Ulster Unionist Labour Association, formed to counter the appeal of Labour: John Harbinson, *The Ulster Unionist Party: Its Development and Organisation* Belfast: Blackstaff Press, 1973, pp. 67–69

[127] *Liverpool Post*, 18 September 1924

[128] Bardon, *A History of Ulster*, p. 506

[129] *Liverpool Daily Post*, 14 July 1925

[130] The Report was finally released on 1 January 1968: R. Lynch, 'The Boundary

From the mid-1920s until the late 1960s the politics of Northern Ireland rarely featured in British politics or the affairs of the Liverpool lodges, but informal social contacts between the Irish and British lodges continued. In February 1923 Enniskillen No. 5 District resumed the practice of authorising Belfast Patriotic LOL 3 to join the Belfast 12 July celebrations and subsequently agreed 'a letter of thanks be sent to the Belfast brethren for their kind reception and welcome to LOL No. 3...' In May 1927 they reciprocated when a Belfast contingent came to Liverpool.[131] In March 1948 Belfast Patriotic LOL 3 were informed that a convalescent member 'had gone over to Ireland for a rest'. On his return the W.M. welcomed him 'back in the lodge and said he had been of good service to us in his travels to and from Belfast...'[132] In January 1953 plans were made for a group from Liverpool Province to visit Belfast, the schedule involving breakfast in Belfast, a bus tour of the city, a visit to the Parliament building and then a train journey to join a Black Institution demonstration.[133] Such informal visiting built up strong personal bonds.

There was a brief flicker of concern over 'Operation Harvest', the IRA campaign of December 1956 to February 1962 in the border areas of Northern Ireland.[134] At its 1957 July meeting Grand Lodge passed a resolution from Liverpool Province that all Irish nationals resident in Britain who had been born after the declaration of an Irish republic in 1949 should either opt for British citizenship or face deportation. Members of Belfast Patriotic LOL 3 expressed concern at 'I.R.A. activities' at a meeting in October 1957,[135] and an indignant member of Stuart McCoy Memorial LOL 2 shared 'a handbill he had been given in Birmingham issued by the IRA asking for donations to buy arms etc. to help take over Northern Ireland...'[136] Once the campaign ended Irish political affairs vanished from lodge meetings. The election of L.P.S. Orr, South Down Unionist MP, as Grand Master of England from 1958 to 1961 may have been a gesture of solidarity with the Irish Order during the campaign.

Commission' in J. Crowley, D. O'Drisceoil and M. Murphy (eds), *Atlas of the Irish Revolution* Cork: Cork University Press, 2017, pp. 28–30

[131] Enniskillen No. 5 District Minute Book 10 May 1911, 14 May 1913, 19 May and 18 August 1927 LRO 306.ORA/7/1/1

[132] Belfast Patriotic LOL 5 Minute Book 24 March, 28 April, 24 May, 25 August 1949 LRO 306.ORA/11/1

[133] Garston True Blues LOL 64 Minute Book 1950–53: 12 January 1953; held at Heald Street Orange Hall, Garston

[134] J. Bowyer Bell, *The IRA 1968–2000: Analysis of a Secret Army* London: Frank Cass, 2000, pp. 289–336; Tim Pat Coogan, *The IRA* (London: Fontana, 1981), pp. 377–418; Richard English, *Armed Struggle: The History of the IRA* Oxford: Oxford University Press, 2004, pp. 73–75

[135] Belfast Patriotic LOL 3 Minute Book October 1957 LRO 306.ORA/11/1

[136] Stuart McCoy Memorial LOL 2 Minute Book 13 October 1957 LRO 306.ORA/12/1

Interest revived from 1968 following the disintegration of the Northern Irish state, growing military conflict between security forces and a resurgent IRA, and outbreaks of sectarian conflict in Londonderry and Belfast, where there were large-scale displacements of population.[137] The Grand Lodge of England made clear its sympathies with its Protestant brethren. In his address to the July 1970 annual gathering the G.M., a Liverpool lodge member, stated that 'I have been over to Belfast and had a meeting with the Grand Lodge Officers of Ireland and stated to them that we are behind them to a man, and if the time comes when they need physical help we will be with them'.[138] In January 1970 Liverpool Province launched a fund-raising campaign in aid of brethren in Northern Ireland with female members well to the fore, Ivy LOL 783 raising £4.20 in its first collection. The following month the lodge discussed a proposal from No. 7 District 'to house some juniors from Belfast'.[139] Provisional arrangements were made against the possibility of an influx of refugees, and a hall for their initial reception and members willing to accommodate them were identified.[140]

On 9 August 1971 internment without trial was introduced in Northern Ireland and security forces conducted raids into those urban areas where the paramilitary leadership cadres were believed to be embedded. Large-scale communal rioting erupted, with 35 violent deaths in August alone, 2,500 Catholics fleeing to camps in the Irish republic and 2,000 Protestants made homeless, the largest displacement of population in western Europe since 1945.[141] The provisional plans discussed by the Order in Liverpool were activated. A group with strong personal links to the Order in Belfast offered accommodation in Liverpool to children and parents until they felt it safe to return.[142] The first batch of about 80 children and 10 adults, travelling by overnight ferry, arrived in the city on 13 August, followed next day by a further 39 children and 18 adults. Initially they were received in the Orange Hall and social club on South Hill Road, Toxteth, where breakfast, clothing and medical care were provided by Order members, sympathisers and local social services. They were then taken to the homes of local Orange Order members. One member of Kirby Defenders

---

[137] Paul Bew, *Ireland; The Politics of Enmity 1789–2006* Oxford: Oxford University Press, 2007, pp. 489–513; Alvin Jackson, *Ireland 1798–1998* Oxford: Blackwell, 1999, pp. 366–77

[138] Loyal Orange Institution of England Report 1970, pp. 9 and 13

[139] Ivy LOL 783, *100 Years of History*, January 1970, p. 38

[140] Niall Gilmartin and Brendan Ciaran Browne, *Untold Journeys: Refugees and Forced Displacement in Northern Ireland's Troubles* Liverpool: Liverpool University Press, 2023, chp. 3: 'Evacuation, exile and resettlement'; I am much indebted to the authors for allowing me access to this material before publication

[141] Bew, *Ireland*, p. 503; Bardon, *History of Ulster*, p. 684

[142] *Belfast–Liverpool: The Refugees Crisis—1971: The Untold Story* Belfast: East Belfast Historical and Cultural Society: undated but probably 2014

Figure 7.4   Enduring connections. Mural in Canada Street, Belfast, commemo-
rating the Liverpool Orange Order taking in Protestant refugees from the Belfast
riots in August 1971.
Source: Author's collection

LOL 300 sent apologies for missing a lodge meeting on 13 August because he
was 'taking in two children from Belfast'.[143] It has been estimated that in all 800
evacuees were received and housed in Liverpool for a few weeks.[144] The report
of the Ladies' Grand Council in 1972 stated that 'this has bound us more closely
together. We are pledged, should the need ever arise again, to be ready within
twelve hours to meet any emergency, to give help and succour to our Brethren
and Sisters in Ulster', clearly indicating that the female lodges had been central
to the project.[145] Whilst this was the largest single project undertaken by the
English Grand Lodge in support of brethren in Northern Ireland, interest in
their welfare persisted and contacts persisted throughout 'the Troubles'.

  But for some Liverpool lodge members financial support and hospitality for
fellow members from Northern Ireland was not enough. In the early 1980s it
became clear that within some lodges there was an element sympathetic towards

[143] Kirby Defenders LOL 300 Minute Book 13 August 1971 LRO 306.ORA/16/1/2
[144] *Liverpool Echo*, 13 and 14 August 1971
[145] Loyal Orange Institution of England Report 1972: Report of the Ladies Grand
    Council, p. 26

the Protestant paramilitary defence groups that had taken root in some urban areas of Northern Ireland and this was exhibited by the display of distinctive flags in processions. When instructed not to do this they refused and the result was a split from which the Independent Orange Order emerged, leading to considerable animosity with the established Order. Some members of both groups argued the schism was a factor in the decline of the Order.[146]

Conclusion

Lodge meetings were dominated by the quite mundane matters common to all organisations; some lodge records contain no political material; political references in female lodges are usually raised by male officers and they are totally absent from juvenile lodge records. Given the origins and the royalist and loyalist outlook of the Order, and the apocalyptic anti-Catholic narrative established by McNeile, his associates and successors such as Wise and Longbottom, it is hardly surprising that the default political posture was to align with the Liverpool Conservatives. That party, for its part, was quick to realise the rich electoral returns from the relationship with the Order, providing a route into significant sections of the Protestant working class whilst the lodges provided a standing pool of workers during election campaigns. The combination of Protestantism, positive policies on housing and working conditions and the deliberate cultivation of an affable, socially inclusive management style by a succession of strong-minded political bosses, created a distinctive political machine yielding several generations of Conservative political hegemony.

But by the late nineteenth century there was growing exasperation in Orange ranks with the realisation that for the Conservatives this was a relationship of electoral convenience that could be side-lined when necessary. Dissatisfaction was reinforced by the tendency of the dominant evangelical element within Liverpool Anglicanism to distance themselves from the militant tactics increasingly deployed by populist anti-ritualist leaders. In the early twentieth century this resulted in the formation of the separatist Protestant Party and the Protestant Reformers' Church which, with its intense infrastructure of devotional, social and leisure-time activities, became a powerful force amongst the working-class Protestant population in the north end of the city, with notable overlap between church, party and Orange Order membership. The gradual development of a political *modus vivendi* with the Conservative Party enabled the Protestant

---

[146] Roberts, *Liverpool Sectarianism*, pp. 105–07

Party to linger until 1974 when it dissolved itself, advising members to support the Conservatives.[147]

Aside from the question of ritualism discussed in Chapter 6, the issue that could be relied upon to rouse grass-roots interest within the lodges was Ireland. The origins of the Order, the activities of generations of Irish clergy in the city, the iconography around the 12 July celebrations and the periodic eruption of Irish issues into the British political agenda proved capable of mobilising large numbers of members. However, following partition, the establishment of the independent Irish state and the Unionist-dominated regional parliament in Northern Ireland, the heat went out of the issue, though fraternal and personal relations were maintained. Within the lodges interest revived with the collapse of the Northern Ireland political state in the late 1960s and was demonstrated by the hospitality offered to refugees, but the broader political landscape was being transformed by deep-seated socio-economic and cultural shifts that increasingly challenged the relevance of many of the Order's fundamental beliefs and preoccupations.

[147] The Conservative government had reformed local government and instructed its local organisations that all seats should be contested

8

Facing Modern Times

Introduction

This chapter notes the decline in the strength and influence of the Orange Order in Liverpool as reflected in the shrinkage of the numbers participating in the 12 July celebrations and the gradual fall in the number of lodges. These developments are attributed to a mix of socio-economic and cultural shifts in British society as they impacted on Merseyside, socio-economic change specific to the Liverpool region and problems within the Order.

Numbers

Chapter One noted how, by the 1930s, the 12 July demonstrations were receiving much less attention in the local press and how those reports that did appear paid less attention to the admittedly rare political speeches and focused instead on the visual and performative impact of the event, with particular attention to the presence and dress of the female and juvenile lodges. It also showed how the strength of the processions in terms of numbers and time taken to pass a fixed point have always been difficult to estimate, thanks to the presence of supporters and spectators and the distractions of colour and music. Recent estimates based on analysis of newspapers and discussion with participants, suggest that a decline in strength was discernible from at least the early 1970s and a similar pattern has been noted in the number of lodges.[1] To some extent these developments reflected the impact of socio-economic change.

[1] Roberts, *Liverpool Sectarianism*, pp. 77–96; Appendix 3.1

Economic and social geography

Though dock-related work still dominated, the years 1918–39 saw the first signs of diversification of the local economy. This was partly in response to the notably high levels of local unemployment during the world depression of the late 1920s and early 1930s, which had provoked strenuous efforts by national and local government to attract new forms of economic activity. Several industrial estates were laid out in peripheral areas of the city and by the late 1930s these had attracted firms specialising in light engineering, food processing, vehicle components and, with the advent of rearmament, military equipment. By the mid-1950s the port had recovered a good deal of its trade, but employment was shrinking due to technological changes in the handling, storage and onward transport of goods. There was something of a second wave of growth and diversification which saw further expansion of the peripheral industrial estates, especially in the manufacture of tyres, sports equipment, chemicals, specialist metals and medical supplies and equipment. This was supplemented by the arrival of branch plants of multi-national enterprises specialising in vehicle components and car assembly. By the mid-1960s manufacturing had, for the first time, overtaken dock work as the most important single employer in the city, and the gender structure of the labour force had been transformed with unprecedented opportunities for women in the growing service and hospitality industries, clerical work, education, administration and health care.

But the economic storms of the 1970s and early 1980s that witnessed a process of 'deindustrialisation' in many Western economies hit the city particularly hard. Problems were exacerbated by the overall shift of British trade patterns from a focus on Atlantic and Commonwealth connections to linkages with the European Economic Community, favouring ports on the south and south-east coasts. Dock work shrank further with the decline of the cruise liner trade in favour of air travel and further mechanisation and containerisation of cargo handling. In addition multi-national industries closed branch plants, with a devastating impact on firms in the supply chains. Both male and female unemployment rose sharply, imposing severe strain on household economies.[2]

Development of the industrial estates was accompanied by large-scale changes in population geography. This was due to a mix of social change, as public and private transport enabled the development of the commuter belt, and shifts in public policy. Liverpool had long been notorious for massive housing problems and from the late nineteenth century the city council became

---

[2] Michael Parkinson, *Liverpool on the Brink: One City's Struggle against Government Cuts* Hermitage: Policy Journals, 1985, pp. 10–15; Pooley, 'Living in Liverpool', pp. 197–98, Table 3.1, p. 252; J. Murden, *City of Change*, chp. 6, pp. 402–09, 428–31

increasingly involved in addressing the problem. Some redevelopment took the form of clearance of existing problem areas and *in situ* replacement by modern housing, but there was also large-scale relocation of inner-city residents to peripheral housing estates. The process entered a new stage of municipal involvement in the 1930s and was resumed after 1945. The result was the development of large 'overspill' estates around the outlying areas of the city.[3]

This was the Liverpool equivalent of a nationwide process of renewal of the housing fabric of British cities, but it has been argued that it played a significant role in the decline of lodge numbers. Undoubtedly, the uprooting of people from neighbourhoods in which successive generations of their family had lived disrupted the dense networks of local organisations making up that intense associational culture that was such a key binding feature of working-class Liverpool life. Some, especially older, Orange Order members are convinced that the clearance and relocation of members to the outlying estates has played a role in the decline of membership. Some have even argued this influenced the decision by the Labour-dominated council of the 1950s under the leadership of Jack Braddock to redevelop the north end districts, so long an Orange Order and Protestant Party stronghold.[4] The strength of this conviction was illustrated in September 1958 when Labour Party leader Hugh Gaitskell came to open a new block of flats on Netherfield Road, named in honour of the Braddocks. A large part of the crowd were women waving lollipops in vivid orange wrappers who kept up a barrage of slogans and Orange songs, and leaflets were distributed bearing the significant heading 'A knife at the heart of Netherfield—Netherfield is being Romanised'.[5] In fact the policy of clearance was launched by the Conservatives and continued by successive Labour, Liberal and Liberal Democrat administrations.

Many more of those interviewed argued in very general terms that the Order's problems flowed from a lack of interest amongst young people. It can be argued that this partly reflects changes in the amount of leisure time available, and real increases in personal income and in the means of spending it. Real disposable income rose in Britain during the second half of the twentieth century, along with increased leisure time in the form of statutory holidays and shorter and more flexible working hours. Partly in response to these developments, there has been a radical commercialisation and professionalisation of the provision of leisure and entertainment facilities and their availability through the mass

---

[3] Pooley, 'Living in Liverpool', pp. 211–18; Murden, *City of Change*, pp. 395–97
[4] Day, 'Pride before a fall', pp. 277–78; Roberts, *Liverpool Sectarianism*, pp. 97–104 and Appendices 4.1 to 4.4, using a larger sample, argues this was a minority view largely confined to older members
[5] *Liverpool Post*, 23 September 1958

media of publishing, film, radio and television.[6] Consequently, the appeal of the lodge-based and church-based socials, and the accompanying dinners and amateur entertainment that traditionally have been central to so much of Orange lodge social life, have suffered by comparison. The availability of home-based entertainment through radio and television, especially with the advent of the video, computer and DVD and streaming services, have had a similar impact.

As discussed in Chapter Four, from its earliest days the Order generated a proliferation of mutual aid societies providing basic forms of insurance against unemployment, poverty, old age and funeral expenses. Originally based on individual lodges, from quite early on the challenge of organising, administering and overseeing them was a considerable burden and there was a gradual trend for these schemes to be devolved upwards to District, Province and in the case of support for widows and orphans, to Grand Lodge. This was one example of a deep-seated trend which saw the insurance industry progressively restructured, with the launch of National Insurance in 1911 and the increasing dominance of the industry by a small number of nationally organised firms, one of which, The Royal Liver Benefit Society, was administered from a striking building overlooking Liverpool pier head. The result was the loss of another key feature of local, lodge-based life, but additional cultural shifts were also under way.

Socio-cultural change

Lodge members were conscious that deep-seated changes within British society were challenging many of their foundational beliefs. This is reflected in dissatisfaction with the mass media, amounting to a conviction of deliberate ill-usage. What was regarded as relatively favourable treatment of the Catholic church drew particular censure. In February 1954 a member of Duke of York No. 6 District shared his concern at 'broadcasts and television studios repeatedly putting on masses & other R.C. propaganda' and the Secretary was instructed to write to the BBC.[7] The Grand Lodge Secretary praised their actions: 'I would like to report that a strong protest has been sent by all the adult lodges in Liverpool to the B.B.C. protesting against the recent television showing of the Roman Catholic High Mass and calling upon those in authority to see that no recurrence takes place'.[8]

This long-running sense of dismay was reinforced with the advent of commercial television and the emergence of regional companies. When Granada Television broadcast Mass in late 1960 Ivy LOL 783 'immediately sent a letter

[6] Pooley, 'Living in Liverpool', pp. 236–45
[7] Duke of York No. 6 District Minute Book 15 February 1954 LRO 306.ORA/13/1/2
[8] Loyal Orange Institution of England Report 1954, p. 16

to the District going on to the Province demanding that one of our services should be shown on tv to keep things fair; of course it never did happen'.[9] The press came in for their share of criticism. In June 1957 members of Garston True Blues LOL 64 were urged to cancel subscriptions to *The People* newspaper and a similar plea was made at Duke of York No. 6 District in August for reasons not specified.[10] At a meeting of Trevor LOL 820 on 5 November 1958 a member

> produced a copy of the *Daily Herald* showing the Pope on the front page and a photograph of the Queen opening Parliament on the inside page. He stated that he did not agree with this and thought it should have been the other way round. All members agreed with him and it was [agreed] that a letter goes to the District [requesting] something be done by them and the Province and also a letter should go to the *Daily Herald* complete with signatures of all persons willing to object.[11]

The local press was the target in November 1981 when LOL 24 wrote to District No. 3 complaining about the lack of coverage of recent Orange parades and demonstrations.[12] The order of precedence of monarch and pontiff caused concern at the highest level. In 1968 the Post Office produced a set of stamps portraying British cathedrals, and Grand Lodge expressed dismay that one stamp had displayed the recently consecrated Liverpool Catholic cathedral with the Queen's head alongside. It was agreed 'that a letter be sent to the Postmaster General pointing out the constitution of the land'.[13]

There was an awareness that traditional means of attracting younger people were under challenge. The availability of surplus cash and leisure time had led to the development of a youth culture in the late 1950s which generated distinctive tastes in dress, food, music and dance styles, all of which were quickly catered for by increasingly market-sensitive entertainment and leisure industries. Lodges struggled to address the challenge but compromised their efforts by narrow definitions of acceptable membership and ethos. When in February 1954 Garston True Blues LOL 64 discussed the possibility of launching new organisations for young people these were named 'Protestant Clubs' and all committee members were to be senior members of the lodge.[14] In early March 1957 Kirby Defenders LOL 300 decided to set up a significantly titled 'Protestant Martyrs Youth Club'.

[9] Ivy LOL 783, *100 Years of History*, p. 31
[10] Duke of York No. 6 District Minute Book 21 August 1957 LRO 306.ORA/13/1/2; Garston True Blues LOL 64 Minute Book 1956–61: June 1957; held at Heald Street Orange Hall, Garston
[11] Trevor LOL 820 Minute Book 5 November 1958 LRO 306.ORA/14/1/2
[12] No. 3 District Correspondence Book November 1981 LRO 306.ORA/3/4
[13] Loyal Orange Institution of England Report 1969, p. 9
[14] Garston True Blues LOL 64 Minute Book 1955–56: 8 December 1956; held at Heald

It was reported 70 girls and some young men from juvenile lodges were willing to join and 'it was hoped they would bring their friends who would eventually join the churches and lodges... Only Protestants to be allowed to join... ages 14–25'. Rules included regulations on church attendance. The club had clearly been opened by early April, when a member reported 'on the previous Wednesday Teddy Boys had been admitted in the club he asked if any Bros. would be present at the next club night'. It was reported that one session had been 'a troublesome night' with 'damage to the premises'.

Similar problems were encountered with use of the hall for dances. At a special meeting of the Hall Management Committee on 1 June recent events were outlined by a member, reporting:

> A large number of young men attended during the evening and everything appeared to be satisfactory until about 9 o'clock when fighting broke out... they continued to fight outside the hall. The police arrived to deal with them, one of the youths had to go to hospital for treatment... Owing to the frequent disorder outside the hall on Saturday evenings the people of the neighbourhood had decided to draw up a petition to have the hall closed for socials.

A committee member stressed the damage done to the reputation of the hall and suggested suspending its use for social events: '[i]f this could be done the people around would not be able to blame the Orangemen... It was very unfortunate that this should happen at this time, owing to the Sunday press also running us down.' The normal June meeting was informed of the proposals, particular note being taken of the bad language and the damage to the good name of the hall. Temporary closure was endorsed by 10 votes to 6.

An open meeting in August was attended by 67 people. It was remarked that there was a general decline in attendance at social events and church services and some older members expressed unhappiness with the 'rock and roll'-style music at the socials. On the youth club, it was argued that part of the problem arose from the lack of adult supervision and failure to enforce the rules requiring church attendance at least once per month. It was decided to recommend to District that the club should be for lodge members only, there should be instruction in the Protestant faith, 'also to have various classes and not all dancing' and that applicants be 'sound Protestants' vouched for by existing members. Only one member queried the value of restricting membership to existing lodge members. By late September the club had reopened with 36 members but by the following

Street Orange Hall, Garston; lack of further mention of this venture suggests it did not endure

March it is clear that problems had resurfaced, the church attendance rule was not being observed and in October 1958 the club was finally disbanded.[15]

Whilst there was a vague awareness of and unease at the social and cultural changes under way in British society, there was a deep lack of understanding of the rival distracting forces at work, especially amongst younger people, which meant the traditional preoccupations, language and ritual of the Order seemed quite incomprehensible and irrelevant to the next generation. Lodge members were simply unable to devise a format that would attract and hold the generality of the young people of the area. Decisions to restrict membership to 'true Protestants' and lodge members meant the clubs were largely duplicating the work of juvenile lodges.

The declining significance of religious belief and practice in British life did much to marginalise the Order. Reliable official data on national religious affiliation was not collected in the census of Great Britain until 2011, rendering temporal comparisons difficult. In 1851 the churches had made an effort to collect information on religious attendance. The results published in 1854 revealed that in Liverpool 45.2 per cent of the population attended of whom 40.7 per cent were Anglican, 32.5 per cent Catholic and 3.2 per cent Welsh Nonconformists. Whatever the deficiencies of the project in terms of organisation, execution and definition of religious observance, this is the only baseline from which to measure subsequent change.[16] The 2021 census recorded that 46.2 per cent of the British population described themselves as Christian, whilst in Liverpool the figure was 57.3 per cent. It should be borne in mind that the 1851 project had inquired about actual Sunday *attendance* whereas the 2021 census should probably be viewed as a question about *cultural affiliation* rather than serious religious conviction.[17] Study of Orange Order members has revealed a notably high level of church attendance and frequent citation of loyalty to Protestantism as the most significant reason for membership.[18]

This slow erosion of traditional religious loyalties and concerns was merely one outworking of a gradual redefinition of Britishness from a traditional Protestant essentialism towards a more inclusive religious and cultural pluralism. Ironically, a key feature of this process was the growth of that British empire in which the Orange Order took such pride. By the early twentieth century the empire was in fact no longer majority Christian, given the presence of large

[15] Kirby Defenders Orange Hall Management Committee Minute Book 5 and 19 March, 2 April, 28 May, 4 June, 11 June, 9 July, 20 August, 30 September 1957, 4 March, 9 September and 28 October 1958 LRO 306.ORA/16/1/1

[16] For an overview of some of the problems, see W.S.F. Pickering, 'The 1851 religious census—a useless experiment?', *British Journal of Sociology*, 18, 1967, pp. 382–407

[17] Office for National Statistics: 2021 Census of Religion in England and Wales

[18] Day, 'Pride before a fall?', pp. 280–81; precisely what respondents meant by 'Protestantism' would require further investigation

Hindu and Moslem populations in India and elsewhere. The imperial population had also come to include considerable numbers of Catholics as both subjects and administrators. Moreover, by the second half of the twentieth century the empire was gradually dissolving into a Commonwealth of independent states, most becoming republics.

The Order was aware of and dismayed by this growing religious pluralism. The meeting of Garston True Blues LOL 64 in August 1922 was informed that the forthcoming revised membership application form would include the question 'Are you a Spiritualist?' and that no spiritualist would be allowed to join 'owing to Spiritualists having no faith in the Bible while our Institution was founded on the Bible...'[19] Grand Lodge had ruled that 'members who are spiritualists must immediately withdraw from the Order, or they will be expelled'.[20] A long-term concern was the decline of Sunday observance by lodge members, provoking a Grand Lodge reminder of the discipline in its very first combined meeting in 1876—this was the first of a series of admonitions.[21] The redoubtable Grand Secretary Touchstone strove to set an example, one of his obituarists noting that in one year alone he had travelled 20,000 miles to address various gatherings 'but never on a Sunday'.[22]

The gradual relaxation of local authority by-laws on Sunday observance particularly dismayed some members. In 1896 Parliament gave the lead when it authorised Sunday opening of national museums and art galleries. In March 1922 Garston Rose of England LLOL 95 expressed its view of a proposal due to come before Liverpool council:

> At our Lodge Meeting of No. 6 District Rose of England Female Lodge No. 95 the following resolution was passed: That we members of the Loyal Orange Institution of England and electors of Garston Ward enter our very strongest protest against the movement afoot to open Lawn Tennis Groups, Parks & Gardens etc. after 2 o'clock on Sundays and call upon our Protestant City Councillors to defeat same as we believe it will be the means of a large number of our children being absent from Sunday School.[23]

But by the late 1940s there is some evidence that not all members were of the same mind. When the topic was raised by the W.M. of Stuart McCoy Memorial LOL 2 at the October 1949 lodge meeting 'a general debate took place and as

[19] Garston True Blues LOL 64 Minute Book 1921–23: 14 August 1922; held at Heald Street Orange Hall, Garston
[20] Loyal Orange Institution of England Report 1922, p. 27
[21] Loyal Orange Institution of England Report 1876, pp. 24–26
[22] Busteed, 'Irish Protestants in nineteenth century Manchester', p. 33
[23] Garston True Blues LOL 64 Minute Book 1921–23: 27 March 1922; held at Heald Street Orange Hall, Garston

one or two of the company became excited the W.M. declared the subject closed until the next meeting'. There is no evidence they returned to the subject.[24] In the early 1960s Ivy LOL 783 strongly opposed any further relaxation of Sunday restrictions on sport and commercial life, commending the work of the Lord's Day Observance Society.[25] The gradual revision of traditional Christian observances in state schools was also deplored. As early as 1906 Everett LOL 108 had expressed concern over the status of bibles in state schools and almost 80 years later a lodge informed District No. 3 that a new version of the Lord's Prayer was being taught to schoolchildren and suggested efforts should be made to discover which schools were responsible.[26]

The Order was particularly challenged by the fact that during the twentieth century relations between the various Christian traditions gradually evolved from animosity and suspicion towards peaceful coexistence, mutual toleration and respect. There was tentative exploration of acceptance of the validity of their respective clergy and governmental structures and exploration of intercommunion. This took institutional form with the establishment of the World Council of Churches in 1948, which included most of the main denominations but not the Roman Catholic Church, though Rome sends official observers to key meetings. In 1967 the Anglican and Catholic churches set up ARCIC, the Anglican-Roman Catholic International Commission, with a mandate to explore theological and doctrinal issues. The thaw in relations was accelerated by the election of the reformist Pope John XXIII in 1958. He launched the Second Vatican Council in October 1962, which concluded its affairs in October 1965. The result was not merely reform of aspects of Catholic ritual, liturgy and government, but a new sense of openness and acceptance in interchurch relations in 'the ecumenical movement'.

In Liverpool from the 1920s onwards there had been gradual shifts in the religious landscape. Within local Anglicanism the diocese retained its evangelical tradition, but the gradual distancing of evangelicalism from ultra-Protestant anti-Catholic polemics that had provoked the Wiseite schisms continued. The agitation against 'ritualism' faded and protests against Anglo-Catholic practices became increasingly low-key. A public meeting in 1924 protesting against the introduction of altar candles and observation of the 'eastward position' in cathedral services by the Anglican Bishop David produced threats of 'gigantic protest under the shadow of the cathedral itself...' but there was no follow-up.[27] Similarly when a Bootle street preacher launched a bitter condemnation of

[24] Stuart McCoy Memorial LOL 2 Minute Book 10 October 1949 LRO 306.ORA/12/1
[25] Ivy LOL 783, *100 Years of History*, p. 34
[26] Everett LOL 108 Signing In Book 20 January 1906 LRO 306.ORA/1/2/1; No. 3 District Correspondence Book August 1982 LRO 306.ORA/3/4
[27] *Liverpool Courier*, 19 February 1924

Catholicism and was in danger of assault by hearers he was arrested and bound over, with no public reaction.[28]

When in September 1962 Toxteth True Blues LOL 548 expressed their disquiet at the form of services at St Margaret's, Toxteth, formerly Bell-Cox's church, they did so with a letter in which the lodge Secretary explained:

> I am instructed by [the lodge] to protest most strongly to the practises [sic] being carried out in your church and school. You all know as well as we that all services in the Church of England are governed by the Book of Common Prayer and the Bible. It is quite obvious that these are being violated and we feel that too many sacrifices have been made in the past to let this matter go. Surely you are not going to let this continue as Good Church of England people which you must be.[29]

Clearly traditional animosity lingered in some of the grass roots. In early 1950 Ivy LOL 783 expressed unhappiness at a very public display of Catholic piety. 'It had been noted by several brethren that several players... were blessing themselves, using the sign of the cross before matches and would ask them to cease please. Unfortunately no record of response from the boys in Blue [Everton FC] is recorded.'[30] In 1958 Archbishop Heenan was stoned by a rowdy Protestant crowd as he went to pay a pastoral visit to a member of St Anthony's parish living off Scotland Road. The incident was universally condemned and when a Catholic church building was vandalised the members of Sons of Victory LOL 80 agreed to send a letter to their District inquiring 'why the officers concerned with press arrangements had not informed the local press that the L.O.I.E had nothing to do with the daubing'.[31] But there were those who, whilst deploring such incidents, were deeply uneasy about the ecumenical movement, which they felt was compromising distinctive Protestant principles and preparing for eventual reunification with the Catholic church and restoration of papal hegemony. Consequently, Protestant church leaders who took part in ecumenical events such as the Week of Prayer for Christian Unity, or discussions with Catholics, and invited Catholics to preach in their churches were regarded with deep suspicion and sometimes subjected to vigorous denunciation in print.

This unease was strongly reflected in the Orange lodges. At the Garston True

---

[28] *Liverpool Echo*, 6 January 1939
[29] Toxteth True Blues LOL 548 to St Margaret's parochial church council secretary, 28 September 1962; I would like to thank Paul Young for gifting me a copy of this letter
[30] Ivy LOL 783, *100 Years of History*, p. 28; Roberts, *Liverpool Sectarianism*, chp. 9: 'Everton and Liverpool Football Clubs: New Gods' for the argument that sporting affiliations and symbols have replaced religious loyalties and sectarianism
[31] Sons of Victory LOL 80 Minute Book 6 August 1967 LRO 306.ORA/18/1/1

Blues LOL 64 meeting in November 1958 the Chaplain noted the election of Pope John XXIII and proceeded to read from the New Testament, 2 Timothy, chapter 3 on the correct qualities of character and behaviour to be sought in ecclesiastical leaders.[32] Early the following year Ivy LOL 783 noted that an interdenominational group of European Protestant churches of various traditions was meeting in Scotland, a gathering that led to the formal establishment of the Conference of European Churches the following year. The lodge sent letters of protest, since, although the Catholic church was not a member, they were convinced that 'as usual they were not far away...', noted the conference's relationship with the European Catholic bishops' conference and concluded 'as usual the main churches seem resolute in their movement away from Luther and towards Rome...'[33] The same feeling surfaced in Garston True Blues LOL 64 in the early 1960s when the lodge Secretary was authorised to meet the vicar of the local parish church to hear his views on the question of church unity–the Secretary reported back that the discussion had been satisfactory. The question returned to their agenda in 1977 when '[a]fter years of supporting the local Church and School the Lodge seriously debated this relationship, due to the church's approach to the subject of unity'. There was a suggestion that they should cease to parade to the church 'but the argument that it was our church and not the Vicar's won the day'.[34] In late 1968 Sons of Victory LOL 80 rejected one church as 'not acceptable' as a host for church parades 'owing to ecumenical talks and being in sympathy with same'. The lodge Secretary admitted he faced personal problems in choice of a church, noting that 'churches in Kirby seemed to be ecumenically minded concerning Roman Catholicism and although a regular church attender when residing in Liverpool [he] did not feel inclined to attend churches in Kirby on account of this ecumenism'.[35]

The arrival in 1975 of Anglican Bishop David Sheppard and in 1976 of Catholic Archbishop Derek Worlock created a challenge for the Order. Building on local ecumenical initiatives that had quietly taken root in previous decades, they developed a warm, cooperative rapport which became close personal friendship.[36] The two were notable not only for participation in each other's services but their joint interventions in the affairs of what in the late 1970s and well into the 1980s was a deeply troubled city.[37] The toxic mix of city problems stemmed

[32] Garston True Blues LOL 64 Minute Book 1956–61: 10 November 1958; held at Heald Street Orange Hall, Garston

[33] Ivy LOL 783, *100 Years of History*, p. 30

[34] *A Glimpse into 125 Years*, pp. 19, 21

[35] Sons of Victory LOL 80 Minute Book 1 December and 2 June 1969 LRO 306. ORA/18/1/1

[36] Andrew Bradstock, *David Sheppard: Batting for the Poor* (London: SPCK, 2019)

[37] Maria Power, 'In pursuit of the common good: David Sheppard and Derek Worlock and the 1981 Toxteth riots', *Crucible: The Christian Journal of Social Ethics*, July

from the economic decline discussed earlier, and included three days of rioting in the deeply deprived Toxteth area in July 1981, considerable political turbulence culminating in the election of a notably leftist Labour Council in 1983 dominated by the Trotskyite Militant element and several years of bruising confrontation with the Conservative government led by Margaret Thatcher.[38]

The remarkable partnership drew much generally appreciative comment, but for the Orange Order it constituted not only a challenge to their traditional beliefs, but deeply unfortunate timing. The schism over displaying sympathies with Ulster Protestant paramilitaries in the early 1980s weakened the Order, not so much through loss of members, but because of the adverse publicity it generated, along with the general impression in the public mind that the entire Order was somehow suspect. But much more adverse publicity arose from a long-running dispute with the Anglican cathedral. The relationship between the Order and the cathedral had been variable. From the earliest days some elements within traditional Protestant ranks had been suspicious of the cathedral project, fearing that services would be dominated by Anglo-Catholic ritual and liturgy. In 1902, before the first sod was turned, that ardent Protestant Party stalwart and Orangeman Robert Griffith had discerned danger, citing reports that 'some of the designs for the Liverpool Cathedral exhibited at the Walker Art Gallery are intended for Roman Catholic chapels'. In 1904, when construction began, he penned a polemic arguing that the current trend in favour of Anglican cathedrals was a symptom of the maturing of the Anglo-Catholic movement, that one recently completed example had become 'a gigantic mass-house... a relic of the Romish dark ages...', stressing it was significant that the design chosen was by the Catholic Gilbert Scott and claiming that 'the tools of Rome—the "altar", candlesticks and Pastoral staff itself have already arrived'.[39] Longbottom took up the theme in 1924 with a petition 'against the ritualistic practices at the Cathedral'.[40]

Yet there was an ambivalence at the heart of this attitude. By 1930 Ivy LOL 783 was encouraging Liverpool Province to approach the Dean and Chapter for permission to hold a parade to the cathedral. Eventually the Province made an approach and Bishop David's letter in response was both cordial and cautious:

> I have an application from 783 Ivy Lodge for a service in Liverpool Cathedral. When we met in the Cathedral I think I told you that the Chapter would consider very favourably an approach from the whole

2014, pp. 26–33; 'Reconciling state and society? The practice of the common good in the partnership of Bishop Sheppard and Archbishop Derek Worlock', *Journal of Religious History* 40,4, 2016, pp. 545–64

[38] Diane Frost and Peter North, *Militant Liverpool: A City on the Edge* Liverpool: Liverpool University Press, 2013, chp. 6: 'Community and Conflict', pp. 123–54

[39] *Protestant Searchlight*, August 1902 and March 1904 LRO H 289 9 PRO

[40] *Protestant Reformers Monthly Magazine*, April 1924 LRO H 289 9 PRO

of the Orange body in Liverpool, but that I was not sure that we would arrange services for single lodges. I will get the matter considered as soon as possible. In the meantime will you tell me what is the membership of your Lodge, and how many you would estimate as likely to attend the service? As to the preacher, you will remember I told you that we select our preachers at all the Cathedral services.[41]

The Ivy history notes with some satisfaction that '[w]ithin a month the Ivy met with the Dean and the parade was held. The parade was a great success and many lodges, Districts and the Province wrote letters of congratulation to the lodge.' The intention may well have been to make a public demonstration of their right to proclaim their traditional Protestantism in what many saw as a ritualistic stronghold. By the mid-1960s the concern was increasingly focused on the impact of the ecumenical movement on relations with the Catholic church. Opinion within the Ivy lodge had shifted to a refusal to participate in any parade to the cathedral 'due to continued movement towards each other by the Anglican and Romanist churches'. The opening of the Catholic cathedral in 1967 further stoked Orange unease. Suspicions were reinforced by the news that it was planned to hold a Catholic Mass in a crypt of Canterbury Cathedral in July 1970, which led some Ivy members to join a coach party travelling down to join a protest led by the Reverend Ian Paisley. When it was learned that an invitation had been extended to Archbishop Beck to speak to a ticketed audience in Liverpool Cathedral in August 1970 on the topic of his hopes for church unity, protests were sent to the cathedral authorities. In the event the address was given by a local priest.[42]

By the end of the 1970s the maturing of interchurch relations had brought about a shift of policy by the cathedral authorities. The Order applied to hold their 1979 Reformation Day service in the cathedral, but Dean Patey wrote to explain why permission was being refused:

> I think we ought to be quite honest with each other and say that we at the Cathedral and you of the Orange Order take such different views about ecumenism that were you to hold a service here it would puzzle many of our friends, not only in the Roman Catholic church, but also amongst Free Churchmen and our fellow Anglicans. Everything that happens here is seen as part and parcel of our ministry and mission. The Church of England does not observe Reformation Day and, I think, rightly so because the perpetuation of a backward-looking view of history which has certainly been overtaken by such events as the formation of the World Council

[41] Sheppard Papers (henceforth SP), 16 November 1930
[42] Ivy LOL 783, *100 Years of History*, pp. 21, 36, 38–39

of Churches, the Anglican/Roman Catholic commission, and the new atmosphere created by the second Vatican Council. We here value our close links with the Metropolitan Cathedral. Unless I am much mistaken these are things which your members deplore, preferring to maintain the divisions of the past.

We do not deny you the right to hold your views, and I know that some Anglicans share them. But I think it would be less than honest to blur the issues by holding a Reformation Day service in the Cathedral. We therefore feel that we are unable to grant your request.[43]

The Order publicised the exchanges in the local press and Grand Master Roberts assured members that 'we will continue our efforts to secure a parade, and let us sincerely hope and trust that there will soon be a return to reformation principles and practices in the Liverpool cathedral'.[44]

Contacts between the Order and the cathedral authorities continued during the following months, but the Dean remained convinced that it was correct to refuse access. In July 1979 he reported:

Our recent meeting with the Orange Lodge officials did not encourage me to go back on our original Chapter decision. The Grand Master tried to soft pedal the anti-roman stance. But the Lodge Chaplain (Mr Mason) seemed to me to present the true Orange Lodge position and this is borne out by the enclosure which I have now received. However much we need to build bridges between Christians of different opinions, I would myself strongly oppose any move on behalf of the Cathedral which appeared to endorse or condone the outrageous sentiments expressed... This would, in my opinion, destroy our whole ecumenical stance. These papers seem to me to support our original decision not to encourage the Orange Lodge to parade here in the Cathedral.

The Dean went on to suggest a possible forum in which a discussion between the Order, the Cathedral authorities and a group of Catholics might be possible, but he was not optimistic and stated that if such an encounter was not possible and if the Order continued 'to make a public fuss about the Cathedral's unwillingness to welcome them here...' he would be quite prepared to publicly denounce what he described as 'the basic evil of the Orange Order approach'.[45]

[43] Dean Patey to J. Evans, Provincial Secretary, SP, 27 February 1979. Reformation Day is 31 October
[44] Loyal Orange Institution of England Report 1979, p. 3
[45] Dean Patey to Canon Gordon Bates, SP, 11 July 1979; Mason was the minister of the Protestant Reformers Memorial Church

A few weeks earlier the incumbent of St George's Church in the heart of the traditional Orange citadel of Everton had sent a remarkably insightful and prescient letter to Dean Patey:

> The Orange Lodge movement in Liverpool, though avowedly anti-Catholic in one facet, is, in my opinion, a movement which gives expression to working class 'folk religion', which results in many not belonging to local congregations, but feel that they support from the side.
>
> There is a reasonably significant group of Orange Lodge members who are conscientious full members of local Anglican congregations and some are Friends and Supporters of the Cathedral. Certainly 95% will be baptized members of the Anglican Church...
>
> There is an articulate and committed caucus of Paisleyite members, only a few of whom are lodge members, but the bulk are members of right-wing Evangelical churches whose theological roots are firmly in the reformed tradition of Calvinism, and are militantly anti-Catholic.
>
> This group will attract Liverpool members of the City Mission, members of the Anglican Church, right-wing Baptists and Protestant Reformed communities. Many of these articulate members do not belong to the Orange Order Movement because they cannot cope with the working-class nature of its belief system and life-style and receive their anti-Catholic theology etc. from ICC in Holland.
>
> As I see it, many 'rank and file' working class Lodge members are very glad indeed of the Cathedral. They are Monarchy/Establishment/Church/ State affirming and this is their moment to have their thanksgiving and celebration. Their aspirations are no different from ethnic groups wishing to have 'black' services or political groups wishing to have services on themes of Justice and peace.
>
> To deny the Orange Movement their service 'puts down' a lot of people who are already, in my terms, oppressed, and I am sure myself that thinking men and women both in the Roman Catholic community and in the Anglican community, will recognise the difficulties that confront you. I hope you will be big minded and big hearted enough to reconsider your decision and make a gesture to the Orange lodge... [I]t is justifiable in that it can be interpreted as a gesture of acceptance rather than rejection.

If they are again rejected, I fear they may be driven to extreme and irrational behaviour, as they would see themselves as having no alternative to demonstrate their dissatisfaction. No doubt you, as well as I, have seen mothers sitting on zebra crossings, trade union men being violent on picket lines venting emotionally their protest. I feel that the Lodge may be driven to such extremism, and whilst this might substantiate the Cathedral in their justification in rejecting the Lodge, I am sure that for the greater peace of Liverpool this would be regrettable.[46]

The Dean's suggestion of an encounter with a group including Catholic represent-atives was rejected by the Order, but tentative conversations with cathedral officials took place in the ensuing months and in December the Dean suggested to Bishop Sheppard that it might be a good idea if he could be present at the next encounter:

As you know, during the past year the Orange Order has made a very consid-erable attempt to 'capture' the cathedral and I think that this is to try to pull us away from our links with the Metropolitan Cathedral, our involvement in the ecumenical movement, and possibly even may have something to do with the visit of the Pope in 1982. Although the Cathedral has been the main target of the Orange Lodge's protest, you have yourself been involved in some of their publicity, and we are very anxious that they should recognise that the kind of ecumenical policy which we pursue is not some idiosyncrasy of the Dean and Chapter, but something to which the whole church is committed. The Chapter is very ready to continue the conversation but we would like to widen this slightly so that it is not simply seen as a Cathedral affair.[47]

Sheppard agreed to be present, but it is clear that the Dean did not have high hopes for the meeting, observing that '[u]nless we are able to find some entirely new formula I am really not very happy about the cathedral associating itself publicly with the Orange Lodge, particularly in view of the proposed visit of the Pope in 1982. I have the feeling the Lodge is trying to "capture" the Cathedral for its cause if it possibly can.'[48]

The encounter took place in January 1981, but that there was no meeting of minds was vividly illustrated by a series of events towards the end of that year.

[46] Canon Neville Black to Dean Patey, SP, 16 June 1979; 10 September 2021 conversation with Canon Black, who kindly allowed me to quote this letter. The ICC (International Council of Christian Churches) is a fundamentalist grouping of ultra-Protestant churches opposed to the ecumenism of the World Council of Churches

[47] Dean Patey to Bishop Sheppard, SP, 2 December 1980

[48] Dean Patey to Bishop Sheppard, SP, 17 December 1980

Determined to make their point, the leaders of the Order informed the cathedral authorities that they planned to bring the lodges to evensong on Sunday 6 December. Cathedral officials decided not to forbid them entry, with the result that a large number of supporters, variously estimated at between 1,000 and 2,000, many wearing regalia, entered the Cathedral. Regular worshippers moved to the Lady Chapel. Lodge members sang hymns, prayed and applauded Grand Master Roberts when he took to the pulpit and explained that the demonstration was primarily intended as a protest against the ban on the Order having a service in the Cathedral and not intended as a protest against the planned visit of the Pope, though in a public statement Dean Patey suggested this was probably a factor.[49] A temporary injunction was obtained from the High Court to prevent a further incursion. In his annual report Grand Master Roberts noted with some dismay that though a rally against the papal visit on the grounds it was a state rather than pastoral occasion had been held in St George's Hall 'we were very disappointed at the turnout of 78 people', a significant indication of the lack of public support or indeed interest outside the Order.[50]

On 24 January 1982 during services launching the week of prayer for Christian unity, members of the Order took further action. A group entered the Cathedral, sat down, put on sashes, proceeded to indicate their displeasure by remaining seated when a Catholic priest read the Gospel and at the end of the service placed a copy of the Prayer Book on the altar, containing a letter detailing their displeasure at the proceedings. Though there was no disorder, the Dean noted the discomfort of members of the congregation. However, in the afternoon things were rather more rowdy when what were believed to be members of the Protestant Reformation Society and some Orangemen displayed anti-Catholic posters and pamphlets at the entrance and during the service barracked the sermon by the Administrator of the Catholic cathedral. That same evening there was a fracas at St George's Church, Everton, where demonstrators with placards gathered outside the church. When the sermon by the guest preacher, the Catholic Auxiliary Bishop, was constantly disrupted, the service was discontinued, the police were called and three arrests were made. In a communication to the Lord Mayor the Dean, whilst pledging to seek a peaceful way forward, stressed that '[t]he relationship between Archbishop Worlock and Bishop Sheppard, and between the two Cathedrals, is too precious a thing to the life of Liverpool to be fractured by events such as these'.[51] Archbishop Worlock was asked to give one of the

---

[49] *Liverpool Post*, 7 December 1981; *Liverpool Echo*, 7 December 1981; statement by Dean and Chapter, SP, 6 December 1981

[50] Loyal Orange Institution of England Report 1981, p. 8

[51] Dean Patey to Lord Mayor of Liverpool, SP, 26 January 1982; *Liverpool Daily Post*, 25 January 1982; conversation with Canon Godfrey Butland, who had succeeded Canon Black

Lenten talks at St Nicholas, the city's parish church, on 9 March 1982. When he rose to speak it was instantly clear that there were about 200 demonstrators in the church who began to heckle and wave banners and eventually stormed out shouting anti-Catholic slogans.[52]

Precisely who had organised the disruption was unclear, Grand Master Roberts being at pains to stress that the Order had always advocated peaceful protest,[53] but it was obvious that the focus of the demonstrations was shifting from Orange Order access to the cathedral to traditional, atavistic anti-Catholicism, centred on the imminent Papal visit. This was clearly demonstrated when the Liverpool-born Archbishop of Canterbury Robert Runcie paid a visit to the city two days later as part of the Lenten programme. As he began a talk in St Nicholas Church groups in the congregation began to shout insults, sing an anti-Catholic song, wave bibles and, as the archbishop abandoned his address and finally left the church, sing 'Land of Hope and Glory'. Other demonstrators with placards had gathered outside and Runcie was jostled as the police escorted him to his car. Grand Master Roberts issued a statement asking militant members to 'cool it', stressing that the Order always believed in peaceful protest, warning against any foolish action when the Pope visited and deploring a recent spate of daubing of Catholic churches, but suggesting that some people felt they were not being listened to.[54] The following day he met Bishop Sheppard and expressed his dismay, being 'very disturbed that some of his members had taken part in this demonstration wearing their regalia against his instructions'. At a subsequent meeting with Sheppard and colleagues, the Grand Master and six other leading Orange leaders shared their fears that in the future the Pope would become the head of the Church of England, 'the Queen would have to move over and our constitution and liberties will be lost'. Sheppard explained what he hoped for from the ecumenical movement, but there was clearly no meeting of minds.[55] Later that week Sheppard and Worlock issued a joint statement deploring the 'ugly scenes', stressing that they would not deter the planned Papal visit and suggesting that the general public was appalled by the events. In this they were definitely correct, as reflected in the editorial and the letters page of a local newspaper.[56]

Amongst the general public the feeling was probably uncomprehending shock along with anger that the city's cathedral and parish church and the local leaders of the two main denominations should have been subjected to such noisy, threatening demonstrations and abuse. There is no evidence in the

[52] *Liverpool Echo*, 9 March 1982; David Sheppard and Derek Worlock, *Better Together* London: Hodder and Stoughton, 1988, p. 243
[53] *Liverpool Daily Post*, 10 March 1982
[54] *Liverpool Daily Post*, 12 March 1982
[55] Sheppard and Worlock, *Better Together*, pp. 243–44
[56] *Liverpool Echo*, 12 March 1982

available lodge records that private lodges took a decision to participate and it is clear that the Protestant Reformation Society was well to the fore. However, there was an undoubted overlap of membership and outlook between some lodge members and the PRS—one of their pamphlets condemning the papal visit was circulating within the lodges from at least mid-1980, when 'it was hoped that copies of the pamphlet would be available to delegates at the Grand lodge',[57] and some demonstrators had worn regalia. In the event the historic Papal visit of 30 May 1982 passed off peacefully.[58]

Subsequently, there were meetings between the Bishop, cathedral authorities and the Orange Order. This was followed by a letter from Dean Patey to the Grand Master, partly to explain why the church had taken out an injunction against unauthorised occupation of the cathedral but also offering an invitation to a planned service of evensong on 20 June when the preacher would be the Dean of Belfast, personal friend of Dean Patey and member of the Orange Order.[59] The service duly took place and the Liverpool Provincial Secretary was clearly impressed, writing '[y]esterday, June the 20th, will long be remembered by our members, not only for the dignity and simplicity of the service, but for the wonderful singing of the choir, and the very inspiring address by the Dean of Belfast'.[60]

In reporting to the Grand Lodge in 1982 the Grand Master made much of the fact that the Order had finally gained access to the cathedral: '[t]his could only be seen as a victory for our members, as we had not moved one inch from our original stand on this matter. Our members rallied round the Grand Master, so much that, on the day, the Cathedral authorities had to hire an extra 500 seats to accommodate us.'[61] However, the history of Ivy LOL 783 contains more than a hint of grass-roots disquiet at the lack of an organised protest by the Order on the day of the papal visit. During 1981 lodge meetings had been:

> mainly taken up with the proposed visit of Pope Benedict [sic] which was set for 1982… this was one of those events which caused as much upset and division within our ranks of our institution as it did outside. There was a feeling of disappointment by the lodge members, when it was agreed that only a silent protest would be held by the lodges in Liverpool… 'without collarettes'… the parade to the cathedral was seen as a 'great victory' by

[57] Loyal Orange Institution of England Report 1980, p. 7
[58] Sheppard and Worlock, *Better Together*, pp. 239–40, 244–45; Bradstock, *David Sheppard*, pp. 213–14; the only protest was a small-scale affair organised by the Reverend Ian Paisley; the Order was particularly concerned that this was a state rather than a pastoral visit
[59] Dean Patey to G.M. Roberts, SP, 15 June 1982
[60] Provincial Secretary to Dean Patey, SP, 21 June 1982
[61] Loyal Orange Institution of England Report 1982, p. 40.

those in the Ivy but was there a deal done somewhere?... many Orange
men and women left the city for the day rather than be anywhere near
all the hoo hah.[62]

It seems much more likely that Orange leaders, realising recent events had been
a public relations disaster, decided yet another such demonstration on the streets
would bring the Order into further disrepute in the eyes of the general public
and decided silent abstention was the better part.

Conclusion

As the twentieth century progressed the Orange Order was faced with the
fact that British society was undergoing profound changes which challenged
or simply side-lined many of their central concerns. At the local level the
structure and geography of the local economy were transformed as dock
work was replaced by manufacturing and service industries, often located in
peripheral estates. Similar radical shifts occurred in the residential population
with the development of overspill estates and suburbanisation, fracturing the
closely bonded neighbourhoods in which local lodges had flourished. There was
large-scale commercialisation and professionalisation of some of the functions
that had previously been at the core of lodge life. Nationally organised health,
welfare and insurance services replaced the lodge, district and province-based
mutual aid societies that had long been a significant feature of lodge appeal.
Similarly, the entertainment once provided by amateur groups at lodge dinners,
dances, bazaars, sales of work and 'smokers' was increasingly provided by professional entertainers of national or international repute and quality who could
be seen in theatres and increasingly at dance halls and cinemas, heard on the
radio or viewed on television. By the second half of the century there was also
a growing moneyed youth culture whose participants, as some lodges learned,
were not attracted to youth clubs designed simply to recruit new lodge members
or church attenders.

The Order was clearly dismayed that the Christian religion no longer
occupied a central place in British national identity and public life and the fact
that relations between the main Christian denominations were markedly less
confrontational than in earlier centuries. This caused dismay within a movement
with traditional Protestantism at its core. At the local level the angry edge had
gradually worn off interchurch relations as expressed in small-scale ecumenical

---

[62] Ivy LOL 783, *100 Years of History*, pp. 45–46; clearly some confusion, since the Pope
in question was John Paul II. Subsequently the Order negotiated a regular cathedral
service on St George's Day

projects and the process was affirmed by the symbolism of the partnership between Bishop Sheppard and Archbishop Worlock. The efforts of local lodges to assert their right to a service in the Anglican Cathedral and the noisy opposition of some groups to the papal visit in 1982 generated a great deal of adverse publicity in the eyes of a largely uncomprehending general public. By the closing years of the twentieth century the dwindling appeal of the Order was largely based on the strong social bonding between members plus family traditions of membership.

Conclusion

Originally a transplant from late-eighteenth-century Ireland imported by returning soldiers and Protestant Irish immigrants, the Orange Order put down deep roots in Liverpool because of its multi-dimensional appeal to a large section of the local, working-class, Protestant population. At one level its fervent Protestant patriotism and royalism tapped into that deep-seated anti-Catholicism that characterised historic English and British popular nationalism, viewing the Roman Catholic church as an autocratic, conspiratorial, subversive foreign 'other'. By the mid-1830s Orange lodges were to be found in the working-class districts of most of the fast-growing urban industrial centres of Britain, but especially in the north-west of England. In Liverpool dock work and religious division rendered the city particularly fertile ground for the Order. The rapid development of the city as one of the premier ports of the United Kingdom and the emerging empire meant that there was a remarkably high level of employment in dock-related work which, well into the twentieth century, was casual, irregular and notably accident-prone. The need to be on hand led to the growth of dense, working-class, residential concentrations close to the docks and stimulated the development of closely bonded neighbourhood groups based on a combination of the extended family, workplace relationships and mutual aid societies. A further distinctive feature was the concentration of Protestants and immigrant Irish Catholics in distinct neighbourhoods, especially in the northern end of the city, and the parallel growth of a dense, frequently parish-based, associational culture.

The Orange lodges fitted nicely into the Protestant neighbourhoods, where the steadily growing levels of Irish Catholic immigration gave local credence to traditional fears. From the 1830s onwards these were articulated by a growing cadre of ultra-Protestant, Irish-born, Anglican clerics of a colourful apocalyptic outlook. Fervent, earnest, eloquent and energetic, they set the evangelical and anti-Catholic tone of the city's Anglican communion for generations, thanks to the appointment of like-minded, often Irish-born, clergy to city livings, the work of a local theological college and the encouragement of successive generations of anti-Catholic campaign groups. They found a ready audience in the Orange lodges, delighted to hear their traditional fears and convictions so eloquently expressed, endowed with an air of respectability and by implication providential endorsement. Throughout the nineteenth and well into the twentieth century issues surrounding education, extension of civil rights to Catholics, Irish home rule and ritualism within the Church of England served to confirm and justify traditional Orange principles and fears.

For its members the Order provided a flattering, exciting, all-encompassing world view expressing their fervent belief in the superior civic virtues inherent in their Protestant faith, but the lodges also attracted and held members for immediate social and material reasons, which combined to make the monthly lodge night a regular feature of life for many working-class men and women. They were attracted by the esoteric secretive world of oaths and passwords and the colourful liturgy and regalia. They enjoyed the socialising after lodge meetings and the dinners, entertainment, outings, leisure-time activities and the public parades in regalia with banners and flags, above all on the twelfth of July, the climax of the lodge year, an opportunity to mark out and confirm residential territorial boundaries and often occasions for sectarian conflict. But they also benefited from the intense sense of fellowship, especially in times of personal crisis, when this was expressed in friendship, emotional support and material aid. From quite early on this was formally organised in benefit societies and burial clubs, originally based on the lodge and later on the District, Province and eventually the Grand Lodge. Support was also provided to members from other lodges migrating in search of work, leading to the development of an Orange diaspora within the framework of the evolving British empire, itself a source of patriotic pride. The result was an intensely bonded, all-encompassing lifestyle, with the lodges penetrating deeply into a significant section of the Liverpool Protestant working class, providing outlets for latent skills of leadership, administration and public speaking and becoming an integral part of the social capital of their communities.

Members were also closely bonded by common social origins. Whilst these varied in detail from place to place depending on the structure of the local economy, available data suggest the great majority were in unskilled or semi-skilled occupations, along with the occasional lower-middle-class member. Their sense of solidarity was further reinforced by unquestioning royalism and a fierce patriotism, expressed in a long tradition of military service proudly commemorated in iconography and regular ceremony. Their Protestantism was equally unquestioned and its boundaries carefully policed to ensure minimal social contact with Catholics, with the ultimate sanction of expulsion and the loss of those intense personal links that flowed from lodge membership.

The Order also became involved in broader public issues. The steady growth of the local Irish Roman Catholic population in numbers, organisational strength and public visibility from the early nineteenth century served to reaffirm historic

Orange concerns and fears. In the early 1830s the local Conservative party, seeking a fresh political path in the face of Parliamentary reform, recognised an electoral opening. They set about crafting a populist, ultra-Protestant, patriotic appeal amounting to a local version of ethno-religious British nationalism unknown outside Ulster, combined with an affable, folksy leadership style and a programme of clientelist municipal welfarism. There was considerable overlap in membership and outlook between Order and party and at election times the lodges were a rich source of ground troops. The result was a strong working-class Conservative vote and a dominance at local and Parliamentary level not successfully challenged until the middle of the twentieth century.

But despite unity on public concerns there were latent cleavages within the Order that were never quite resolved. The more devout were never happy with the boisterous socialising of working-class life and on 12 July, particularly the consumption of alcohol. This reached crisis level in the 1950s and 1960s when shortage of funds led to the organisation of lodge-based social clubs and applications for alcohol licences, resulting in litigation, resignations and expulsions. There has also been chronic ambiguity over the place of women within the Order. They have clearly played a key role in the social side of lodge life, displaying considerable skills in catering, organising social events and taking a leading role in the oversight and welfare of the juvenile lodges, but the process of achieving formal recognition has been contested and hesitant.

The Order has not always been satisfied with either the state church or the Conservative Party in their response to the development of the Anglo-Catholic element within the Church of England. In both cases there has been a sense that those in authority have not acted with sufficient firmness to suppress developments in doctrine, ritual, liturgy, clerical dress and internal church embellishments that, for members of the Order, seem to represent the infiltration of Catholicism into the state church. Historically, the resulting strains have led to public sectarian clashes and schism, with the emergence of independent ultra-Protestant churches of which the Protestant Reformers was the most notable and a distinctive Liverpool Protestant Party, both well supported by lodge members, though many have remained with mainstream churches.

The Order has been uncomfortable with the social and cultural shifts in British life in the second half of the twentieth century that gradually redefined the nature of Britishness as a more inclusive social construction. That belief in the superior spiritual and civic virtues inculcated by Protestantism, which lies at the heart of the Order's self-definition, no longer has widespread acceptance. In particular the gradual acceptance of Roman Catholics as full and trustworthy citizens, the incorporation of Anglo-Catholicism into the Anglican spectrum, the decline of religious belief and observance, together with the end of empire and the realignment of political loyalties on class lines combined to erode the public significance of many of the Order's defining concerns. Whilst the Northern

Ireland situation could still pull on the mystic chords of Orange memory and fraternity, the issue did not resonate with the general population. The world view and tactics of past populist leaders seemed increasingly anachronistic, lacking in credibility, irrelevant and distasteful. Moreover, increasingly elaborate social services replaced the welfare role of the lodges, the commercialisation and professionalisation of entertainment and leisure-time activities, the advent of the mass media and the rise of a popular youth culture replaced many of the traditional social and leisure attractions of the lodges, whilst the role allocated to women seemed increasingly arcane. In Liverpool radical changes in social and economic geography fractured the local loyalties and kinship networks so basic to lodge life. Moreover, the distancing of mainstream evangelicalism from militant anti-Catholicism, improvement in relations between the major Christian denominations, the development of ecumenical projects at the parish level and strong local leadership saw a gradual ebb of sectarian feeling and its partial sublimation into football loyalties. That combination of context, contingency and agency which had enabled the Order to establish a long-lived, distinctive role in the city had gradually unravelled.

Bibliography

Primary Sources

Held in Liverpool Record Office (LRO) unless otherwise indicated

1. Bishop David Sheppard Papers (S.P.)

2. Minute Books

Liverpool Province

Processions Committee 1959–73
Provincial Grand Secretary's Report 1905 (Museum of Orange Heritage, Belfast)

Liverpool Districts

No. 3 District 1904–26; Correspondence Book 1979–89
Enniskillen No. 5 District 1909–30
Duke of York No. 6 District 1948–53; 1953–62
No. 6 District Hall Management Committee 1959–62 and 1962–65

Male Lodges

Everett LOL 108: 1882–98, 1898–1902, 1903–08, 1908–13
Cromwell LOL 94: 1884–94, 1894–1905
Sons of the Boyne LOL 28: 1907–20, 1920–28
Garston True Blues LOL 64: 1921–23, 1927–29, 1950–53,1953–55, 1955–56, 1957–61; Distress Committee 1921–23; Hall Committee 1921–25; Building (Hall) Committee 1939–54; Building Committee 1954-62 (held at Heald Street Orange Hall, Garston)

Pride of West Derby LOL 5: 1936–54, 1955–62 (meeting jointly with Belfast Patriotic
    LOL 3 1944–49)
Belfast Patriotic LOL 3: 1949–57
Stuart McCoy Memorial LOL 2: 1946–68
Trevor LOL 820: 1948–52, 1952–61
Protestant Martyrs LOL 35: 1955–59, 1959–61
Sons of Victory LOL 80: 1958–69
Kirby Defenders LOL 300: 1965–68, 1968–71, 1971–82
Old Swan Arch Purple Heroes LOL 810: 1914–22
Kirby Defenders Orange Hall Management Committee 1956–59
Ivy LOL 783: 1905–34, 1945–2005 (circulated privately on disc)

Female Lodges

Kirkdale's Glory LLOL 80: 1904–12, 1913–23
Ladies (Lady 1907 onwards) Stanley LLOL 97: 1905–13, 1913–54
Daughters of Victory LLOL 11: 1924–30, 1930–35
Protestant Martyrs LLOL 91: 1967–77

Juvenile Lodges

Old Swan Star of the East Female Juvenile Lodge LOL 105: 1956–60
Pride of West Derby Male and Female Juvenile Lodges LOL 11 and 12: 1962–64,
    1964–70

3. Annual Reports, Rule Books

Auxiliary of the Protestant Reformation Society Report 1878
First Annual Report of the Liverpool Protestant Association   Liverpool: Davenport,
    1836
Grand Protestant Association of Loyal Orangemen of England, Half Yearly Meeting
    3 February 1834, Appendix 5
Laws and Ordnances of the Loyal Orange Institution of Great Britain   Liverpool.
    Printed by Order of the Grand Lodge, 1842
List of Warrants of the Grand Protestant Association of Loyal Orangemen of Great
    Britain   Chowbeat: 1850; Museum of Orange Heritage, Belfast
Liverpool Protestant Association Annual Report 1836
Liverpool Provincial Grand Secretary's Report 1905   Museum of Orange Heritage,
    Belfast
Liverpool Workingmen's Protestant Reformation Society First Annual Report
    1853–54
Loyal Orange Institution of England Annual Reports (private collection)
Loyal Orange Institution of England Burial Service for Departed Members of the
    Orange Order, undated
Report of the Auxiliary of the Protestant Reformation Society 1878

Report of Proceedings, The Grand Protestant Association 1864

Rules and Regulations to be observed by the Members of the Loyal Orange Benefit Society Lodge No. 14. Held at Liverpool. Liverpool: Reston, 1843

Rules of the Benefit Society of Loyal Orange Association Lodge No. 13 Liverpool: Braithwaite: *c.* 1842

Rules of the Funeral Fund Association of the Order of Loyal Orangemen, Liverpool District Liverpool: Shaw, 1843

4. Miscellaneous and Ephemera

100 Years of History Ivy LOL 783; privately available on disc; covers period 1905–2005

Belfast–Liverpool: The Refugee Crisis—1971: The Untold Story Belfast: East Belfast Historical and Cultural Society, *c.*2014

Garston True Blues LOL 64: A Glimpse into 125 Years History of Garston True Blues LOL 64 Privately published: 2001

Henderson, R.F., *George Wise of Liverpool: Protestant Stalwart Twice Imprisoned for the Gospel's Sake* Privately published: 1960

Junior Orange Lecture enclosed with Garston True Blues LOL 64 Minute Book October 1953–July 1955; held at Heald Street Orange Hall, Garston

Metropolitan Cathedral Archives Series 2: Elections and Voter Registration: Municipal Elections

Orange Vision No. 5, January–March 1960 Author's collection

Regulations and Ceremonies of the Juvenile Branch

5. Contemporary Publications

Bell, Peter, *Liverpool and Birkenhead in the Twentieth Century: Contemporary Biographies* Brighton: publisher unknown, 1911

Bullock, C., *Hugh McNeile and Reformation Truth* Publisher unknown, *c.*1881

Evans, J., *Lancashire Authors and Orators* London: Houlston and Stoneman, 1850

Falloon, Hugh, *Memoir of William Marcus Falloon* Liverpool: J.A. Thompson, 1893

Heiser, F.B., *The Story of St Aidan's College 1847–1947* Chester: Phillipon and Golder, *c.*mid-1880s; Special Collections, Sydney Jones Library, University of Liverpool

Kay, James Phillips, *The Moral and Physical Condition of the Working Classes Employed in the Cotton Manufacture in Manchester* London, 1832; new edition with preface edited by W.D. Challoner: London: Cass and Co., 1970

Liverpool Pamphlets 1797–1860: Religious No. 20

Orchard, B.G., 'Rev. Richard Hobson', in *Liverpool's Legion of Honour* Liverpool: Marples & Co., 1893

Report of the Select Committee Appointed to Inquire into the Origin, Nature, and Tendency of Orange Institutions in Great Britain and the Colonies. With the Minutes of Evidence, Appendix and Index, 1836

St Aidan's Theological College, Prospectus Special Collections, Sydney Jones
   Library, University of Liverpool
Statistics of Vauxhall Ward, The Condition of the Working Class in Liverpool in 1842.
   Compiled and edited by John Finch; a facsimile report, prepared and introduced
   by Harold Hikins Liverpool: Toulouse Press, 1986

6. Dissertations

Bullough, Oliver, '"Remember the Boyne": Liverpool Orange Processions
   1919–1939', MA dissertation, Department of British and American History,
   University of Warwick, 1990; copy Liverpool Record Office
Wardle, J.A., 'The Life and Times of the Reverend Hugh McNeile, B.D.,
   1795–1879', MA dissertation, Department of Ecclesiastical History, Joule
   Library, University of Manchester

7. Newspapers, Periodicals

Cowdroy's Manchester Gazette and Weekly Advertiser
Garston and Woolton Reporter
Liverpool Albion
Liverpool Chronicle
Liverpool Courier
Liverpool Daily Post
Liverpool Echo
Liverpool Evening Express
Liverpool Journal
Liverpool Mail
Liverpool Mercury
Liverpool Review
Liverpool Times
Orange Vision
Protestant Reformers Church Monthly Magazine
Protestant Searchlight
Protestant Times
The Porcupine

Secondary Sources

Akenson, Donal Harman, *Discovering the End Time: Irish Evangelicals in the Age
   of Daniel O'Connell* Montreal: McGill-Queens University Press, 2016
Asher, Michael, *Khartoum: The Ultimate Imperial Adventure* London: Penguin,
   2006
Bardon, Jonathan, *A History of Ulster* Belfast: Blackstaff Press, 1992

Barnard, Toby, 'The uses of 23 October 1641 and Irish Protestant celebrations', *English Historical Review*, cvi, 1991, pp. 889–920

Bartlett, Thomas, *Ireland: A History* Cambridge: Cambridge University Press, 2010

Belchem, John, *Irish, Catholic and Scouse: The History of the Liverpool Irish* Liverpool: Liverpool University Press, 2007

––– (ed.), *Liverpool 800: Culture, Character and History* Liverpool: Liverpool University Press, 2006

–––, *Merseypride: Essays in Liverpool Exceptionalism* Liverpool: Liverpool University Press, 2000

–––, *Popular Politics, Riots and Labour: Essays in Liverpool History 1790–1940* Liverpool: Liverpool University Press, 1992

–––, '"The church, the throne and the people: ships, colonies and commerce": popular Toryism in early Victorian Liverpool', *Transactions of the Historic Society of Lancashire and Cheshire*, 143, 1993, pp. 35–55

–––, 'The immigrant alternative: ethnic solidarity and sectarian mutuality among the Liverpool Irish during the nineteenth century', in O. Ashton, R. Fyson and S. Roberts (eds), *The Duty of Discontent: Essays for Dorothy Thompson* London: Mansell, 1995, chp. 11, pp. 231–50

–––, 'The Liverpool Irish enclave' in D. MacRaild (ed.), *The Great Famine and Beyond: Irish Migrants in Britain in the Nineteenth and Twentieth Centuries* Dublin: Irish Academic Press, 2000, chp. 5, pp. 128–46

––– and MacRaild, D., 'Cosmopolitan Liverpool' in Belchem, *Liverpool 800*, chp. 5, pp. 311–91

Bell, J. Bowyer, *The IRA 1968-2000: Analysis of a Secret Army* London: Frank Cass, 2000

Bew, Paul, *Ireland: The Politics of Enmity 1789-2006* Oxford: Oxford University Press, 2007

Blackstock, Allan, '"A dangerous ally": Orangeism and the Irish Yeomanry', *Irish Historical Studies*, xxx,119, 1997, pp. 393–405

–––, 'A forgotten army: the Irish Yeomanry', *History Ireland*, 4,4, 1996, pp. 28–33

–––, *An Ascendancy Army: The Irish Yeomanry, 1796-1834* Dublin: Four Courts Press, 1998

–––, '"The invincible mass": loyal crowds in mid Ulster, 1795-96' in P. Jupp and E. Magennis (eds), *Crowds in Ireland c.1720-1920* Basingstoke: Macmillan, 2000

Blake, Robert, *Disraeli* London: Eyre and Spottiswoode, 1967

Bohstedt, J., 'More than one working class: Protestant and Catholic riots in Edwardian Liverpool', in Belchem, *Popular Politics, Riots and Labour*, chp. 8, pp. 173–216

Bradley, J., 'Wearing the green: a history of nationalist demonstrations among the diaspora in Glasgow' in Fraser, *The Irish Parading Tradition*, chp. 7, pp. 111–28

Brady, Liam, *T.P. O'Connor and the Liverpool Irish* London: Royal Historical Society, 1983

Bradstock, Andrew, *David Sheppard: Batting for the Poor* London: SPCK, 2019

Bruce, Steve, *No Pope of Rome: Militant Protestantism in Modern Scotland*   Edinburgh: Edinburgh Publishing Company, 1985

Bryan, Dominic, *Orange Parades: The Politics of Ritual, Tradition and Control*   London: Pluto Press, 2000

Bryson, Ann, 'Riotous Liverpool' in Belchem, *Popular Politics, Riots and Labour*, chp. 5, pp. 98–134

Busteed, M., 'Irish Protestants in nineteenth century Manchester: the truly invisible minority', in S. Brewster and W. Huber (eds.) *Ireland: Arrivals and Departures*   Trier: Wissenschaftlicher Verlag, 2015, chp. 3, pp. 25–36

–––, 'Nationalism: historical geography of', in R. Kitchen and N. Thrift (eds), *International Encyclopaedia of Human Geography*, vol. 7   Oxford: Elsevier, 2009, pp. 255–60

–––, *The Irish in Manchester: c. 1750–1921: Resistance, Adaptation and Identity*   Manchester: Manchester University Press, 2016

Butcher, Deborah, 'The changing demographics of Scottish women's Orangeism', *Journal of Orange History*, 1, 2015, pp. 18–33

Cesarani, David, *Disraeli: The Novel Politician*   New Haven, CT: Yale University Press, 2016

Colley, Linda, *Britons: Forging the Nation 1707–1837*   London: Pimlico, 1994

Coogan, Tim Pat, *The IRA*   London: Fontana, 1981

Croft, M., 'Richard Hobson and the Anglican church in 19th century Liverpool', in J.A. Davies and J.E. Hollinshead (eds), *A Prominent Place: Studies in Merseyside History*   Liverpool: Liverpool Hope Press, 1999

Davies, John, 'Irish narratives: Labour in the 1930s', *Transactions of the Historic Society of Lancashire and Cheshire*, 148, 1999, pp. 31–62

–––, '"Rome on the Rates": Archbishop Downey and the Catholic schools question 1929–39', *North West Catholic History*, 18, 1991, pp. 16–32

–––, 'Sensible economy? Sectarian bigotry? The Liverpool Catholic schools question 1938–9', *Transactions of the Historic Society of Lancashire and Cheshire*, 155, 2006, pp. 85–120

Davies, Sam, *Liverpool Labour*   Keele: Keele University Press, 1996

Davis, Graham, *The Irish in Britain 1814–1914*   Dublin: Gill and Macmillan, 1990

Day, P., '"Pride before a fall?": Orangeism in Liverpool since 1945', in M. Busteed, F. Neal and J. Tonge (eds), *Irish Protestant Identities*   Manchester: Manchester University Press, 2008, chp. 19, pp. 273–88

Devlin, C., 'The Eucharistic Procession of 1908: the dilemma of the Liberal government', *Church History: Studies in Christianity and Culture*, 63,3, 1994, pp. 407–25

Donnelly, James jr, *The Great Irish Potato Famine*   Stroud: Sutton Publishing, 2002

Doyle, Peter, *Mitres and Missions: The Roman Diocese of Liverpool 1850–2000*   Liverpool: Bluecoat Press, 2005

Dunn, S. and Morgan, V., 'Series editors' preface', in Fraser, *The Irish Parading Tradition*, pp. vii–viii

Dutton, D.J., 'Lancashire and the new unionism: the Unionist Party and the growth of popular politics 1906–14', *Transactions of the Historic Society of Lancashire and Cheshire*, 130, 1980, pp. 131–48

Dye, R., 'Catholic protectionism or Irish nationalism? Religion and politics in Liverpool, 1829–1845', *Journal of British Studies*, 40,3, 2001, pp. 357–90

Edwards, Ruth Dudley, *The Faithful Tribe: A Portrait of the Loyal Institutions*   London: Collins, 2000

English, Richard, *Armed Struggle: The History of the IRA*   Oxford: Oxford University Press, 2004

Farrell, Sean, *Rituals and Riots: Sectarian Violence and Political Order in Ulster, 1784–1886*   Lexington, KY: University of Kentucky Press, 2000

Fitzpatrick, David, *Descendancy: Irish Protestant Histories since 1795*   Cambridge: Cambridge University Press, 2014

–––, 'Exporting brotherhood: Orangeism in South Australia', *Immigrants and Minorities*, 23, 2005, pp. 277–310

Forker, Martin, 'Ritual and metaphor in the Orange Order', *Journal of Irish Studies*, 28, 2013, pp. 68–77

Foster, Roy, *Modern Ireland 1600–1972*   London: Allen Lane, 1988

Fraser, Antonia, *The King and the Catholics: The Fight for Rights 1829*   London: Weidenfeld and Nicolson, 2018

Fraser, T.G. (ed.), *The Irish Parading Tradition: Following the Drum*   London: Macmillan, 2000

Frost, Diane and North, Peter, *Militant Liverpool: A City on the Edge*   Liverpool: Liverpool University Press, 2013

Furnival, John, *Children of the Second Spring: Father James Nugent and the Work of Child Care in Liverpool*   Leominster: Gracewing, 2005

Gallagher, Tom, *Glasgow: The Uneasy Peace*   Manchester: Manchester University Press, 1987

Geoghegan, Patrick, *Liberator: The Life and Death of Daniel O'Connell 1830–1847*   Dublin: Gill and Macmillan, 2010

Gilley, Sheridan, 'The Garibaldi riots of 1862', *The Historical Journal*, 16,4, 1973, pp. 697–732

Gilmartin, Niall and Browne, Brendan Ciaran, *Untold Journeys: Refugees and Forced Displacement in Northern Ireland's Troubles*   Liverpool: Liverpool University Press, 2023

Gray, Tony, *The Orange Order*   London: The Bodley Head, 1972

Haddick-Flynn, Kevin, *Orangeism: The Making of a Tradition*   Dublin: Wolfhound Press, 1999

Hamilton, Malcolm B. 'Sociological aspects of Christian millenarianism', in S. Hunt (ed.), *Christian Millenarianism from the Early Church to Waco*   London: Hurst and Co., 2001, chp. 1, pp. 12–25

Harbinson, John, *The Ulster Unionist Party: Its Development and Organisation*   Belfast: Blackstaff Press, 1973

Harrison, John, *The Second Coming: Popular Millenarianism 1780–1850*   London: Routledge and Kegan Paul, 1979

Hempton, David, 'Evangelicalism and eschatology', *Journal of Ecclesiastical History*, 31,2, 1980, pp. 179–84

---, *Religion and Popular Culture in Britain and Ireland from the Glorious Revolution to the Decline of Empire*   Cambridge: Cambridge University Press, 1995

Henderson, R.F., *George Wise of Liverpool: Protestant Stalwart Twice Imprisoned for the Gospel's Sake*   Privately published, 1967

Hikins, H.R., 'The Liverpool transport strike, 1911', *Transactions of the Historic Society of Lancashire and Cheshire*, 113, 1961, pp. 169–95

Hill, Jacqueline, 'National festivals, the state and Protestant ascendancy in Ireland 1790–1829', *Irish Historical Studies*, 24, 1984, pp. 30–51

Hill, Myrtle, *The Times of the End: Millenarian Beliefs in Ulster*   Belfast: Belfast Society, 2001

Hilliard, D., 'Unenglish and unmanly: Anglo-Catholicism and homosexuality', *Victorian Studies*, 25,2, 1982, pp. 181–210

Hirst, Catherine, *Religion, Politics and Violence in Nineteenth-Century Belfast: The Pound and Sandy Row*   Dublin: Four Courts Press, 2002

Hobson, Richard, *What God Hath Wrought*   London, 1913; Banner of Truth reprint 2003

Horwood, T., 'Public opinion and the 1910 Eucharistic Congress', *British Catholic History*, 25,1, 2000, pp. 120–32

Hughes, K. and MacRaild, D., *Ribbon Societies in Nineteenth-Century Ireland and Its Diaspora: The Persistence of Tradition*   Liverpool: Liverpool University Press, 2018

Hunt, Tristram, *Ten Cities That Made an Empire*   Harmondsworth: Penguin, 2014

Hurd, Douglas, *Robert Peel: A Biography*   London: Phoenix, 2008

Hurd, Douglas and Young, Edward, *Disraeli, or Two Lives*   London: Vintage, 2016

Hyde, Montgomery, *Carson: The Life of Sir Edward Carson, Lord Carson of Duncairn*   London: Constable, 1987

Jackson, Alvin, *Colonel Edward Saunderson: Land and Loyalty in Victorian Ireland*   Oxford: Clarendon Press, 1995

---, *Ireland 1798–1998*   Oxford: Blackwell, 1999

Jackson, Daniel, '"Friends of the Union": Liverpool, Ulster and home rule 1910–1914', *Transactions of the Historic Society of Lancashire and Cheshire* 152, 2003, pp. 101–32

--- and MacRaild, D., '"The conserving crowd": mass Unionist demonstrations in Liverpool and Tyneside, 1912–13', in D.G. Boyce and A. O'Day (eds), *The Ulster Crisis, 1885–1921*   London: Palgrave, 2005, chp. 12, pp. 229–46

Jackson, John Archer, *The Irish in Britain*   London: Routledge and Kegan Paul, 1963

Jarman, Neil and Bryan, Dominic, *From Rights to Riots: Nationalist Parades in the North of Ireland*   Coleraine: Centre for the Study of Conflict, University of Ulster, 1998

Jeffrey, Keith, *Ireland and the Great War*   Cambridge: Cambridge University Press, 2000

Jenkins, Roy, *Asquith*   London, Fontana Collins, 1967

---, *Gladstone*   London, Macmillan, 1996

Jess, Mervyn, *The Orange Order*   Dublin: O'Brien Press, 2007

Kaufmann, Eric, *The Orange Order: A Contemporary Northern Irish History*   Oxford: Oxford University Press, 2007

Kelley, T. and Lunney, L., 'Hugh Boyd McNeile', in J. McGuire and J. Quinn (eds), *Dictionary of Irish Biography*, vol. 6   Cambridge: Cambridge University Press, 2009

Kelly, J., 'The emergence of political parading 1600–1800', in Fraser, *The Irish Parading Tradition*, chp. 1, pp. 9–26

Kennaway, Brian, *The Orange Order: A Tradition Betrayed*   London: Methuen, 2007

Keogh, Dermot, *Twentieth-Century Ireland: Nation and State*   Dublin: Gill and Macmillan, 1995, chp. 2, pp. 64–107

Kinealy, Christine, *This Great Calamity: The Irish Famine 1845–52*   Dublin: Gill and Macmillan, 1994

Lane, Tony, *Liverpool: Gateway of Empire*   London: Lawrence and Wishart, 1987

Lees, Lynn Hollen, *Exiles of Erin: Irish Migrants in Victorian London*   Manchester: Manchester University Press, 1979

Longmore, J., 'Civic Liverpool 1680–1800' in Belchem, *Liverpool 800*, chp. 2, pp. 113–69

Lowe, W.J., *The Irish in Mid-Victorian Lancashire: The Shaping of a Working Class Community*   New York: Peter Lang, 1989

Lynch, R., 'The Boundary Commission', in J. Crowley, D. O'Drisceoil and M. Murphy (eds), *Atlas of the Irish Revolution*   Cork: Cork University Press, 2017

Lyons, F.S.L., *Charles Stewart Parnell*   London: Fontana, 1977

MacPherson, James, *Women and the Orange Order: Female Activism, Diaspora and Empire in the British World, 1850–1940*   Manchester: Manchester University Press, 2016

––– and MacRaild, D., 'Sisters of the Brotherhood: female Orangeism on Tyneside in the late nineteenth and early twentieth centuries', *Irish Historical Studies*, 35,137, 2006, pp. 40–60

MacRaild, Donald M., *Culture, Conflict and Migration: The Irish in Victorian Cumbria*   Liverpool: Liverpool University Press, 1998

–––, *Faith, Fraternity and Fighting: The Orange Order and Irish Migrants in Northern England, c.1850–1920*   Liverpool: Liverpool University Press, 2005

–––, *Irish Migrants in Modern Britain, 1750–1922*   Basingstoke: Macmillan, 1998

–––, 'Networks, communication and the Irish Protestant diaspora in Northern England, *circa* 1860–1914', *Immigrants and Minorities*, 23, 2005, pp. 311–37

–––, 'The associationalism of the Orange diaspora', in D.A. Wilson (ed.), *The Orange Order in Canada*   Dublin: Four Courts Press, 2007, chp. 1, pp. 25–41

–––, 'The Irish and Scots in the English Orange Order in the later nineteenth century', in L. Kennedy and R.J. Morris (eds), *Order and Disorder: Ireland and Scotland 1600–2001*   East Linton: John Donald, 2005

–––, '"Wherever Orange is worn": Orangeism and Irish migration in the nineteenth and early twentieth centuries', *Canadian Journal of Irish Studies*, 28,2/29,1, 2002–03, pp. 98–117

McArthur, W.P., 'Medical history of the famine', in R.D. Edwards and T.D. Williams (eds), *The Great Famine: Studies in Irish History 1845–52*   Dublin: Lilliput Press, 1994, chp. 5, pp. 262–315

McAuley, James W., Tonge, Jonathan and Mycock, Andrew, *Loyal to the Core? Orangeism and Britishness in Northern Ireland* Dublin: Irish Academic Press, 2011

McCormack, A., '"That ultra-Protestant nursery": Trinity College Dublin and the supply of Anglican clergy to England', in T.P. Power (ed.), *A Flight of Parsons: The Divinity Diaspora of Trinity College, Dublin* Eugene, OR: Pickwick Publications, 2018, chp. 8, pp. 143–61

McFarland, Elaine, 'Marching from the margins: twelfth July parades in Scotland 1820–1914' in Fraser, *The Irish Parading Tradition*, chp. 4, pp. 60–77

–––, *Protestants First: Orangeism in 19th Century Scotland* Edinburgh: Edinburgh University Press, 1990

Machin, G.I.T., 'The last Victorian anti-ritual campaign', *Victorian Studies*, 25,3, 1982, pp. 277–302

Major, S., 'New crowds in new spaces: railway excursions for the working classes in north west England in the mid-nineteenth century', *Transactions of the Historic Society of Lancashire and Cheshire*, 116, 2017, pp. 120–35

Marshall, William, *The Billy Boys: A Concise History of Orangeism in Scotland* Edinburgh: Mercat Press, 1996

Marston, S., 'Space, culture, state: uneven development in political geography', *Political Geography*, 23,1, 2004, pp. 1–16

Milne, G., 'Maritime Liverpool' in Belchem, *Liverpool 800*, chp. 4, pp. 257–309

Munson, J., 'The Oxford Movement by the end of the nineteenth century: the Anglo-Catholic clergy', *Church History: Studies in Christianity and Culture*, 44,3, 1975, pp. 382–95

Murden, J., '"City of change and challenge": Liverpool since 1945', in Belchem, *Liverpool 800*, chp. 6, pp. 393–485

Navickas, Katrina, *Loyalism and Radicalism in Lancashire 1798–1815* Oxford: Oxford University Press, 2009

–––, *Protest and the Politics of Space and Place 1798–1848* Manchester: Manchester University Press, 2016

Nead, L., 'The secret of England's greatness', *Victorian Culture* 19,1, 2014, pp. 161–82

Neal, Frank, *Black '47: Britain and the Famine Irish* Basingstoke: Macmillan 1998

–––, 'Manchester origins of the English Orange Order', *Manchester Region History Review*, iv, 2, 1990–91, pp. 12–24

–––, *Sectarian Violence: The Liverpool Experience 1819–1914. An Aspect of Anglo-Irish History* Manchester: Manchester University Press, 1988

–––, 'The Birkenhead Garibaldi riots of 1862', *Transactions of the Historic Society of Lancashire and Cheshire*, 131, 1982, pp. 87–112

Nicolson, Harold, *King George V* London: Constable, 1984

Noonan, Gerard, *The IRA in Britain, 1919–1923* Liverpool: Liverpool University Press, 2014

Ogborn, Miles, 'Ordering the city: surveillance and the reform of urban policing in England 1835–56', *Political Geography*, 12,6, 1993, pp. 505–22

O'Leary, S., 'Re-thinking popular Conservatism in Liverpool: democracy and reform in the later nineteenth century', in M.J. Turner (ed.), *Reform and Reformers in Nineteenth Century Britain* Sunderland: Sunderland University Press, 2004, chp. 9, pp. 158–74

O'Mara, Pat, *The Autobiography of a Liverpool Slummy*   New York: Vanguard Press, 1933

O'Murchadha, Ciaran, *The Great Famine: Ireland's Agony*   London: Continuum, 2011

O'Neill, Michael, *St Anthony's Scotland Road, Liverpool*   Leominster: Gracewing Press, 2010

Pakenham, Thomas, *The Boer War*   London: Abacus, 1979

Parkinson, Michael, *Liverpool on the Brink: One City's Struggle against Government Cuts*   Hermitage: Policy Journals, 1985

Paz, D.G., *Popular Anti-Catholicism in Mid-Victorian England*   Stanford, CA: Stanford University Press, 2004

Pedersen, Susan, *Eleanor Rathbone and the Politics of Conscience*   New Haven, CT: Yale University Press, 2004

Pelling, Henry, *Social Geography of British Elections 1885–1910*   London: Macmillan, 1967

Pickering, W.S.F., 'The 1851 religious census—a useless experiment?', *British Journal of Sociology*, 18, 1967, pp. 382–407

Pooley, Colin, 'Living in Liverpool' in Belchem, *Liverpool 800*, chp. 3, pp. 171–255

–––, 'Residential differentiation in Victorian cities: a reappraisal', *Transactions of the Institute of British Geographers* New Series, 19,2, 1984, pp. 131–44

Power, Maria, 'In pursuit of the common good: David Sheppard and Derek Worlock and the 1981 Toxteth riots', *Crucible: The Christian Journal of Social Ethics*, July 2014, pp. 26–33

–––, 'Reconciling state and society? The practice of the common good in the partnership of Bishop Sheppard and Archbishop Derek Worlock', *Journal of Religious History*, 40,4, 2016, pp. 545–64

Ralls, W., 'The Papal Aggression of 1850: a study in Victorian anti-Catholicism', in G. Parsons (ed.), *Religion in Victorian Britain*, vol. 4: *Interpretations*   Manchester: Manchester University Press, 1995, pp. 115–34

Roberts, Keith, *Liverpool Sectarianism: The Rise and Decline*   Liverpool: Liverpool University Press, 2017

Romer, John, *History of Ancient Egypt from the First Farmers to the Great Pyramid*   London: Penguin, 2013

Salvidge, Samuel, *Salvidge of Liverpool: Behind the Political Scene 1890–1928*   London: Hodder and Stoughton, 1934

Scott, G., 'The times are fast approaching', *Journal of Ecclesiastical History*, 36,4, 1985, pp. 591–604

Senior, Hereward, *Orangeism in Ireland and Britain 1795–1836*   London: Routledge and Kegan Paul, 1966

Shallice, A., 'Liverpool Labourism and Irish nationalism in the 1920s and 1930s', *Bulletin of the North West Labour History Society*, 8, 1981, pp. 19–28

Sheppard, David and Worlock, Derek, *Better Together*   London: Hodder and Stoughton, 1988

Smith, J., 'Class, skill and sectarianism in Glasgow and Liverpool', in R.J. Morris (ed.), *Class, Power and Social Structure in British Nineteenth-Century Towns*   Leicester: Leicester University Press, 1986, pp. 158–215

---, 'Labour tradition in Glasgow and Liverpool', *History Workshop Journal*, 17, 1984, pp. 2–53

Storch, R.D., 'The policeman as domestic missionary: urban discipline and popular culture in Northern England 1850–80', *Journal of Social History*, 9, 1975, pp. 481–509

Taplin, Eric, 'Dock labour at Liverpool: occupational structure and working conditions in the late nineteenth century', *Transactions of the Historic Society of Lancashire and Cheshire*, 127, 1977, pp. 123–74

---, 'False dawn of New Unionism? Labour unrest in Liverpool, 1871–73', in Belchem, *Popular Politics, Riot and Labour*, chp. 6, pp. 135–59

---, *Near to Revolution: The Liverpool General Transport Strike of 1911* Liverpool: Liverpool University Press, 1994

---, 'The history of dock labour, Liverpool', in S. Davies (ed.), *Dock Workers: International Explorations in Comparative Labour History*, vol. 2 Aldershot: Ashgate, 2000, chp. 21, pp. 442–70

Thompson, Eric, *The Making of the English Working Class* Harmondsworth: Penguin, 1968

Toon, P. and Smout, M., *John Charles Ryle: Evangelical Bishop* Cambridge: James Clark and Company, 1976

Urquhart, Diane, 'Unionism, Orangeism and war', *Women's History Review*, 27,3, 2018, pp. 468–84

Walker, G., 'The Protestant Irish in Scotland', in T. Devine (ed.), *Irish Immigrants and Scottish Society in the Nineteenth and Twentieth Centuries* Edinburgh: John Donald, 1991, chp. 3, pp. 195–211

Walker, Robert, 'Religious changes in Liverpool in the nineteenth century', *Journal of Ecclesiastical History*, 19, 1968, pp. 195–211

Waller, P.J., *Democracy and Sectarianism: A Political and Social History of Liverpool 1868–1939* Liverpool: Liverpool University Press, 1981

Whittingham-Jones, Barbara, *The Pedigree of Liverpool Politics: White, Orange and Green* Liverpool: privately published, 1936

Wolffe, John, *The Protestant Crusade in Great Britain 1829–60* Oxford: Clarendon Press, 1991

Wright, A.R., and Lones, T.E., *British Calendar Customs: England* London: Folk Lore Society, 1936

Index

Printed in the USA
CPSIA information can be obtained
at www.ICGtesting.com
CBHW080422170724
11681CB00011B/490

9 781837 645084